William Henry Gilder

Ice-pack and Tundra

An Account of the Search for the Jeannette and a Sledge Journey Through Siberia

William Henry Gilder

Ice-pack and Tundra
An Account of the Search for the Jeannette and a Sledge Journey Through Siberia

ISBN/EAN: 9783744799973

Printed in Europe, USA, Canada, Australia, Japan

Cover: Foto ©Andreas Hilbeck / pixelio.de

More available books at **www.hansebooks.com**

Ice-Pack and Tundra

AN ACCOUNT OF

THE SEARCH FOR THE JEANNETTE
AND A SLEDGE JOURNEY THROUGH SIBERIA

BY

WILLIAM H. GILDER

CORRESPONDENT OF "THE NEW YORK HERALD" WITH THE RODGERS SEARCH
EXPEDITION; AUTHOR OF "SCHWATKA'S SEARCH"

WITH MAPS AND ILLUSTRATIONS

London
SAMPSON LOW, MARSTON, SEARLE, & RIVINGTON
CROWN BUILDINGS, 188, FLEET STREET
1883

[All rights reserved.]

CONTENTS.

CHAPTER I.
	PAGE
AT SEA	1

CHAPTER II.
OFF KAMTCHATKA 13

CHAPTER III.
PETROPAULOVSKI 23

CHAPTER IV.
ST. MICHAEL'S 45

CHAPTER V.
IN ST. LAWRENCE BAY 60

CHAPTER VI.
WRANGEL ISLAND 67

CHAPTER VII.
ROUND THE ISLAND 83

CHAPTER VIII.
IN THE ICE FIELDS 95

CHAPTER IX.
EETEETLAN 102

CONTENTS.

CHAPTER X.
LOSS OF THE RODGERS.................................. 115

CHAPTER XI.
PROSPECTS OF RELIEF 129

CHAPTER XII.
THE FATE OF PUTNAM................................. 137

CHAPTER XIII.
ACROSS SIBERIA 148

CHAPTER XIV.
ON THE ROAD.. 161

CHAPTER XV.
MIDDLE KOLYMSK 172

CHAPTER XVI.
APPROACHING THE LENA............................... 186

CHAPTER XVII.
THE DIARY OF DE LONG............................... 198

CHAPTER XVIII.
HOW THE BODIES WERE FOUND........................ 217

CHAPTER XIX.
THE VOYAGE OF THE JEANNETTE...................... 227

CHAPTER XX.
THE RETREAT 240

CHAPTER XXI.
Bennett Island 259

CHAPTER XXII.
Nindermann and Noros 275

CHAPTER XXIII.
Among the Yakouts 299

CHAPTER XXIV.
Caught by the Floods 319

CHAPTER XXV.
End of the Journey 331

LIST OF ILLUSTRATIONS.

	PAGE
THE JEANNETTE SEARCH PARTIES IN YAKOUTSK..	*Frontispiece*
From a photograph.	
ST. MICHAEL'S	43
From an Esquimaux drawing.	
HUNTING SCENE	53
From an Esquimaux drawing.	
THE TRAPPER	57
From an Esquimaux drawing.	
PARROT-BILL GULLS	59
From an Esquimaux drawing.	
TCHOUKTCHI YOUTH	63
From a pencil sketch by the author.	
TCHOUKTCHI GIRL	70
From a pencil sketch by the author.	
HERALD ISLAND	74
From a sketch by the author.	
PLACING RECORDS ON HERALD ISLAND	77
From a sketch by the author.	
CAMP AT EETEETLAN	102
From a sketch by the author.	
THE BURNING OF THE RODGERS	121
From a sketch by Ensign Hunt.	
"ONE-EYED RIELY"	126
From a sketch by the author.	
TCHOUKTCHI CHILDREN	155
From a pencil sketch by the author.	
SIBERIAN LANDSCAPE	173
From a photograph.	

LIST OF ILLUSTRATIONS.

	PAGE
COSSACK FORT	177
From a sketch by a political exile.	
YAKOUT FISHERMEN	178
From a pencil sketch by the author.	
INTERIOR OF A STAROSTA'S HOUSE	182
From a sketch by the author.	
INTERIOR OF POVARNNIAR	188
From a sketch by the author.	
REINDEER	190
From a sketch by the author.	
NICHOLAI CHAGRA'S HOUSE	192
From a sketch by the author.	
NICHOLAI CHAGRA	193
From a pencil sketch by the author.	
WERCHOJANSK	195
From a photograph.	
THE PLACE WHERE THE BODIES WERE FOUND	199
From a pencil sketch.	
FINDING DE LONG	201
From a pencil sketch.	
MONUMENT HILL	217
From a pencil sketch.	
DIAGRAMS OF TOMB	221
From drawings by Bartlett.	
POSITION OF THE BODIES	224
From a sketch by Bartlett.	
THE JEANNETTE SURVIVORS IN YAKOUTSK	225
From a photograph.	
DIAGRAM OF POSITION OF THE JEANNETTE	228
From a sketch by Captain De Long.	
ARRANGEMENT OF CAMP	234
From a sketch by Captain De Long.	
DIAGRAM OF SHORE LINE	266
From a sketch by Captain De Long.	
NINDERMANN AND NOROS	276
From a photograph.	

LIST OF ILLUSTRATIONS.

	PAGE
TUNGUSES	289
From a photograph.	
KUSMAH	295
From a pencil sketch by the author.	
YAKOUTSK	297
From a photograph.	
YAKOUT HORSE	302
From a sketch by the author.	
GROUP OF BORIAKS	304
From a photograph.	
ROAD PASS	305
Reduced fac-simile.	
ORDER FOR HORSES	306
Reduced fac-simile.	
BRIDGE OF EXILES	309
From a photograph.	
LAGOON CAMP ON THE ALDAN	317
From a sketch by the author.	
VIEW ON THE UPPER LENA	320
From a photograph.	
NISHNI NOVGOROD	329
From a photograph.	
TOMSK	335
From a photograph.	
GOLD MINES OF WITEM	339
From a photograph.	
GENERAL ANOUTCHINE	341
From a photograph.	
LAKE BAIKAL	343
From a photograph.	
MAYOR OF TOMSK	344
From a photograph.	

LIST OF MAPS.

CRUISE OF THE RODGERS IN SEARCH OF THE JEANNETTE IN THE SUMMER OF 1881 .... *To face page* 1

WRANGEL ISLAND .... *Page* 65

GENERAL MAP OF NORTHERN SIBERIA AND EUROPE, SHOWING THE AUTHOR'S ROUTE ACROSS THE CONTINENT.
At end of the volume

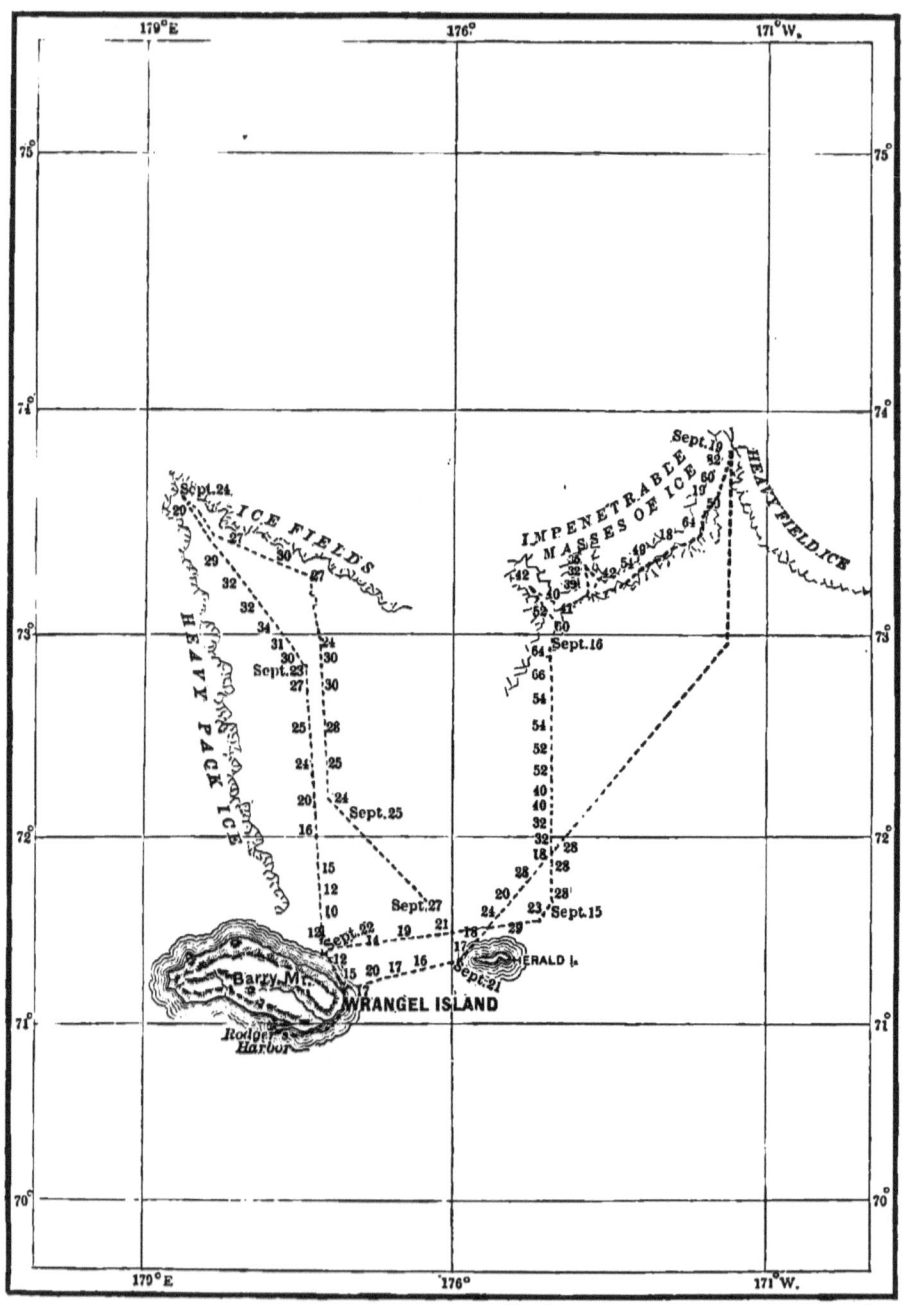

CRUISE OF THE RODGERS IN SEARCH OF THE JEANNETTE
IN THE SUMMER OF 1881.

ICE PACK AND TUNDRA.

CHAPTER I.

AT SEA.

On Board U. S. S. *Rodgers*,
June 27th, 1881.

AFTER numerous delays from various unexpected causes, the United States *Jeannette* Relief Expedition at last finds itself upon the broad Pacific Ocean, about 1,000 miles from San Francisco, and were it not for a half gale that is blowing most of the time, and kicking up a very rough sea, its individual members would have time for serious reflection. But for some reason or other the *Rodgers*, though a staunch and seaworthy craft, has a habit of pitching and rolling most mercilessly, and the component parts of the relief expedition are anxiously awaiting a change of weather to bathe their aching limbs and bruised bodies. As I write, the sun is shining, but the sea is running very high, and now and then an unusually big wave sweeps the main deck, and would carry away the deck-load of lumber were it not securely lashed, or, perhaps, rising aloft, douses the officer on the quarter-deck in an ocean of spray.

This sea, however, is moderate in comparison with what we encountered almost immediately after leaving the headlands at the entrance of the Golden Gate. The very first night out found us tempest-tossed on the heaving breast of the so-called Pacific Ocean. More than one of those accustomed to life upon the billowy deep were seeking the retirement of their state-rooms, not to sleep, but to hide their feelings from public gaze. No one need expect sympathy in sea-sickness. It seems to be the usual thing for the strong to laugh at the weaker stomachs. No tender hand is there to smooth the aching brow, or to bathe the throbbing temples of the sick one, and yet, perhaps, no sickness is more agonizing to the sufferer. My room-mate, a handsome young Cuban, who though aware of the fact that he is sick almost all the time he is at sea, has pluckily chosen the profession of a surgeon in the navy, was most terribly handled by the relentless sea. But there was no sympathy for him in the ward-room. All the encouragement he would get would be the cheery laugh and raillery of his comrades as they called upon him to "brace up" and "have some style"; and when three days had passed, during which he was unable even to think of food, they came to him with rusty hard bread, and advised him to eat it with plenty of mucilage to make it stick. Despite his agony he smiled good-naturedly, and expressed his disgust at his weakness. Said he, "Just look at me, a big strong man, and yet so weak that I can't walk or eat. It is simply disgusting. And yet I tell you I feel so utterly nerveless that if I were to fall overboard, I don't believe I would try to swim."

But where is Dominick all this time? Dominick Boocker is the steward, who came way from Louisville, Ky., to gain the glory of being the first colored man at the north pole. He is a faithful fellow, but, oh! so slow.

Perfectly satisfied with his prospective distinction, he acts as though that were all he had to do in this world. At Mare Island and in San Francisco he was supremely happy. A cabin full of "gemmen" to wait upon, an Italian cook to prepare the meals that he ordered, and all dependent upon him—what else was there in life to be desired? But launched upon the heaving breast of the broad ocean in one of her angriest moods, and called upon to cast up his accounts, a change came over him. From the grinning good nature that had previously distinguished him, he became thoughtful and morose; and finally a look of such utterly helpless misery settled upon his face, that it was absolutely touching. The first-class Italian cook, imported from New York at the expense of the officers' mess, had also succumbed to the weather, and the ship's cook, with the assistance of the blacksmith, had to do all the work for both ends of the vessel. There was not much that could be done, though, for the vessel rolled and pitched so that it was next to impossible to cook any thing. Perhaps a little coffee, that generally came to grief somewhere between the galley and the ward-room, or a boiled potato and some hard bread, comprised the meal which had to be eaten while grasping some convenient projection along the wall of the cabin, or with one leg wound around the leg of the table and the other braced against a handy bulkhead. In the meantime nearly all the crockery was broken, and the mess kit was in a very dilapidated condition when viewed after the storm subsided. The night of Sunday, the 19th, and the three following days, were most delightful. The sea was perfectly smooth and the wind so light that steam was ordered, and we moved by the propeller until Thursday morning, when the wind freshened sufficiently to dispense with steam. Since then a strong wind has prevailed which necessitated shortening sail.

We have been somewhat disappointed in the sailing qualities of the vessel, or rather in the speed she has been able to develop. But she is deeply laden, carrying about one hundred tons more than was anticipated, and is heavily sparred. This causes her to roll considerably, and assists in deadening her headway. Dragging her screw propeller through the water also has a tendency to check her speed, and the sheathing to protect her from the ice has a similar effect. Upon the whole, however, her officers are thoroughly satisfied with her, and consider her one of the finest vessels, if not indeed the best, that ever entered the Arctic. She showed more speed under steam than was expected, having reached five and a half knots, without any assistance from the sails, on Wednesday the 22d. This was a knot better than had been anticipated; and the chief engineer has since said that he hopes to improve upon that record before reaching Petropaulovski.

We have a splendid crew of men, selected chiefly from volunteers from the regular navy. Young men accustomed to discipline, well trained in their duties, and full of animal spirits. It is a pleasure to see them at work about the ship, singing the tarry songs of the briny deep as they heave upon the ropes. Their songs are of various kinds, but may be divided into the two general classes of working and loafing choruses. There are those in quick measure, when they haul rapidly hand over hand, in time to the music, and others with a long, dismal, monotonous solo, with a chorus at rare intervals of "Haul, boys, haul away," when they put the strain on the ropes. This is the loafing song.

Some of the men are so full of life that it is impossible to restrain them. They despise the ratlings, but go aloft, hand over hand, by any convenient rope. The other night, while taking in sail during a squall, one of the men had occasion to go from the upper top-sail to the lower yard, and, instead of going by the ratlings, let himself down by a rope, and after completing his task would not even return in the regular way, but went up, hand over hand, by the same rope. The rolling of the vessel swung him clear out over the angry waves, but he paid no attention to the apparent peril of his position. Not so, however, the officer of the deck. It was too good an opportunity to do some swearing, and he cursed the daring fellow's recklessness roundly. The men do not appear to do such things in a spirit of bravado, but simply with implicit reliance upon their powers. It is the unanimous opinion that there never was a finer crew assembled upon any vessel. Strong, young, skilful, good-natured and under thorough discipline, they possess all the qualities to make for themselves a noble record when their skill and daring are called upon in the approaching conflict with the ice floes and storms of the polar sea. Several of them have seen service in the north before this trip. Payer considers enlisted men with Arctic experience rather a detriment than an advantage to the force of an Arctic cruiser, as they are apt to consider such experience as an offset to the skill, judgment and intelligence of their officers. With us, however, are several officers who have had more or less experience in that country, so that the men cannot and do not claim any superiority on that score. It is a pleasure to see the alacrity with which the orders of the officers are obeyed, and it is also gratifying to see the judgment and skill displayed by these youthful officers, as has already been evinced more than once during the exceedingly severe weather already experienced.

It had been remarked in San Francisco before we left that if there was any weakness in the equipment of the *Rodgers*, it was the extreme youthfulness of her officers. But it has already been demonstrated that the careful training of intelligent minds in a course such as is pursued at the United States Naval Academy develops competent officers more rapidly than the mere school of experience can possibly accomplish. With such a vessel as the *Rodgers*, officered and manned as she is, it is not surprising that friends at home expect great results from this voyage. This feeling was liberally displayed in the escort tendered us on the day of our departure from San Francisco, the 16th of June. Many ladies and gentlemen went down the bay on our vessel, and a large steamboat and several tugs accompanied us as far as it was safe or convenient for the ladies, who attended in great numbers. As we passed the forts in the harbor, the army tug came out to meet us, and steamed for some time alongside, the fine military band of the Fourth Artillery playing several appropriate and inspiring selections. On one tug that kept close beside the *Rodgers* in her progress down the bay, were Paymaster A. S. Kenney, purchasing officer of the expedition, and Pay-Director Caspar Schenck, of San Francisco, with numerous invited guests, who drank to our safe and successful return, waving their glasses and the festive demijohn toward us in the most tantalizing manner, considering that they were enjoying a privilege denied to us, though such deprivation is a self-imposed obligation, to be broken only on high days and holidays, or the finding of any of the *Jeannette's* party. Several of the yachts of the San Francisco squadron joined the escort, and, in the stiff breeze that comes in through the Golden Gate every afternoon, sailed merrily around us, the ladies waving their handkerchiefs and the gentlemen their hats, and shouting words of encouragement whenever they came near us. It was a scene of intense excitement, and it is perhaps unnecessary to say that not a man or officer on board our vessel but felt his bosom swell with pride and satisfaction at the genuine heartiness of the God speed tendered us. There was manifest in every individual on board the *Rodgers* the consciousness that he had started upon a perilous expedition with a humane object in view—a rescue; and his determination to do something worthy of the cause was strengthened by the very evident appreciation of friends and strangers.

Finally the hour arrived when the guests on board the *Rodgers* must leave, for there was already quite a heavy sea, and delay would make the disembarking more and more difficult of accomplishment. The little revenue cutter, *General Irwin*, drew alongside, and though both vessels kept bobbing up and down on the waves, the large party of ladies and gentlemen was safely transferred, and crowded the upper deck of the cutter, much to the dismay of their friends upon the *Rodgers*. Again and again cheers and the last parting words were exchanged, and hearts were close to the mouths of many on board both vessels. The last good-bye came from the signal station on Telegraph Hill, where in the dim distance we could see the Stars and Stripes dipping from the flag-staff. This signal was answered, and we steamed slowly and silently past the headlands of the Golden Gate, and were out upon the boundless deep. The pilot left us at half past seven that evening, and carried back a few hastily written words of parting to distant friends;

and as the white-haired old mariner stepped over the rail into his tiny boat, that was to take him to his pretty craft close by, his eyes were dimmed by emotion we scarcely expected in one whose interest in us we had believed to be only mercenary.

Soon an ugly swell made the *Rodgers* roll heavily, and the wind springing up, we began to miss one and another of the ship's company who had retired to the privacy of their state-rooms or the friendly support of the hand rail. Mark Twain has said that nothing makes a man so conceited as to have his stomach behave itself when others are experiencing the pangs of sea-sickness. I remembered this, and tried to appear modest; in fact I was not certain how long I might enjoy immunity from this dread ill, as the sea was getting rougher continually. But though during this and the succeeding two days I experienced the worst weather I ever encountered, I had no cause to complain of that useful member of my physical economy. I tried to pity my poor room-mate, and offered my services to do anything for him, but he was beyond the reach of human aid for relief, and just then I caught sight of Dominick, and if there ever was a picture of repentance he was the model.

"What river is this?" said he, after we had been out of sight of land about three days.

"This is the ocean, Dominick."

"Well, whars de land?"

"It will be many days before you see land again, old fellow."

There was no reply to this. Poor old Dominick retired to the forecastle, and was not seen for several days, when, during a storm which kept the vessel wet from stem to stern by the seas she constantly shipped and leaked through the seams above the water-line, one of the officers asked a sailor if he knew what had become of Dominick.

"I guess he's drowned, sir," was the reply. "I saw a box washed out from under a bunk in the forecastle this morning and Dominick came floating out behind it, and he looked as if he were dead then, or wished he was."

But a few days of pleasant weather brought all the sick ones to their feet, and Dominick was again on duty. He never was a racehorse, and the rough handling he had encountered while at sea had not increased his activity. There was an uncertainty in his every motion that was particularly annoying. It was not surprising perhaps that he should be confused with half a dozen officers calling him in different directions at the same time, and upon entirely different errands; but such is the daily experience of a ward-room steward, and it requires a habitude that he had not acquired to get along under such circumstances. Among the officers is a jovial youth from South Carolina, who takes especial delight in confusing poor Dominick. He keeps calling him constantly, and insists that he shall "come a running," something he probably never did in his life. A few days ago he rebuked him in sailor terms for his lack of energy, and Dominick apologized by saying he did not feel well, and, when he was sick that way, he was "dull and stupid." "Well," said Stoney, "if that's the case, I guess you've been at the point of death ever since I knew you." I have an impression that Dominick would give at least a month's pay if he had never seen this "river."

Our young South Carolinian has taken a most decided fancy to the colored steward, and his affection is reciprocated. The one is reminded of home by having a genuine Southern darkey to bull-doze with good-natured raillery, and the other is similarly reminded of home in being bull-dozed.

"Dominick, you've got to come and live with me after this cruise," said the ensign, the other morning. "You'll never have to do another stroke of work as long as you live. All you'll have to do will be to hold my children on your knee, and lie to them about this trip."

"Have you got any children, sir? You look like you was too young a man," said Dominick.

"No, not yet," was the reply; "but if some one remains of the same opinion when I return as when I left, I hope to have one of these days."

There are no married men among the officers. All are young, hopeful, and ambitious. Most, and perhaps all, have some one at home for whose sake they hope to win a name, and the thought that fervent prayers are daily offered for the absent, and that loving eyes are eagerly looking for news of them, nerves every arm, and will inspire men with greater courage in the hour of danger. The lonely night watch gives plenty of time for such reflections, unless foul weather occupies the entire attention of the officer of the deck.

The routine on board the *Rodgers* is conducted with all the regularity of a man-of-war, and cheerfulness predominates under the most trying circumstances. The evenings in the cabin are passed pleasantly in games of cards, chess, back gammon, and the like, and in reading works of scientific interest or lighter literature. Dumb bells and Indian clubs engage attention on the quarter-deck during pleasant weather, and the men forward take turns in pummelling each other with a set of boxing-gloves.

A pair of black pigs enjoy the freedom of the deck below the top-gallant forecastle, and are named respectively Michael Angelo and Raphael. Three kittens and a puppy, of parentage so involved as to puzzle a committee from any kennel club in the country, are the pets of the sailors, and sustain names that would make them proud if they only understood their significance. The kittens are Phryne, Aphrodite and Proserpine; while the dog responds to the name of Billee Stuart. It is becoming a sad reflection that either Michael Angelo or Raphael will have to die to provide us with a fitting thanksgiving dinner. The ship is so well provisioned that one might imagine there would be no necessity for such a sacrifice, but nothing can withstand the keen edge of a salt air appetite. Where are now those dainty palates that refused the delicacies of the San Francisco restaurants, the Occidental Hotel, the California House, Marchand's, and the "Poodle Dog"? Where are those appetites that had to be stimulated with a cock-tail before breakfast and absinthe before dinner? I wouldn't even trust Billee Stuart to run at large were other food lacking. Unless we should have the misfortune to lose our vessel it will be a long time before we are reduced to any strait for food. Beside the regular navy rations for two years and a half, we have on board about two years' full rations of specially selected food, purchased with the Congressional appropriation. In other words, there is food for four or five years at least upon the *Rodgers*. This is perhaps much more than we will require for our own use, but not too much should we have to reprovision the *Jeannette* and the missing whalers. We may not meet any of them, but that is the object of our expedition, and it is proper to be prepared for such an event. All of the food on board is of superior quality, except perhaps the canned meats, which had to be purchased very hurriedly to replace the provisions of that class prepared at the Brevoort House in New York, and supposed to be of the very best put up, but which spoiled in transit from that city to San Francisco on the overland freight trains. It was a great disappointment to lose these goods, for their excellence seemed to be admitted wherever known. The Naval Board in Washington, to whom specimens had been sent, approved of the purchase after testing them in their families. The fame of the chef of the Brevoort House is world-wide, and to dine in the arctic upon such soups and meats would simply be taking all the romance of arctic life out of the trip. There you expect walrus meat and blubber, and to get turtle soup and *tête de veau en tortue* instead, is altogether wrong, for it admits of no excuse for dirty hands and blue shirts. It is fortunate, though, that the condition of these meats was developed before they reached the hold of the vessel, so that they could be replaced with others, though not of so good quality as these were supposed to be. It has been already discovered that some of the canned meats bought in California are somewhat tainted, but the probability is that most of them will be found in good condition when required for use.

We had the pleasure of exchanging signals with an English bark, apparently bound for San Francisco, last Thursday morning. The weather was thick and a high sea running, so that there was no effort made to visit, or "gam," as it is familiarly called.

Sunday, the 26th instant, the wind was very fresh and squally. The waves were running high, but we carried sail until the lee rail was under water, and though butting into a heavy swell we made nine knots an hour. Quite satisfactory speed under the circumstances.

CHAPTER II.

OFF KAMTCHATKA.

PETROPAULOVSKI, KAMTCHATKA,
July 23*d*, 1881.

THE *Rodgers* reached this port on the afternoon of the 19th instant in one of the heavy fogs that distinguish this portion of the world. The evening before our arrival we were only about sixty miles from the shore, and, as the weather was very thick, Lieutenant Berry deemed it advisable to heave-to until daylight, as this is a disagreeable coast to approach in unpropitious weather. Shortly after three o'clock in the morning we started again slowly toward the land, the commanding officer constantly on deck to personally guide and direct the movements of his vessel, as is his custom when danger threatens. About half-past eight, though the land was about forty miles distant, and still concealed by the fog, we could distinctly smell the grass and moss of the Kamtchadal mountains. We at last "picked up" the land, as the sailors term it, about half-past ten o'clock, and after taking the bearings of several headlands, established our position as about twenty miles south of the entrance of Avatcha Bay. We therefore steamed up the coast against a head wind, catching occasional glimpses of the land, and toward evening could make out the little light-house on one of the bluffs, and had no further difficulty in making our way into the snug little harbor of Petropaulovski, the closer landmarks being easily recognized as we passed. When nearer the town we could see by the aid of our glasses that there were two large steamers in ahead of us, and a small boat brought Mr. Green, first officer of the Alaska Commercial Company's steamer *Alexander* to us, under whose guidance we secured a fine anchorage outside the sand spit, and about half a mile from the town. He told us that we were expected, and that the other steamer was the Russian steam corvette, the *Strelock*, Commander De Livron, which had come to anchor that morning. The *Alexander* had arrived the previous day from Behring Island, and was discharging her cargo preparatory to continuing her trading voyage, or rather her sealing operations on the Commander Islands.

Soon a cutter from the Russian man-of-war brought one of her officers, with the compliments of his commanding officer, saying that he would take an early opportunity to call, and that he would gladly furnish us any assistance in his power to further the object of our expedition. About the same time another boat arrived with Captain Sandman, of the *Alexander*, together with Captian Hunter and Mr. Mulawansky, residents of the village, who also tendered their services to the extent of their ability. Captains Sandman and Hunter, though personally strangers, were familiar to most of us through the books of Kennan and Bush, of the Russo-American Telegraph Company, who had met them here while engaged in their Arctic work in the interest of that enterprise. Captain Sandman was the commander of the brig *Olga* that brought the American party from San Francisco, and Captain Hunter, then as now, a resident of this place, had materially aided them with wise counsel derived from his experience in the country. After a short but pleasant visit our guests departed, promising to devote themselves to the task of securing for us such articles of Arctic outfit as could be procured here, and which had been the object of our visit to this town of one yearly mail.

The following morning, with our newly-found friend, Captain Hunter, as interpreter, Lieutenant Berry and your correspondent paid a visit to Commander De Livron, of the *Strelock*, and learned from him that he had been directed by his government to aid us to the extent of his ability, and to make a summer cruise in Behring Sea and the Arctic in aid of the search for the *Jeannette*. He further said that he would like to know our route from here, and the points where we would stop in prosecuting our search, so that he could go to other localities, thereby making the search as extended as possible. He also told Lieutenant Berry that there was a deposit of 500 tons of coal in Plover Bay, placed there by the Russian government, and that he was at liberty to use as much of it as he desired. He begged Lieutenant Berry to command his services at any time, and subsequently furnished him with his intended route after leaving this port to Cape Serdze Kamen, from which place he would bring whatever mail matter we had, and transmit a despatch from the nearest point of telegraphic communication in Asia, where he expected to arrive in the latter part of September. The following day the officers of the *Rodgers* were entertained at breakfast by the officers of the *Strelock*, and during our entire stay here they have extended the most cordial hospitality toward us. The *Strelock* is a steamer of about 1,400 tons, manned by twenty officers and one hundred and fifty men. She has a battery of heavy breech-loading guns, and can make twelve knots under full steam. Captain De Livron is expecting the arrival here, within a week, of the Russian Admiral of the Pacific fleet, with three other vessels of war of the Imperial Russian Navy. This will be a matter of unusual importance in the history of this very quiet, and, to all appearances, unimportant post. This morning the *Kamtchatka*, a steamer of 1,400 tons. burthen, belonging to Mr. A. E. Philippeus, a Russian merchant, arrived here, and is about to proceed on a trading tour to the mouth of the Kamtchatka River and the various ports in the Ochotsk Sea. Captain Hunter, who is the local agent and representative of the owners, will accompany the vessel upon this trip.

Through the active interest of Messrs. Hunter and Mulawansky and the co-operation of the Ispravnik, or chief magistrate, Mr. Sarabrenekoff, we have succeeded in securing forty-seven fine dogs from the people of this neighborhood, but were unable to procure as much dried salmon for dog food as we require. It is too early in the season to find dried fish, though fresh salmon are taken daily in immense quantities. We have obtained a large amount of reindeer skin clothing, which will be invaluable during our sledging operations in the Arctic. The clothing obtained is far superior in quality of workmanship and dressing to that of the Esquimaux, and is much more ornamental. There seems also to be a difference in the quality of the fur to that of the American reindeer, the clothing made from which has to be renewed each year, while this, though having been used a long time, is apparently as good as the day it was made. I have noticed a striking difference in the management of the dogs. These are much more kindly treated than are those of the Esquimaux, and are carefully trained as draught animals. They are driven by the voice instead of a whip, and, instead of being harnessed each with a separate trace, are all attached in pairs to a long line with one leader, who minds the word of command, and turns to the right or left as the driver desires. The Siberian dogs are trained to make rapid journeys, and will readily accomplish eighty or a hundred miles a day for four or five days in succession if regularly fed and watered. I am inclined to believe, however, that they will not equal the Esquimaux dogs in pulling heavy loads over rough ice or land. A load that they can draw easily they will take with great rapidity, but as soon as it drags heavily they all stop. This is, in a great measure, the result of their training, as the driver, when he gives the command to halt, plunges a strong staff into the snow, so as to impede the progress of the sled as much as possible as a further indication of his desire to stop, so that when the dogs feel this heavy drag they stop and lie down. We will probably, however, have an opportunity this fall and winter for practice in the sort of work to be done in the spring. The female dogs are never used in harness in this country, and the males selected for the teams are all emasculated before their training commences. They are evidently of the same species as the Esquimaux dog, and bear a strong resemblance to them in size, color, and shape. The mode of driving is much the same noisy process on both continents, though the words of command are different. When the Kamtchadal wishes his dog to turn to the right he says "Kah-kah" or "Sundah," to the left "Houch" or "Ho-gee, Ho-gee," and it sounds much like the grunting of a pig. When he desires them to start he either whistles or says "Heigh-Heigh," and to stop "Nah-n-a-h."

The sledges of the Kamtchadal are very different in construction from the Esquimaux sledges, which are heavier and better adapted for carrying weight than for rapid transit. Nothing could better combine lightness with strength than the sleds of the people of Petropaulovski; and they have one style upon which the occupant (for it can carry but one person) sits astraddle, which very well corresponds with the sulky of civilized race-courses. It has broad but thin wooden runners, turned up in front, with a frame-work upon which perches a basket-like shell, and its various parts are held together with thongs of seal or bear-skin. A team of six dogs will take one person in a sled like this eight or ten miles an hour over a good road, and their estimate of the power of their dogs is 600 pounds for a team of nine good animals. An Esquimaux team of equal numbers will carry a load of 1,800 or 2,000 pounds fifteen or twenty miles a day for weeks and even for months.

We found no reindeer meat at Petropaulovski, but have taken on board six cattle, which, with a deck-load of lumber and cord-wood and our forty-seven dogs, makes it quite lively for one who has to go from one end of the vessel to the other. This is the second night since the embarkation of our dogs, and the whole interval has been filled with one prolonged howl that makes the nights especially something to be remembered to the end of one's existence. We expect to leave for St. Michael's in Alaska to-morrow morning, there to take on board two hundred tons of coal, which has already been shipped for our use by the Alaska Commercial Company's steamer *St. Paul;* but where it is to be put is a question that would puzzle the most experienced stevedore that ever stowed a cargo. About one hundred tons can be used to replenish the coal-bunkers in the hold, and the remainder must go on deck—but where? The cows are forward of the foremast, and the lumber and the dogs fill the intervening space from the foremast to the quarter-deck, while the rigging is all hung with salmon, which is drying for dog-food. Fortunately we need not anticipate much heavy weather inside of Behring Sea or the Arctic Ocean; and it will be only a short time comparatively before we will be compelled to seek winter quarters either upon Wrangel Land or the adjacent Siberian coast. Some such weather as we had upon our trip from San Francisco would make sad havoc with our deck-load.

The Fourth of July was a stormy day, and the vessel rolled and pitched considerably; the spirit of the occasion was manifested in the band of young and patriotic officers. We could not kill a fatted calf, for we had none to kill, but the fatted pig, Michael Angelo, furnished the ship's company with a pleasant repast of fresh meat that would have made him feel that he had not died in vain, had he known how he was appreciated after death. One of the officers opened a box that had been sent to him for the occasion by some lady friends, in which each officer was remembered by the bestowal of some toy or gift; and the merriment that followed the discovery of a baby rattle, a top or whip, was unbounded. The box itself was an especial source of amusement, in view of a label which suggested the nursery quite as thoroughly as did the toys which it contained. Dominick, the colored steward, though scarcely able to keep his feet under him, arose to the occasion, and produced a meal which would have done credit to a first-class restaurant on a firm foundation. After the cloth had been removed, Dr. Jones, the senior surgeon, read an appropriate address expressing his views of those who go down to the sea in ships, Arctic research, and the duty of patriotism. The Italian cook was induced to make some chocolate, which, being neither tea nor coffee, was appreciated as a pleasant change of diet. I overheard the conversation that led to the chocolate, and recorded it as a curiosity of international communication. Said the caterer of the mess: "You know chocolate?"

"Oh, yes; me know him well."

"How long it take to make it?"

"About so long, I guess"—(measuring off about eighteen inches of air between his two hands).

"No, I mean how long time?"

"Oh, yes," with a smile beaming with intelligence and evident delight at having caught the meaning exactly. "How long time? About two weeks, I guess."

"Confound it!" said the now exasperated caterer, "Haven't you any brains? I want to know if we can have chocolate for breakfast."

"Oh, yes, me make him quick now."

So we had our chocolate, and enjoyed it all the more when it was told how much patience and tact our caterer had exhibited in securing it.

The night of July 4th we had a succession of squalls, and one which passed a little to leeward of the ship that the officer of the deck said would have wrecked us if it had hit us fairly. He said he saw it coming, and that it flattened the waves down in its course so that it seemed to cut a furrow right through the sea, and that a cold gray light attended it that made everything look pale and sepulchral like the green light in the death scenes of some emotional plays. He had never felt so insignificant as when he saw that pass, and knew how utterly powerless he was to do anything in case the vessel had stood in its path. It did not, and therefore we live to tell the tale.

On the 9th of July we sighted Oonalaska's high mountains, and the next day passed within fifty miles of Umnak, and saw the peak of its snow-crested volcano, 5,000 feet high, burst through a cloud and tinged with the glory of the setting sun. It was a gorgeous spectacle, and one that will live long in the memory of all who saw it. It was a most perfect representation of Fusiyama, the sacred mountain of Japan, so familiar by its reproduction in all Japanese works of art. Near it we saw the smoke arising from one of the burning volcanoes of the Four Mountains. The following day, the 11th instant, we passed into Behring Sea through the so-called "172d pass," upon the 172d meridian, between Amoughta and Seguam islands, and found a smooth sea almost immediately. It was a pleasure to sail upon such water after so rough a passage, and we scarcely minded the fog that hung about us all the time. Indeed, we had but five days' fair weather since we left San Francisco.

Thursday, the 14th of July, we crossed the 180th meridian, and were in east longitude. Here is where the mariner takes up one day when sailing toward the west, or drops one if going east. As we return in a few days and re-cross the same meridian, we would have to make two changes in our calendar, but Lieutenant Berry concluded that we might as well retain our old reckoning. The only difference it made is that we found the religious people of Petropaulovski holding service on Saturday instead of Sunday, and we are constantly in doubt as to whether to-day is really to-day or to-morrow. And yet this constantly dropping and taking up a day every time we cross the 180th meridian, would make it exciting for us in case of wintering on Wrangel Land, as that meridian passes directly through the island; so that we would be constantly crossing and re-crossing it, involving ourselves and our journals in the most inextricable confusion. We could not go hunting and reach the hunting-grounds until the next day, no matter how short the time occupied in the journey, and, in returning, would always arrive the day before we started. No well-balanced mind could exist under such circumstances.

I am not at all sorry to have finished this letter, for while writing here in the ward-room of the *Rodgers* I have been a perfect martyr to those interminable pests of the Arctic —the mosquitoes. One would scarcely expect to meet them here, but here they are in such numbers as to make life a burden to the sojourners in these latitudes.

CHAPTER III.

PETROPAULOVSKI.

U. S. S. *Rodgers*, BEHRING SEA.
July 28*th*, 1881.

WERE it not that during the Crimean war the allied enemies of Russia saw fit to attempt the capture of the place, and thus gave it dignity that it would have been difficult otherwise to acquire, one would believe Petropaulovski to be of little importance in the world. But when in August, 1854, the combined fleets of England and France, consisting of six frigates, assembled before the town and landed a large force in its rear, they found it fortified and defended by a small but determined band of Russians and Cossacks, who, aided by topographical advantages and palpable errors on the part of their adversaries, defeated them most ignominiously with the loss of most of the English and French officers, and about one hundred and twenty men. On a hillside near the earthwork, where the engagement took place, is a cemetery about twenty feet square, within which are two mounds surmounted by wooden crosses, bearing inscriptions in the Russian language, which cover the remains of those who fell on both sides during the fight. The cemetery is surrounded by a neat paling fence, painted white, and is not lacking in picturesque effect, at the foot of the high, rugged hill, and flanked by the grass-grown ruins of the fort, and the powder magazine.

Petropaulovski is correctly pronounced with the accent on "paul," and gently sliding over the remaining syllables. It is situated in a valley between high hills, with wooded slopes on the sides least exposed to the prevailing winds. Its houses are small, and chiefly made of roughly hewn logs, the poorer ones thatched with straw. Many of the government buildings, the warehouses of the Russian Fur Company, and the dwellings of the principal citizens, are of boards imported from foreign ports, and neatly painted. There is but one street that could properly be so called, and that is but about thirty feet wide. The houses are apparently not arranged with any reference to the so-called street, but are erected wherever the convenience or whim of the builder suggested. There are two church buildings, the old and the new. The former a dilapidated but picturesque edifice of hewn logs, with many angles and projections, and surmounted by a green cupola, of curious design, somewhat oriental in its architecture. The new church is of boards, painted white, with a flight of broad, new stairs leading up to the front door. It is situated in a miniature park, through which trickles a mountain rivulet, whose banks are studded with tombstones, amid which, gloomy and peculiar, stands the black iron pillar commemorating the death of the Russian explorer, Vitus Behring, whose tomb is upon the island, about two hundred and fifty miles away, where his vessel was wrecked in the year 1741, and he subsequently died. In the same graveyard, on the opposite side of the church, is a tombstone of black marble inscribed in Russian characters, showing that it was erected to the memory of the officers and crew of a small Russian trading vessel, wrecked some time ago upon one of the Kurile islands, all on board perishing. The tombstone was sent out from Russia to be erected at the place of the disaster; but as it would probably never be seen there, it was thought better to give it the wide publicity of the grave-yard in Petropaulovski, which has about four hundred inhabitants, and one overland mail each year.

The new church was built and is kept in repair by the Russian Fur Company, which is really but another name for the Alaska Commercial Company, enabling them to enjoy the same privileges of the seal fisheries on Behring and Copper islands, under the Russian jurisdiction, as are accorded to them by the United States government upon the Aleutian islands. This church is occupied for services in summer only; and the smaller and more easily warmed old church accommodates the few who desire the comforts of religion in the long winter, when the building is entirely covered with snow, and is entered through a long passage way excavated through the drift. The services are conducted by a priest and two deacons, all of whom are occasionally to be seen about town, always dressed in long silken gowns which reach to their heels, and are belted at the waist with a band of the same material. A tall black felt hat is worn over long hair, and flowing beards adorn their faces. The priest wears around his neck a long golden chain, to which is attached a large golden crucifix, presented to the wearer by the late Emperor of Russia. Not very long ago the resident Archbishop of the Greek Church on the Pacific coast of the United States paid a visit to Petropaulovski, and, as Captain Hunter told me, had much difficulty in securing recognition from the inhabitants, because he did not wear long hair and beard, and discarded his churchly raiment when not engaged in conducting services.

There is only one store in town, but as there is no money

among the inhabitants, except the government officials, military and clerical, and the foreign residents, one store is at least sufficient. General sympathy would naturally be with the storekeeper, and the wonder be how he makes a living. But Mr. Mulawansky, the storekeeper, a native of Russian Poland, who speaks English and French with equal fluency as his native tongue, is an enterprising fur trader, and during the winter months makes several extended sledge journeys into the interior, thereby accumulating a large stock of the most valuable skins to be obtained ; as through long experience he has become one of the most expert judges of furs in the land. He sends all his trade to London for a market, and can never be prevailed to sell a single skin to a visitor.

"Why wouldn't you sell me that sea-otter skin for one hundred dollars? You say it will bring you only that in London, and by selling it now you would not have to wait so long for your money," said Lieutenant Berry.

"Because," said Mulawansky, "I want to retain your friendship. I would gladly do anything I can to aid you or to accommodate you in any way, and am always happy to entertain you to the extent of my ability. If, however, I were to sell you that skin, even for what it cost me, or a little more, when you took it to a furrier at home to be dressed and made up he would naturally ask where you got it and what you paid for it. He would then, inspired perhaps by jealousy, assert that it was not worth so much, and you would therefore think Mulawansky had cheated you. Then I would lose your friendship."

This seemed reasonable enough and an unanswerable argument, and the subject was not continued, especially as the Lieutenant was not anxious to become a purchaser, but asked merely for information.

Previous to settling in Petropaulovski, Mr. Mulawansky had led a very adventurous life among the Indians of the Pacific coast in British Columbia and Alaska, and many are the hair-breadth escapes that he has encountered among his warlike and treacherous customers. Several times he has been shot at, and he now bears two ugly gun-shot wounds, obtained at the hands of the Indians while living among them, one upon his left fore-arm and another upon his left leg. Resolution and courage, backed by a thorough knowledge of the ways of the savages, and the best means of conciliating them when necessary, have carried him through many adventures which he would not readily encounter again, since he has become accustomed to the comforts of a peaceful life with a wife and children growing up around him. He has amassed a large fortune in his business, and is liberal in his dealings with others. Indeed, without the assistance of such people as Mulawansky and Captain Hunter, the poorer citizens would find it hard to pull through the long winters when food is scarce, for, like most uncivilized people, the Kamtchadals are improvident, and make no provision for the season when game and fish are scarce.

The morning after our arrival, Lieutenant Berry and I, accompanied by Captain Hunter, called upon Mr. Sarabrenekoff, the Ispravnik, or Military Governor, who lives in a centrally-located house, one story high, of white painted boards and the customary red roof, put up at the expense of the government for the use of its representatives. It is quite a comfortable residence for that country, and is heated, as are all the larger houses, by an oven or "Peachka," as it is called, made of bricks, and containing arched flues to allow the heat to circulate throughout the structure. A wood fire is built within, and when the smoke has escaped through the chimney it is closed, and small apertures about three inches in diameter are opened into each room adjoining the peachka, through which the heat pours into the room. The bricks have by this time become thoroughly heated, and retain their caloric a long time, thus with very little fuel keeping the building at a pleasant temperature throughout the day. As the climate, even in the severest weather, is not colder than about twenty degrees below zero, unusual means would not be necessary for securing heat were it not that wood is scarce, and has to be brought from across Avatcha Bay, a distance of about twelve miles. We entered the Ispravnik's house by a vestibule, where we hung up our hats, and, without the formality of knocking, walked into the parlor, a pleasant room with painted floor and modern furniture, plain but comfortable. The governor's wife, a comely little woman, shortly afterward joined us, and, when shaking hands, expressed, I presume, her pleasure at meeting us, but this impression was derived rather from her smile than from what she said, of which I did not understand a word. She, however, passed around some "papyrosa," that is, Russian cigarettes, and, lighting one, seated herself for a comfortable smoke. Presently her husband entered, clad in a green, double-breasted military coat trimmed with red cord, with gilt shoulder-knots upon his shoulders and two rows of white-metal buttons down his breast. He evidently meant to be pleasant, though dignified and formal; but conversation was neither general nor brilliant. He, however, informed us that an earthquake had shaken the town about an hour before we called; but it must have been slight, as we had not noticed it upon the water. After a brief call, during which he renewed his assurances of assistance, we bade the Ispravnik and his pretty wife good day, and went to Captain Hunter's residence near by, where we had been invited to dine. We had a pleasant and bountiful meal, with fresh beef and vegetables grown in our host's own garden, and plenty of rich milk, which was especially gratifying.

We called later upon Mr. Mulawansky, where, as everywhere else in the town, we were regaled with tea made from a "Samowar," which is pronounced Samovar, the last syllable accented. Whenever you see the letter "w" in Russian you must call it "v." For instance, I found difficulty in explaining to some Russian officers, most of whom spoke at least a little English, and some quite well, what I meant by Wrangel Land until I pointed out the place on the map, when they exclaimed as with one voice, "Vrangel Island, yes." Why tea from a samowar should taste better than when made any other way I am at a loss to explain, and yet its universal use in Russia, a nation of tea-drinkers, would seem to confirm such an impression. The samowar is only a vessel wherein to boil the water of which the tea is made. It is an urn, usually of brass lined with white metal, and with a hollow cylinder passing vertically through the centre. Into this cylinder is put a quantity of burning charcoal, the space surrounding it being filled with water which is heated thereby. In order to create more draft for the burning charcoal, a chimney, which is also of brass, is put on over the cylinder, and after the gases have entirely escaped, the chimney is removed, and in its place is put a circular cover so made as to admit of a small China tea-pot resting upon it, in case it be desirable to keep it warm. Into the tea-pot is put the requisite amount of tea, and when the water is boiling hot a small quantity is drawn off upon the leaves in the pot, thus in a few minutes producing a strong essence of tea. I was cautioned against filling the tea-pot more than half full of water, as by so doing a large part of the aroma would be lost. It was also enjoined that the shorter the time required for steeping the leaves the more fragrant would be the tea. When the essence of tea is ready a small portion is placed into glass tumblers, and diluted, according to the taste of each guest, with water from the samowar. Great stress was laid upon the advantage of using tumblers instead of tea-cups, as it was thus easier for the lady of the house to gauge the exact amount of tea essence required for each person. If the tea in the tea-pot is to be kept warm for others, or to replenish the glasses of the guests, it is allowed to rest upon the circular holder over the cylinder of the samowar, but the choicest beverage is that served without submitting the tea-pot to other heat than is derived from the hot water. It may have been an overwrought imagination that inspired the thought, but it seemed to me that I never drank such delicious tea as was everywhere tendered me from the samowars of the hospitable people of Petropaulovski. Before the *Rodgers* left, my newly acquired friend, Mr. Mulawansky, presented me with one of the magic urns, and I hope to put it to good use when we reach our winter quarters on Wrangel Land.

This curious little town presents one strange feature in being a community of between four and five hundred people who can get along pleasantly without lawyers and without courts of justice. I was told by an old resident, who is quite familiar with life in more civilized portions of the globe, that during the past eighteen years not a single crime has been developed in this neighborhood that required magisterial interference. There are no police there except the few Cossacks, who are distinguished from the civilians by red cording around the edge of their caps. On landing at the beach, where a miniature plank dock leads from the deck of a sunken hulk that serves as a wharf to the shore, I had noticed a small box, large enough to hold a man erect, built against the wall of a warehouse, locked and bearing the seal of the imperial government. I wondered at the time for what purpose it was intended, but did not find out until two or three nights afterward, when, returning from an entertainment in town, I was startled by a salute in a deep bass voice which seemed in the darkness to have come out of the bowels of the earth, but which to my relief I found emerged through the tawny beard of a Cossack who stood within the sentry box guarding the town against surprise by another invasion of hostile fleets. The structure had looked to me like a sentry box, but I could not realize the necessity for sentinels here upon the outskirts of civilization.

I said I was returning to the ship from an entertainment, and I will endeavor to describe the fête, as not without interest in showing how the people amuse themselves in such a place as Petropaulovski. There are a few people residing here who are not natives, but have acquired education and cultivation in the customs of polite society in other parts of the world. They have been drawn here chiefly by the attraction of profitable business in the fur trade, and some have taken root by marrying into the native or the Russian element. Among these are, beside Captain Hunter and Mr. Mulawansky, Captain Lugebil, agent of the Alaska Commercial Company; Mr. Sandylane and Dr. Federer, the schoolmaster; for in rear of the new church edifice is a small school-house, built and maintained by the Russo-American Fur Company. Captain Sandman, of the steamer *Alexander*, was also temporarily residing in town, with his wife and family, and his bluff, hearty good nature proved an attractive feature of every entertainment. The people assemble in the early evening at the house to which they are invited, and with the giddy excitement of four large steamers in the harbor, there was a social gathering every night while we were in port. The officers of all the other vessels were nearly all Russians, and perfectly at home in society where I could only show my civilization by smiling and accepting every thing that was offered in the way of eating and drinking. I won a high place in the esteem of my hostess on several occasions by the hearty manner with which I devoured raw herring and pickled salmon. Nothing inspires your Russian entertainer with greater respect than the exhibition of unusual powers of digestion and perfect readiness to partake of raw fish, radishes, milk, pickled salmon, tea, brown bread and caviar, at a moment's notice. I did not know half the time what I was asked to eat, but I did not intend to show my ignorance by inquiring, or any lack of interest by declining. Most of the fare was indeed delicious, and especially so to one just from the monotonous diet of canned meats and vegetables on ship-board. In nearly every house, too, I found some one who spoke English, and could always express my ideas when necessary. Lieutenant Berry and I attended a reception and ball at Captain Lugebil's residence on Friday night. The captain is a Russian by birth, but became a citizen of the United States by the transfer of Alaska. He was in the employ of the Alaska Commercial Company for a long time, and went to Petropaulovski to represent the company's interests there. As he felt that he could not be a good citizen without adopting some line of politics, he has taken sides with the Democrats, and, together with Captain Hunter, a former resident of Baltimore, who is also a Democrat, mourns the defeat of General Hancock at the last election. Captain Hunter has not visited his native land for twenty-three years. He speaks the Russian language fluently, is married to a Russian lady, and has an interesting family of children, none of whom speak English. Upon his parlor walls, as well as in Captain Lugebil's house, hangs a photographic likeness of the late President Andrew Johnson, who probably never knew that even in a little Kamtchadal town, upon the borders of the Arctic world, were those who recognized and admired his genius. Captain Lugebil's house, which was erected by the company he represents, is the most civilized and pretentious dwelling in town, even more so than the new one of the Ispravnik, which that functionary will occupy when his deputy comes out next spring; for arrangements have already been made for enhancing the importance of the place by increasing the government detail there, and making it also a military post. This will be a good thing for the town by bringing more government money into circulation.

As we passed through the churchyard on the evening of Captain Lugebil's reception, our ears were greeted by the cheerful strains of music and the tripping of merry feet to the accompaniment of the " Babies on the Block," played with great spirit upon a large parlor organ by our gray-haired host, who exerted himself to the utmost to promote the cheerfulness of his guests. When he wearied of playing, for no matter how devoted he might be he was only mortal, there needed to be no cessation of dancing, for the accompaniment was immediately taken up by a hand-organ, vigorously ground by a volunteer from among the guests, which merely substituted "What Kind of Slippers do the Angels Wear?" and, with organized relays of grinders, could keep it up indefinitely. The social spirit of the worthy old captain could not be restrained even when relieved from the responsibility of acting as orchestra, but, rushing to the crank of the hand-organ, he stirred the dancers up to a livelier measure, and encouraged them to greater enthusiasm by himself dancing up and down with extraordinary vigor as he industriously plied the handle of the groaning instrument. Among the guests were several of the officers of the Russian man-of-war, who were ubiquitous and exceedingly friendly. They were in uniform; and it is needless to say were very popular, especially among the ladies. The female society, without which all balls are "flat, stale, and unprofitable," consisted of Mrs. Lugebil, her three handsome daughters—who have experienced the refining influences of San Francisco society; Mrs. Captain Sandman, who has enjoyed the same privilege; Mrs. Mulawansky, Mrs. Sarabrenekoff, and several young ladies whose cards I have mislaid, and whose names I am sure could never be recorded with the limited supply of consonants in the English alphabet. They were all good natured and anxious to entertain, but, in the absence of a general means of communication, conversation at times flagged. But then there was the never-failing source of amusement—dancing; and some one always on the floor, or ready to accept an invitation. I should not omit to mention that the table that supported the hand-organ was spread, and often replenished during the evening, with cold meats, raw and pickled herring and salmon, beets, cheese, black and white bread, fresh butter, caviar, and other delicacies. There was also a liberal supply of light California wines, whiskey, bottled Milwaukee beer, and home-made small beer—somewhat tart and spicy, and very agreeable to the taste. Cigars and Russian cigarettes of fine Turkish tobacco abounded, and ladies and gentlemen all smoked with the most comfortable freedom. Captain Lugebil, who speaks English perfectly, insisted upon our regaling ourselves at pleasure, and himself set the example. The Russians are among the friendliest of people. If ever one raised his eyes to glance about the room, glasses must be clinked all around; and on meeting and parting you are expected to shake hands with every one present, even though it be a dozen times a day. Lieutenant Berry and I had to depart early, but the festivities were kept up until about two o'clock in the morning.

The next evening a ball was given on shore by some of the officers of the *Strelock*, with whom we have established the most friendly relations, and several of the officers of the *Rodgers* accepted the cordial general invitation extended to us, and indulged in a merry-making such as they never before witnessed. A number of the young ladies of Petropaulovski society lent the charm of their presence to the occasion, and the countenance of many of the older dames was not wanting. Unfortunately, my duties required my attention on board the vessel, where I was engaged in writing at half-past three o'clock, when the revellers returned. It was unnecessary for me to ask if they had enjoyed themselves. That fact was sufficiently apparent in the moistened locks and wilted collars of the dancers. The fun had been fast and furious, and though many of the figures of the dance were new and most difficult of execution, they had not faltered in the attempt. Indeed during the latter part of the evening nothing but "ground and lofty tumbling" would answer, and even the staid and dignified members of the search expedition did not hesitate to follow the example of a pious-looking lieutenant of the Russian frigate, who exhausted his English in exclaiming, "God save the Queen," turned two somersaults in the middle of the floor, and drank to "Russia and America" amid loud shouts of applause and the clinking of many glasses.

Although we arrived at Petropaulovski in a drizzling rain, which continued for a day or two afterward, such is not the usual climate of the harbor. Indeed Captain Hunter told me that this was the first rain they had been blest with for more than a month, and prayers had been offered up in the church for rain. The last two days of our stay were delightful, or would have been were it not for the heat and the mosquitoes. We had the pleasure of seeing the volcanoes that surround the bay in all their grandeur. Through a gap in the hills to the north of the town rose the snow-clad peaks of Korianski, Avatcha, and Koselska, the first named eleven thousand five hundred feet high, the second over nine thousand, and most always in action, while the last has attained the no mean altitude of five thousand three hundred feet. About thirty miles to the southward stands Wiluchinski, its crest over seven thousand feet above the level of the sea. It not only serves to add interest to the landscape, but is said to be a most perfect barometer, and as such is constantly watched by the residents of Petropaulovski. When its entire outline is clearly cut against the sky, it is an indication that the following day will bring fair weather, and the approach of storms or foggy weather is foretold by clouds that hide the peak merely, or conceal the entire mountain from view. These peaks are never devoid of snow, although the soil in the valleys is susceptible of a high state of cultivation, and is very fertile. The people, however, have no ambition to become farmers, even though the prospect of good crops is so flattering. Their chief dependence for food is upon fish, which abound in the waters of the harbor and the bay. During the season, a net cast anywhere near the town, and at any time of the day, can be hauled in full of salmon, tom-cod, smelt, bass, and herring. Large quantities of salmon are dried during the summer months for food for the people and their dogs, and when thus prepared are called "yukal." A fish and a half of the average size are counted as a day's ration for each dog when working. Before being hung up to dry they are cleaned and salted, but later in the season vast quantities are buried in the ground and covered over without cleaning, to be used when the prepared food is exhausted. It thus becomes tainted, but, as with the Esquimaux, the bad smell and taste is not objectionable to a hungry Kamtchadal stomach. Along the shores of the harbor, as well as upon the neighboring bay, could be seen numbers of picturesque drying-sheds, thatched with straw, the sides open to the wind, and sunburnt men, women, and children salting and hanging the fish beneath the shelter. Often considerable annoyance is occasioned by the onslaughts of blue-bottle flies, which deposit their larvæ in the fish, and after that they soon become food for worms.

The pasturage for cows, horses, and sheep is found upon the neighboring hillsides and in the streets of the village, and consequently an ordinance of the town prohibits dogs to run at large on pain of death, as they worry the cattle and kill the sheep. They are therefore kept chained up in the vicinity of the town, but far enough away to prevent their constant howling disturbing the repose of their owners at night. Horned cattle and horses were seen everywhere about the village; but some time before our advent a dog got loose and drove a flock of sheep belonging to Mr. Mulawansky to the mountains, where, by this time, he says, they have become wild, and can only be captured by shooting them.

Bears are numerous in the neighboring mountains, and have been known to approach the village during the winter and destroy the cattle in the very streets. The skin of the bear has an excellent quality of fur during the winter. It is of a light brown color, and available for making rugs, but has no commercial value. It is a singular phenomenon that, together with all the wild animals of the Arctic regions, the dogs, horses, and cows of this country have, during the winter, a heavy coating of woolly fur under the hair that covers their bodies, as an additional protection against the rigors of the climate.

Since reaching the northern waters, Drs. Jones and Castillo have been very active in securing "specimens," for scientific analysis and classification, from sea and land. The drag net is nearly always astern, and the dredge was used in Petropaulovski harbor with "valuable results," as they informed me; but my unpractised eye could only discover a quantity of black mud with a squirming mass of hideous insects. Several birds were secured and suffered martyrdom in the cause of science at the hands of the medical men, who preserved the skins and bones for "setting up," as they say when they mean stuffing. One or two of these birds were probably rare, and undoubtedly beautiful. Day after day, Dr. Jones,

Mr. de Tracie, the ship's carpenter, with Mr. Bulger, chief engineer of the *Alexander*, who is well acquainted with the country, trudged over the neighboring hills in search of something to kill and skin, and were sometimes rewarded with "valuable specimens." Dr. Castillo, my room mate, is an inveterate "bug hunter," and has lost all consideration for insects of every kind except as entomological specimens. His most familiar attitude is with one eye screwed up and the other gazing through the tube of a microscope in search of "animal life," as he says, in the phosphorescent sea water. In this way he has unconsciously contracted a very extraordinary expression—similar to that of a person addicted to the use of a single eye glass. In making inquiry concerning the sanitary statistics of Petropaulovski, Dr. Jones found that the prevailing ailments were of a scrofulous nature, resulting from disease said to have been introduced by the sailors of La Perouse's vessel when he visited this coast in the latter part of the eighteenth century. There are also several cases of leprosy in town, probably from the same cause. The government caused to be erected some time ago a hospital for the treatment of the diseases peculiar to the locality, and sent a physician, who is a political exile, to take charge of it. But the hospital is at present empty, and the surgeon has gone upon a trip to the lower part of the peninsula of Kamtchatka. This is not owing to any diminution of the disease, but rather to the laxity with which government affairs are administered at such great distances from the throne.

The second day after our arrival Lieutenant Berry sent two boats across Avatcha Bay in charge of Mr. Putnam, the senior watch officer, to bring back some dogs and dried fish from a settlement about twelve miles distant, and

Chief Engineer Zane and Dr. Castillo went along to obtain an idea of roughing it in the northern "bush." They were accompanied by the native to whom most of the dogs belonged, who is said to be a fine hunter and one of the richest and most enterprising citizens of the country. When they were about to start, Mr. Mulawansky sent them a mosquito net, which had naturally been omitted from the outfit of the boats, and as they would have to camp out over night he knew they would find it useful. It was fortunate for them that he had been so thoughtful, otherwise they would have been severely tormented, and, as it was, were not altogether exempt from the attacks of the little pests. Even Dr. Castillo lost his patience, and slaughtered "interesting specimens" without mercy. A few of the natives from the village near by gathered around them and performed many friendly offices, such as bringing wood and water for the camp, and giving the strangers plenty of nice fresh milk. In return, our people shared their food with the simple-hearted Kamtchadals, and established relations of friendship with them. They were not sorry, however, to return to the ship, and bade adieu to their new friends and the mosquitoes without a tear. They brought twenty-one dogs back with them, and it appears to be a very fine collection, perhaps not the best, but good, serviceable young dogs. Altogether we secured forty-seven full-grown dogs and several puppies, which will be available for the teams next spring. The price of a dog was established at fifteen roubles, that is, seven dollars and a half, but we bought two fine animals the night before we left Petropaulovski for twenty roubles (five dollars apiece). Lieutenant Berry, Dr. Castillo and I went to the nearest beach with the man who offered them for sale, to see how they would work in harness. It was amusing to see the almost frantic anxiety of the animals to be harnessed when they saw the sled brought out, and heard the rattle of the harness-chains. Fletcher, the owner, drove them without much trouble, and they dragged him with great speed over the rank grass and weeds. Then he invited Lieutenant Berry to get on and ride, but, before he got fairly into the seat, the dogs broke away from Fletcher, and dashed at full speed down the sand spit. I expected they would keep on without stopping until they got to the town or maybe the next village; but before long some misunderstanding arose between two of the dogs, and they stopped to fight it out, when Fletcher caught them again and brought them back. It was amusing to hear this man Fletcher talk. He is an Englishman, born in London, where his father at one time kept an ale house; but he has lived in Kamtchatka so long that he speaks his native tongue very imperfectly, and with the broken accent peculiar to the coast where he now lives. His father, now very old and feeble, also lives in Petropaulovski.

There is very little circulating medium in this country. The standard of exchange is the "rouble" and the "coppick," valued in round numbers at fifty cents and half a cent respectively. Fletcher says that times are hard now; he don't make any money though he works hard. He says he used to make sometimes two hundred roubles a day. I think, however, he was exaggerating the truth somewhat in order to impress us with the value of his acquaintance, for I don't believe he would make as much as that now in ten years. Fresh salmon sell for two coppicks (one cent) each, and herring for one coppick. There is not a very lively fortune in that market I am sure.

At Petropaulovski we secured about twenty-five "Kuklankers," which are coats of reindeer skin with a hood to cover the head, the whole garment being almost identical with the "Koolitar" of the Esquimaux, but of finer workmanship, and altogether more ornamental. They cost from sixteen to forty roubles each, but will prove an inestimable blessing during the approaching winter. We also obtained a quantity of fur boots, stockings, and gloves, which, with what we may find among the natives further north, will comprise a complete outfit for the entire crew. In compliance with written instructions from their principals, the Alaska Commercial Company, Captain Lugebil and Captain Sandman refused any remuneration for what they supplied our vessel, hay for the cattle, and several cords of woods for kindling purposes, and offered anything in their stores.

We got under way at five o'clock of the afternoon of the 24th instant, and steamed out into the bay, the vessels in the harbor dipping their flags as a parting salute, and Wiluchinski smiling his assurance of fair weather. Notwithstanding his promise, however, we found the usual fog awaiting us at the entrance of the bay; but as we had our bearings and knew our course it made little difference other than depriving us of a fine view of the mountains we had anticipated enjoying as we steamed up the coast. One circumstance annoyed rather than surprised us ever since leaving San Francisco, and that is the remarkable prevalence of head winds. From San Francisco to Petropaulovski we had north-west winds most all the time, and from Petropaulovski to St. Michael nothing but north-easterly winds. But then I suppose it was about time it should change.

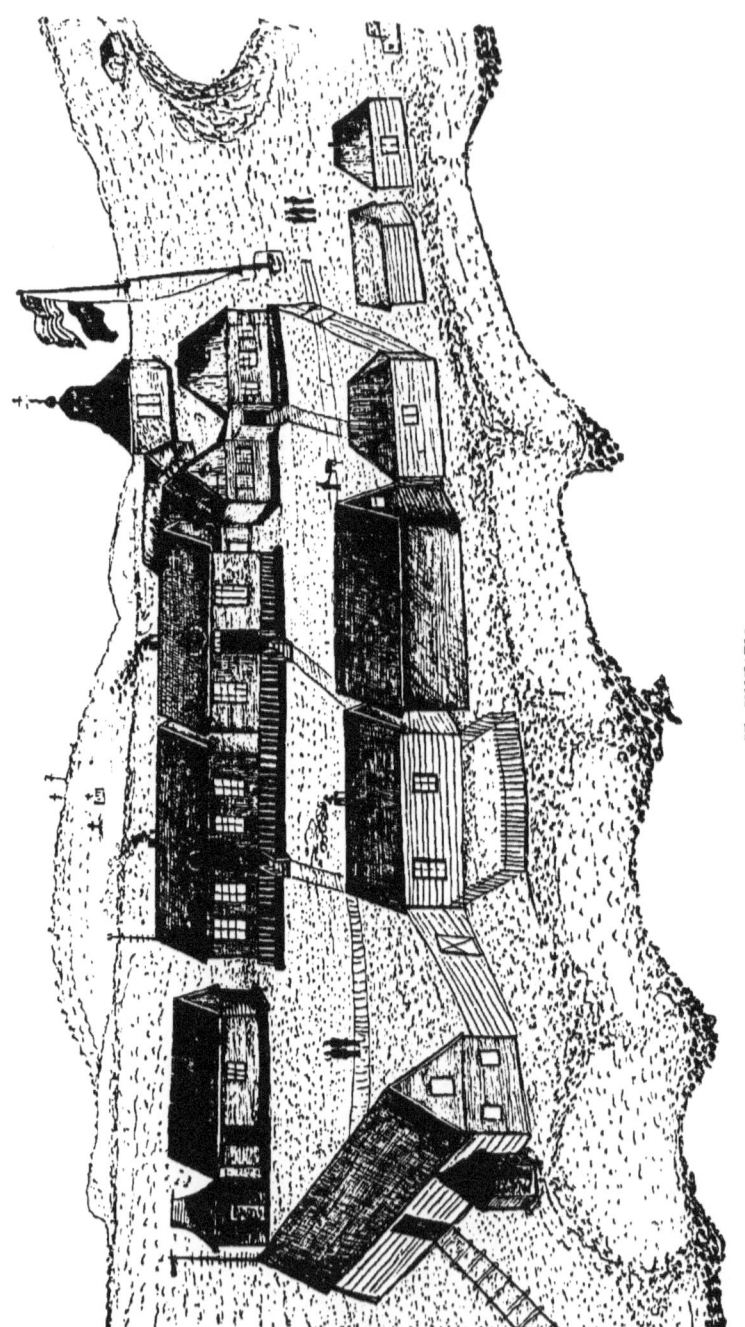

ST. MICHAELS.
From an Esquimaux drawing.

CHAPTER IV.

ST. MICHAEL'S.

U. S. S. *Rodgers*, ST. MICHAEL'S, ALASKA TER.,
August 10*th*, 1881.

IT was blowing a gale from nearly the direction of our course, and we were anxiously looking for land when we sighted Stuart Island, in Norton Sound, on the afternoon of August 3d. We would have seen the island sooner had it not been for the mist that hung over the horizon to windward, and made the navigation of poorly surveyed waters, in search of an unfrequented harbor, a dangerous task. The sea was running very high when we came to anchor, at dark, under the shelter of Stuart Island, to wait for daylight to aid us. About five o'clock the following morning we got under way, and steamed slowly on our course in a dismal rain and fog. The lead was kept going constantly, the quartermaster calling in a dreary, monotonous voice the depth of water found at each cast of the lead. Again we were compelled to drop anchor on account of shallow water and the concealment of the few known landmarks under the mist. About eleven o'clock the fog lifted a little, and we could see the little settlement of St. Michael's, about seven miles distant, and shortly afterward dropped anchor beyond the point of land that forms a shelter for the harbor, a few antiquated iron guns bellowing forth a salute. Soon a boat was descried putting off from the beach near the fort; and in a little while Mr. Lorenz, agent of the Alaska Commercial Company, and Sergeant Leavitt, United States signal observer, came on board to welcome us and receive the mail matter we had brought for them from San Francisco.

They informed us that the revenue cutter *Thomas Corwin* had been here twice, and had left for the Arctic on the 9th of July, since which time they had not heard from her. They also gave the very welcome intelligence that last winter had been unprecedentedly mild, and the present was an unusually open season. The whaling fleet had been exceedingly successful, and already several vessels had returned to the United States with full cargoes. The *Corwin*, before her first visit here, had landed a sledge party on the Siberian coast, about Plover Bay, they believed, to investigate the rumor that came through the natives there that the wreck of a vessel had drifted ashore on the northern coast, about the vicinity of Koliutchin Bay. In the mean time they had spent five days at St. Lawrence Island collecting further information and relics concerning the fatal famine on that island during the winter of 1879–80. A large number of skeletons were taken on board the *Corwin*, to be deposited in the Smithsonian Institute. This was the occasion of quite an interesting scene on board that vessel. Mr. Nelson, the previous signal observer at St. Michael's, had obtained permission to accompany the *Corwin* in her present cruise, and had taken with him, as an interpreter, a native of the tribe of Esquimaux whose village is within a quarter of a mile of Fort St. Michael's. The Esquimaux are a very superstitious people, as your correspondent has had occasion to observe in other parts of the Arctic world, and nothing, in their belief, will produce such universal misery as to disturb the mortal remains of any of their nation who have died. When, therefore, this poor savage saw the scientists of the *Corwin* coming on board the vessel with their arms filled with the bones of the victims of the famine on St. Lawrence Island, he was beside himself with horror, and endeavored to kill himself by plunging a knife into his heart. Fortunately his hand was arrested by some bystanders before he had inflicted mortal injury upon himself. This, however, did not prevent a second attempt at suicide, which he made by jumping into the sea. Again he was rescued, and, for the time being, his mind averted from *felo de se*, but it is highly probable that he will make another and more successful effort when he returns to his former home. Upon returning to the Siberian coast to pick up their sledging party, the *Corwin* learned that they had visited the scene of the wreck, and from a careful inspection it was believed to have belonged to the lost whaler *Vigilant*. Among the *débris* were portions of a forecastle, and several articles within it marked with a letter "V." My informants believed there was nothing found to indicate the escape of the crew, and the supposition was that the ship had been crushed in the ice, and all on board had perished.

The finding of these relics seems to indicate that the natives of the northern coast of Siberia are observant, and that the wind or currents have, at times at least, a tendency to make that coast a depository of wrecks in that portion of the Polar Sea; in which event news would soon be obtained of disaster to the expeditionary vessel *Jeannette*. Should, therefore, nothing be heard of her through the sea-coast Tchouktchis, there remains a gratifying presumption of her safety and probable harborage upon Wrangel Land.

Mr. Lorenz told us that two hundred tons of coal had come for us by the *St. Paul,* and was now on the beach near his warehouses; but as we could not get within about three-quarters of a mile of the wharf, and the coal had to be towed out in a lighter that could carry but about ten tons, we had little prospect of getting away within a week or ten days. This delay was exceedingly galling after hearing of the open season further north, but every one set to work with the determination of hastening our departure as much as possible. All hands were called at four o'clock in the morning, and work continued daily until about eight o'clock. In the meantime, Mr. Lorenz set about the task of supplying the deficiency in fur clothing. Mr. Grenfield, the agent of the Western Fur Trading Company, also furnished what clothing he could spare, and to-morrow when we leave this place we will be pretty well supplied with the necessary Arctic outfit.

I went ashore with Mr. Lorenz in his boat with a crew of natives, and had a very pleasant visit; while Mr. Stoney and Mr. Hunt, in two of the ship's boats, spent several hours in sounding the harbor for a closer anchorage to the settlement. They succeeded in finding a channel and anchorage in three and a quarter fathoms of water, about a quarter of a mile nearer the coal deposit; but as the harbor is open to the north-east, a heavy blow from that direction would produce a sea that would compel us to get up steam and move out to deeper water. In fact, yesterday afternoon we were treated to a storm from that quarter, which at low tide bumped us against the soft muddy bottom, and fires were quickly made under the boilers; but before steam could be made the sea abated, and by the time of high water we were again floating comfortably, though very close to the bottom. Lieutenant Berry, however, ordered the fires under the boilers to be banked during the remainder of our stay here, so that we can run from danger at a moment's warning.

It was indeed a surprise as well as a pleasure to find the residence of Mr. Lorenz, within the enclosure, not only comfortable but elegant, and to see everywhere evidences of the refining influences of female society. Seated in a handsomely furnished parlor, I found Mrs. Lorenz, a young and pretty woman, who has dared the severity of the north, and has passed a winter in a higher latitude than any other woman from the temperate zone. She is a native of the State of Maine, and came here with her husband last year. Her husband is a Russian, from Odessa, who has been the agent of the Alaska Commercial Company here for the past eight years. Last year he took a holiday, and went to the United States, where he visited a friend in Maine. There it was that he lost his heart and found a partner for life. His wife is a cultivated and intelligent lady, and a small, but well selected library gave token of refined taste in literature. One would naturally be surprised, here, beyond the limit of civilization, to find a house with walls covered with Morris paper, and carpet and chairs in keeping with that style of decoration, so that I scarcely felt at ease there in my coarse sailor garb. The welcome I received was cordial, notwithstanding; and it was not difficult to understand that visitors from lower latitudes, brimful of later news, would be welcome guests. I cannot say that it was disagreeable to me, either, to have conversation invaded by the merry tones of two canary birds, who poured forth their welcome from their gilded cages with a heartiness that was not in the least forced. Pots of flowers in bloom filled the windows of the dwelling, and among them were roses and camellias, together with other plants, that brought me nearer home than I had felt myself to be since leaving San Francisco.

The fort of St. Michael's, as it is called, is an enclosure of dwellings and warehouses, the interstices filled with a high wooden fence that was originally erected as a protection against the assaults of hostile Indians. The fence of the present day is, however, maintained rather as a shelter against the winds than to guard against savages. The neighboring tribes are mild and peaceful, unless under the influence of liquor, which they still procure at exorbitant prices in exchange for furs and whalebone from whaling vessels and traders in violation of the existing laws, which are so strict that the agents of the American trading companies cannot even bring any kinds of liquors, wines or beer here for their own use. Mr. Lorenz says that, while he cannot land beer for his table or cartridges for breech-loading guns for his own use, he can buy liquor or cartridges from the natives at any time. He would have to pay heavy prices, however. I asked him how this illegal traffic could be carried on while a government vessel, sent here to prevent it, was constantly cruising in Behring Sea and adjacent waters. He replied, that it appeared to him as if the cruisers were maintained as much for the purpose of collecting scientific specimens for the Smithsonian Institute as for anything else. He also says that the quality of liquor brought by the whalers and traders was the cheapest and vilest stuff that can be procured; and that in order to make it strong enough to gratify the savage palate, after it has been watered sufficiently to gratify the cupidity of the poachers, it is doctored with cayenne pepper, tobacco juice, and other powerful ingredients, until the wonder is that those who drink it are not killed at once. Its ultimate effect can easily be predicted.

Several of the buildings within the enclosure are quite old, having been erected by the Russians when the post was first established, nearly half a century ago. They were all built of drift-wood logs, roughly tongued and grooved into each other, and calked on the outside and inside. The result is an exceedingly strong and comfortable structure, impervious to the wind. Loose dirt is piled up around the outside of each building to the height of about three feet, and boarded over to protect it from the rains. This keeps the wind from entering beneath the flooring, and adds greatly to the comfort of the occupants. Wood alone is used for fuel, and an abundant supply for that purpose is found upon the neighboring coast, constantly drifted down from the interior of Alaska by the currents of the great rivers emptying into Behring Sea. Outside of the enclosure is a neat little church of the Greek faith, also of logs, and surmounted by a red painted cupola and wooden cross. Behind the kitchen is a small kitchen-garden, where is raised, without much trouble, a goodly supply of radishes, lettuce and turnips, the excellent quality of which I can heartily affirm. This is the last place in the direction of our wanderings where the comforts of a Russian bath can be secured, and through the courtesy of the kind-hearted agent all of the ship's company who desired it were enabled to enjoy the blessed privilege. He gave me a receipt, however, for a Russian bath which may prove a real blessing in the far north. It is as follows: Take a quantity of stones, and erect an oven-like structure, within which make a fire of drift-wood. When thoroughly heated put up a tent over the stones, and close all apertures as much as possible. Go inside, remove your clothing, and throw water upon the stones until steam is generated, which will soon fill the tent like a laundry on Monday morning. Continue this application until perspiration is induced to the necessary degree, and finish the process with a sponge and tub of water, followed by brisk friction with coarse towels. The result will be a blissful feeling, that must be experienced to be appreciated. This bath is practicable in any climate.

Adjoining Mr. Lorenz's residence is the dwelling occupied by Mr. Leavitt, the signal officer, and Mr. Newman, Mr. Lorenz's assistant. Their quarters are both commodious and comfortable. The life of a signal observer in these latitudes is necessarily exceedingly monotonous, but Mr. Leavitt has set himself the entertaining and exciting task of acquiring the Russian language, under the guidance of Mr. Lorenz. The difficulties to be surmounted in this undertaking will perhaps furnish him with all the mental occupation he desires, and may in a measure compensate him for his isolation from the usual comforts of ordinary civilization. The rules of the service require him to record synchronous observations with all the other signal posts, and thus he is compelled to investigate the state of the wind and weather at 1:20 A.M.; an exhilarating duty in an Arctic winter, but one he will scarcely be envied. His predecessor was an indefatigable naturalist, and sent to the Smithsonian Institute not only hundreds, but thousands of specimens of the flora and fauna of this interesting locality.

The only other white men at the post are a tall white-haired and white mustached Russian workman, and a gray-haired individual, who resides in the Esquimaux

HUNTING SCENE.
From an Esquimaux drawing.

village near by, and is the Arctic representative of the "squaw man" of the American frontier. Both have native wives, and a colony of half-breed children to inherit their poverty.

I noticed that the natives were apparently both of Esquimaux and Indian extraction. I was greatly pleased to see such perfect similarity of features and general appearance between the natives of this section and the Esquimaux of the Eastern coast of America. I had been told that these people were all Indians, and spoke an entirely different language from the Cumberland Inlet and central tribes, and that even the people from a few miles further north could not talk with them. I had also heard entirely different names for familiar objects in nature, such as the seal, whale, walrus, reindeer, etc., and the examples given as the names used by the natives of this coast. My surprise and pleasure may be imagined, then, when, after being with these people for several days and only communicating with them through an interpreter, I asked one of the men if he understood the Inuit language, and saw his look of surprise, and heard his quick reply "Armelar" (yes). We then opened quite a lively conversation, and found less difficulty in understanding and being understood than with many of those whom I met in Hudson Bay and the vicinity of King William's Land. Some words were identical in both sections, and the similarity of all was quite sufficient to be readily understood. Since then I have talked with many of them who had never heard white men speak their language, and I was not surprised when one of the interpreters told me one of them had just asked him if I was a Kavearamute, that is, an Esquimaux of one of the more northerly tribes.

Those of the people who lived near the post I found to have acquired many habits of civilization, living in rudely made houses rather than in tents, and cooking food after our own fashion. Indeed, the cook of Mr. Lorenz, the agent of the company, was an Esquimaux named Joe, who not only was an excellent chef, but quite an artist with the pencil. At my request he made a few sketches of native life, which he was particularly anxious should be given to the world; and I insert them here.

Several of the officers accompanied Mr. Lorenz to the "Kashine" in the Esquimaux village to see a native dance, which was procured by the inducement of a sack of flour. The "Kashine" is a sort of town-hall for the use of the male members of the tribe. It is built almost entirely underground, and with a roof covered deeply with earth. It is lighted through a skylight in the roof, and entered by a passage-way and an opening which can only be passed by crawling on hands and knees. It is constructed of logs of drift-wood, and the dirt roof supported by ingenious interweaving and without columns. Mr. Lorenz told me of one he had seen similarly constructed, fifty feet square, and the roof sustained without the support of columns. In the centre of the room is a deep pit, where in winter a fire is built to heat the building, after which it is closed, and the heat retained for an entire day. In this building the men live most all the time. Here they sleep and eat, and they seldom rest in the bosom of their families. They have little of the home feeling or parental attachment, and until lately used to get rid of surplus babies by wrapping them up and leaving them on the moors while still living, to become food for foxes and wolves.

When we entered the "Kashine" we saw a few of the

men sitting stretched asleep upon a shelf, about eighteen inches wide and four feet high, which extends all around the room against the wall. One young man prepared himself for the dance, by stripping off all his clothing except his trousers and putting on a pair of reindeer mittens. Three old men perched upon the shelf, and armed

THE TRAPPER.
From an Esquimaux drawing.

with drums made of thin skin stretched over hoops, and beaten with a stick, kept up a rhythmic measure, at the same time singing a dismal chant in unison and without words. The nearly naked youth leaped across the pit in the middle of the room, and commenced a series of gyrations in time to the music, straining his muscles to their fullest tension, and throwing himself into attitudes of the chase and battle. Meanwhile he kept shouting as if wrought to the highest pitch of excitement; but soon paused, as the exertion was too great to be continued for any length of time. When rested he recommenced, and was shortly joined by several children and another young man. The children were in full evening costume, that is, had on nothing but their mittens. The dance had more of the character of Indian performances than any I had ever previously seen among the Esquimaux. The entertainment was resumed after intervals of rest, and lasted about half an hour, when the reward of meal was brought in and portioned out to the participants. None of the women joined in the dance or mingled their voices with the orchestra, but several were interested spectators, a sort of Esquimaux wall-flower at the ball.

The men are good watermen, and use a skin kyack similar to that of the eastern Esquimaux, but broader and deeper, though not so long. Some are made with two and even three holes for rowers, who use a single-bladed paddle with great dexterity. They are said to be good sea-boats, and able to ride out a very strong gale without danger to the occupant.

Several of the officers went upon a hunting excursion while here, and shot a large number of ducks, snipe, and partridges. Dr. Castillo added largely to his ornithological collection, and Dr. Jones succeeded in securing some fine photographic views of people and places.

The *Rodgers* received her last load of coal this afternoon, and will sail to-night or early to-morrow morning. The entire amount of coal here was not taken aboard, because, in order to receive it, it would be necessary to

ST. MICHAEL'S.

throw overboard the cattle, the dogs, or the deck-load of lumber; but as none of them could well be spared the coaling was stopped when the bunkers and deck were filled to their utmost capacity.

Messrs. Lorenz and Leavitt, as well as Mr. Neuman and Mr. Grenfield, have done everything possible to make our visit an agreeable one, and to provide for our future comfort. Our return will be looked forward to as a source of pleasure, not only to these good people but to ourselves as well.

PARROT-BILL GULLS.
From an Esquimaux drawing.

CHAPTER V.

IN ST. LAWRENCE BAY.

On Board U. S. S. *Rodgers*,
St. Lawrence Bay, Siberia,
August 18*th*, 1881.

The sail from Plover Bay to this anchorage was about the pleasantest and the briefest trip the *Rodgers* has yet made. It was blowing hard when we weighed anchor yesterday morning, but we felt there was no time to be lost if we meant to accomplish anything in the Arctic this season. Already we had been delayed most annoyingly, and, though the weather bid fair to be boisterous, Captain Berry determined to start. As soon as we reached the open sea, after leaving Plover Bay, we noticed the fog was rising, and soon the mists rolled away from the mountains along the coast line and revealed a most gloriously picturesque country. The sun now broke through the clouds, and our good ship bowled along nearly ten knots an hour. It was really exhilarating after the tedious monotony of fog and rain with head-winds, which had been our portion for so many weary days. All the officers were on deck most of the day, and a bracing air, with a temperature of 42°, made us pity the poor fellows at home who were at the same time trying to cool their fevered pulses at Long Branch and Coney Island. Before midnight we were so near the entrance of St. Lawrence Bay that Captain Berry thought it advisable to heave-to and wait for daylight to enter the harbor.

We had expected to meet Captain De Livron and the Russian frigate *Strelock* at Plover Bay, but found that he had waited there for us several days, and left a note with one of the natives, saying he would await us at St. Lawrence Bay, if he did not find us there already; our unfortunate delay at St. Michael's, caused by the difficulty experienced in taking on board the necessary coal, having led him to believe we had omitted Plover Bay from our schedule. Captain De Livron came on board soon after our arrival, and gave us some news of so sensational a nature that, meagre as it is, and coming in so roundabout a way, I repeat it with great regret. It is a fair sample of the tales which reach the ordinary traveller in the Arctic ice-fields.

Day before yesterday the schooner *R. B. Handy* came into St. Lawrence Bay, having on board the master of the whaler *Daniel Webster*, which had been wrecked this season on the coast near Point Barrow. From him and others Captain De Livron had learned that a wreck was found by native Tchouktchis, a short distance west of Cape Serdze Kamen. The vessel was water-logged, and nearly filled with ice. In the forecastle were the bodies of four of the crew who had perished, and a figure-head of reindeer antlers was recognized as that of the lost whaler *Vigilant*. The Esquimaux at Point Barrow had given information that this spring they had seen four white men travelling along the northern coast of America, in the direction of the Mackenzie River, and that they had found some huts of snow where they had been living during the winter. At these places they had also found several dead bodies, and had seen sledge tracks, with the tracks of dogs and men travelling along. Capt. De

Livron added that he had been informed that the impression prevailed that these poor stragglers were from the *Jeannette*. In the absence of the information upon which this impression is based it is impossible to form a conclusive opinion in the matter, but it would seem almost incredible that members of the *Jeannette* expedition would be travelling toward the Mackenzie River instead of toward Behring Strait, where they would be sure to find friendly Esquimaux, and meet the whaling fleet as soon as the season opened; while in the other direction they were going into the country of notoriously warlike and vicious natives, and under the most favorable circumstances would encounter untold of hardships in an overland journey to where they could obtain relief, with the chances very great against their reaching any settlement whatever. It would appear much more probable that this party was composed of sailors from one or the other of the missing whalers, who might be ignorant of the route they were travelling over. Captain Berry will make every effort possible to investigate this affair, and I trust that I will yet be able to send some authentic information before the summer is ended.

Captain De Livron and the subordinate officers of his vessel have been unremitting in their attention to us, and have offered assistance in any possible way, even to the extent of towing the *Rodgers* to Cape Serdze Kamen, for the purpose of saving the consumption of our coal; so if the sea be smooth to-morrow when we sail we will be attached to the *Strelock* by an eight-inch hawser, otherwise that vessel will bear us company on the journey.

The Krauss brothers, the two German scientists who came to Siberia this summer for the purpose of making observations in the natural history of this coast, are living in a tent on the northern shore of St. Lawrence Bay, and will go upon the *Strelock* to-morrow as far as East Cape, where they will await the return of the *Strelock* from the Arctic Ocean, and go with her to Plover Bay, where they will be left to spend the winter months in the pursuit of their studies.

The passage of the *Rodgers* from St. Michael's to Plover Bay was made in rain and fog, and against head

TCHOUKTCHI YOUTH.

winds; but on the afternoon of the 14th instant the lookout on the top-gallant forecastle heard breakers on the port bow, and the ship was immediately put about. Just then the fog lifted, and showed the bold, rocky coast of Siberia near Cape Tchaplin. Shortly afterward Dominick, the colored steward, came on deck, and seeing the vessel headed away from the precipitous cliffs that were so close to the stern, was somewhat confused, and expressed his surprise in the inquiry: "Tell me how we came through that place, Mr. Waring?" But Mr. Waring couldn't tell. Though but about forty-five miles from Plover Bay we did not reach it until the afternoon of the 16th, owing to fogs and head-winds. We found the chart very inaccurate, and the soundings particularly erroneous, probably indicating a very uneven bottom. We had hopes to find here a native Tchouktchi known as "John Cornelius" who was represented as a thorough pilot for Behring Strait, a good dog-driver and interpreter, who speaks English remarkably well. He had already gone to the Arctic Ocean with Captain Owen.

While in Plover Bay I had the pleasure of seeing the Tchoucktchis for the first time, and noticed a striking dissimilarity between them and the American Esquimaux. They are of lighter complexion and much fatter than the Esquimaux, and speak the most astonishing lingo I ever heard. The Pay Yeoman of the *Rodgers* had wintered at this place, and knew these people very well. I asked him to inquire if there were any reindeer in the vicinity, and he immediately addressed a native with extraordinary gesticulation as follows: "Reindeer here, man-come" to which came the reply, "No, tah pah;" and I was told by the interpreter that it meant the reindeer were a long way off. This is a fair specimen of the jargon used as means of communicating with the white visitors. I found that some of them knew a little of the Esquimaux language, but not sufficient to aid me in understanding them with facility.

To-morrow morning at six o'clock we expect to get away to the Arctic Ocean, to investigate the sensational rumors heard here.

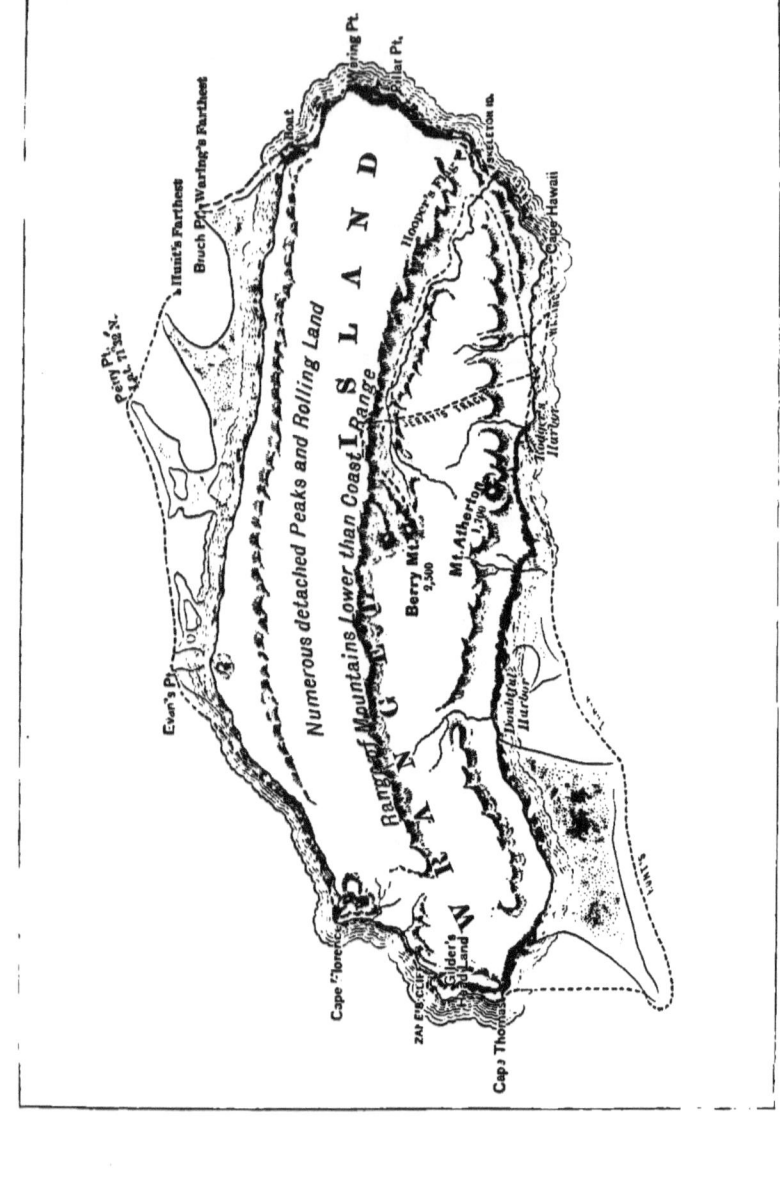

CHAPTER VI.

WRANGEL ISLAND.

ON BOARD U. S. S. *Rodgers*, WRANGEL ISLAND,
Sept. 2nd, 1881.

IT is a great pleasure to be able to date a letter from this mysterious and heretofore unknown land. We dropped anchor within half a mile of the shore at 10 o'clock on the night of August 25th, after having landed on Herald Island the previous day. Three separate expeditions have examined the coast line and interior of this island for indications of the previous visit of the *Jeannette*, and many specimens of the flora and fauna have been collected. Magnetic observations have been continued throughout the sixteen days of our stay, and the coast line and harbor accurately surveyed. Observations have been made of the winds, currents, and tides, and the movements of the ice carefully noted, and so much of our work has been successfully accomplished. Were Wrangel Island a continent, as many have supposed, and our object a survey of the country, or a northern sledge journey, we could not desire a better base of operations. We are, fortunately, ensconced in a secure harbor, the only one on the island; but the knowledge of its existence may prove a great blessing to some whaler that has been caught in the pack and carried toward these forbidding shores.

No traces of the *Jeannette* were found, though the entire coast has been skirted by our boats, and no evidence of former inhabitants or previous visits of human beings were found anywhere, except the record left by Captain Hooper about two weeks before. The only animals existing upon the island are a few foxes and field mice, if we except the occasional visits of Polar bears, three of which were killed by our people during our sojourn here. No indications that reindeer or musk-oxen have ever been upon the island were found, and the probability is that they never were here. We have, therefore, failed to confirm the statement of Captain Dallman, who claims to have landed upon Wrangel Land where he found vegetation plentiful, and saw the tracks of reindeer and musk-oxen. The probability is that he landed somewhere else, or mistook the footprints of wild fowl and Polar bear for the tracks of the animals he named. When we parted with the *Strelock* in St. Lawrence Bay we had expected to meet again at Cape Serdze Kamen, and to transfer our latest mail to the care of Captain De Livron, but we failed to see his vessel again, except for a while the following morning, near Cape East, where it had gone for the purpose of landing the Drs. Krauss with their boat and boatmen. Our stay in St. Lawrence Bay had been but a short one, reaching anchorage on the morning of the 18th of August, and sailing the evening of the 19th. It had been very foggy all day during the 19th, lifting occasionally but settling again, and very unpropitious for departure. Everything was ready on board the *Rodgers* to move out at short notice, and the fires were banked all day long. The Drs. Krauss came over and spent the evening with us until half-past 8 o'clock, when Captain De Livron sent word that if the weather continued as at present, the fog then lifting, he would be ready to sail in an hour and a half. In less than an hour the *Rodgers* was under way, and steamed out of the harbor into the billowy sea of Behring's Strait. An hour later the *Strelock* got under way and soon overtook and passed us, going under half steam about eight knots an hour, while we were under full steam and making little over four knots.

The 20th was very stormy and blowing very hard from the northwest, so that we could scarely make any headway against it. We could see the *Strelock* working in shore, but finally lost sight of her while beating to windward, and saw her no more. The following morning was clear and pleasant when we passed the Arctic Circle, and soon came in sight of Cape Serdze Kamen; which we could readily recognize from the picture in Captain Hooper's report of his cruise in the *Corwin* during the summer of 1880. In the early morning, while near the land, a skin boat filled with Tchouktchis came along-side for the purpose of trading. They had nothing that we wanted, and could give us no valuable information, because we had no interpreter except two Tchouktchi dog drivers whom we brought with us from St. Lawrence Bay, and though they could talk fluently enough with the strangers, we could not understand them. Presently we picked up another boat-load of natives, among whom was one who could talk sufficiently to impart vague information concerning sleds and dogs and two white men on the shore not far away, and a steamer that had been there, but now was "powk," which means "gone," but not indicating whether steaming away or destroyed. This, of course, demanded investigation, and they took us to a place which seemed to be Koliutchin Island and bay, where there is a large Tchouktchi settlement. Lieutenant Waring, Ensign Hunt, Doctor Jones, and your correspondent went ashore and found a large number of dogs which were pointed out and said to belong to "steamer with two masts." Finally, they brought out a piece of board on which were carved the names of Lieutenants Herring and Reynolds, and Coxswain Gissler, of

TCHOUKTCHI WOMAN SEWING.

the *Corwin;* and then it was clear enough that that vessel had been there earlier in the season and landed her dogs, so as not to be inconvenienced by having them on her deck while cruising during the summer, but holding them where they could be reached without much trouble should it be decided to spend the winter in the Arctic Ocean.

The beach was a difficult one to land upon, owing to heavy surf, but there seemed to be a fair harbor between the island and the mainland, should we be compelled to winter upon that coast ; and the discovery of this fact was considered a sufficient recompense for the delay caused by the necessity of following up information so vague and so incomprehensible as is that which can be gained from these people without an interpreter. Dr. Jones gathered some specimens of the flora near the beach, and we had an opportunity for the first time to see the Tchouktchis in their native abodes.

The village consisted of seven large circular dome-like tents of about twenty feet in diameter, made of seal skins sewed together and supported by an intricate arrangement of poles of drift-wood. On the side opposite the entrance were arranged three or four sleeping apartments, shut off from the main tent and each other by curtains of reindeer skins. These were the separate tenements of as many families, the savage semblance of flats and an apartment house. The skin drapery of several of these rooms was raised, and upon the beds, which were also of reindeer skins and covered the entire floor of each, sat women engaged in household duties, or attending to the wants of a colony of dirty half-nude children. The savage odor of dirt and blubber seemed to bear me back to Hudson Bay and the tents of the Esquimaux ; but I found no similarity in the dialect, so that I was unable to converse with these people except in the unsatisfactory medium of sign language and the few English words they had acquired by association with the whalers. Almost the entire populalation of the village followed us to the boat, and the majority attempted to get into the boat with us, so that our efforts to be rid of them may have appeared rude, while necessary, as we intended to sail away without delay. Our guests were appeased with a few gifts, and dropped astern as we headed our course toward Herald Island.

I noticed that the custom of tattooing prevailed among the Tchoukchi women as with the Esquimaux; with the difference that with these people the girls were tattooed, while among the Esquimaux this mark was an indication that the young wife had reached that age when she must depart from the parental roof and join her husband's fortunes. Another distinction was apparent in the diversity of pattern; the style of adornment for the cheeks seeming a matter of individual taste. The decoration of the chin was, however, in every instance I noticed, identical with that of the Esquimaux females of every tribe.

To one accustomed to the accurate surveys of southern coasts, the irreconcilability of Arctic shores to the chart lines is somewhat bewildering, and a discrepancy of from forty to sixty miles in the location of Koliutchin Island by the various charts made it rather doubtful that we had reached that point. Knowing the name to be the native one for the position, I appealed to our guide and asked him if it was Koliutchin Island. At first he seemed to be in doubt, but, after consultation with his friends ashore, he came to me and pointing at the island pronounced the name. I was then satisfied that he was correct, but his mere assent to my question, I felt, amounted to nothing; he would undoubtedly have said "yes" had I asked him if it were Staten Island. His volunteered information was much more satisfactory; but, like all these good-natured savages, he seemed willing to agree to anything suggested to him. We had a fair wind that night and next day. Sounding with the deep-sea lead was continued at intervals of an hour, finding the depths of water to correspond generally with those given on the charts. Drift-wood was seen occasionally, moving usually with the current in a northerly and westerly direction.

On the 22d the commanding officers and crew were assigned to each boat, and all preparations made so that in case of necessity for abandoning the ship it could be effected with as little delay and confusion as possible. It was very foggy all next day until about seven o'clock, when we were called on deck to get our first view of Wrangel Land; but when we saw it, it looked so much like a fog bank that considerable discussion was provoked as to whether it was the much-desired land or not, but such it proved, and a rapid falling of the temperature of the water, a difference of seven degrees being recorded within three hours, indicated the vicinity of ice. A little later it was visible from the masthead to the northward and westward, and soon after could be seen from the deck. The wind was directly from the ice and damp, so that it felt very cold to those from the temperate latitudes, though the thermometer registered 37° F. Still later what appeared, through the many telescopes directed toward it, to be a dismantled vessel, housed over and covered with snow, was seen, and the steamer was headed toward it, to investigate it. Shortly after entering the ice we could see this object more distinctly, and found it to be merely a large cake of ice covered with mud, but the illusion was well preserved until quite near it. All the ice we encountered was apparently old and rotten, though it had evidently been very heavy. Our vessel was then put upon her course, but being still in the ice, and darkness having settled upon the sea, we lay-to, in order to avoid as much as possible coming in contact with the many heavy masses. Even in spite of such precautions we received several hearty thumps that shook the heavy timbers of the *Rodgers*, but did her no injury.

Early the next morning the weather was clear and cold, with Herald Island and Wrangel Island both in plain view. At noon we reached Herald Island, and found it clear of ice, and attempted to pass to the westward of it. We found, however, the sea breaking over a dangerous reef that extended about two miles from the island in a southwesterly direction by compass. We therefore lay-to

HERALD ISLAND.

about three miles south of the western extremity of the island, and sent a whale-boat ashore to search for any evidence of the *Jeannette*, and to leave a record of our visit. There was a heavy sea running at the time, but the landing was effected near the western end, where a small extent of beach was partially protected by the reef, over which the sea was breaking furiously. The boat was in charge of Acting-Lieutenant Waring, and was accompanied by Ensigns Hunt and Stoney, Surgeons Jones and Castillo, and your correspondent. A large plank was erected near the summit of the western ridge, inscribed with the name of the vessel and the date. While this duty was being performed some of the party scaled the ridge and walked along to the centre and highest point of the island, while others were shooting specimens of waterfowl or gathering mosses and flowers for classification by the scientists. The island was found to be a narrow ridge between five and six miles long, and not over a quarter of a mile wide at the base. The crest of the western half of the island was so narrow that one could straddle it, while the eastern portion was lower and more rounded at the top. The portion visited by our party was composed of a slaty shale, with occasional croppings of granite in the hill sides. The ascent was precipitous and very difficult, owing to the nature of the soil, and could only be effected by crawling on hands and knees and catching hold of projections of the shale, which were loose, and threatened an avalanche that would carry the venturesome climber to the bottom at any moment. The island is not more than about six hundred feet high at the highest point, but from it, the atmosphere being perfectly clear, we could see a long distance. Wrangel Island was in plain view, but no land could be seen to the northward of it as far as the eye could reach.

Difficult and dangerous as was the ascent, still more critical was the descent, until when near the bottom, where the small, loose particles of shale were piled up a great height. Down this some of the party came with a run which carried them far out upon the beach before the gathered momentum was exhausted, while others descended more safely but not more gracefully by sitting down and sliding to the bottom with a velocity not to be exceeded by the runners. Upon the beach was found large quantities of drift-wood, and a brisk fire was started there by some of the crew. Over the breakers hovered a large flock of gulls, some of which were secured, together with a few ducks, dorekies, and snipe. After completing our task we returned to our boat, which had been hauled up on the shore, and as the wind had turned and rolled the surf on the beach we had no difficulty in launching the boat, which was half filled with water in the effort; the sea was very rough by this time, and nearly every wave poured a portion of its water into our little craft, which was only kept afloat by constant bailing. Our ship steamed toward us, and picked up the thoroughly drenched party about a mile and a half from the shore, much to their gratification. We found it would be almost impossible to land on the eastern end of the island at this time, and the vessel steamed along the coast, keeping a sharp lookout for cairns. None were to be seen with the glasses, although we subsequently learned, from a record left on Wrangel Island by the *Corwin*, that a party from that vessel had landed and deposited a record there previous to our visit.

After passing the eastern end of the island the *Rodgers* was headed toward Cape Hawaii on Wrangel Island, and at ten o'clock the next morning that point was in plain view, with ice packed along the eastern shore and extending to the northward as far as we could see. We kept on to the south and west, and headed up to the ice pack, which we entered at half-past four o'clock, and steamed slowly toward the land, which was distant about twelve miles. As we drew closer and closer to the land the excitement on board the *Rodgers* increased, and when open leads were found, as at several times was the case, long stretches of clear water were encountered, and we moved forward at full speed, the keenest pleasure was manifest in every member of the expedition. Several times, however, the mighty strength of our vessel was felt to be of advantage, as we had to force our way through heavy loose ice that frequently cut us off from the open water. Near the land the water was clear of pack ice, with nothing but large loose cakes which could easily be avoided,

PLACING RECORDS ON HERALD ISLAND.

and at ten o'clock we dropped anchor in seven fathoms of water within between a half and three quarters of a mile of the shore. Two boats were lowered at once, and several of the officers landed on a low gravelly beach and gave three hearty cheers, which were responded to by those on board. Two sky-rockets were sent aloft, and when the party returned one of the officers opened his heart and cut a Christmas cake in honor of the event.

When about to send up the sky-rockets Lieutenant Waring called for "Liverpool" and "Cockney," our two Tchouktchi assistants, and asked them if they knew what they were.

"Yes, me sabe," was the reply, and the match was applied as they stood by and closely watched the effect. They were very much amused when they saw the preliminary fizzing of the fuse; but when the rush and whirring of fire shot out toward the deck, and the little harmless missile went roaring into the firmament in a streak of flame, their terror and amazement were most amusing to behold. With one impulse they grabbed their hair, as if to hold it on their heads, and made a most surprising backward leap, then stood panting and breathless, gazing at the many-colored stars that dropped leisurely downward after the rocket exploded in the heavens. It was quite evident that they knew nothing of "Fourth of July."

At half past six o'clock the following morning a boat was sent in to examine a lagoon or bay which had been reported by the landing party as existing between the shore where they had stood and a higher coast line beyond; and a fine harbor was thus discovered behind a long, low sand spit, with water enough to allow a vessel as large and heavily loaded as the *Rodgers* to swing with the tide and ride safely, with firm holding bottom. Upon the return of the boat we steamed into our harbor, and at once commenced preparations for exploring the land for traces of the *Jeannette* or the missing whalers.

Three parties were organized, one under Captain Berry, to proceed overland to the northern coast, or some mountain from which a general view of the land and water might be obtained; another, under Acting-Lieutenant Waring, to skirt the eastern coast in a whale-boat; while Ensign Hunt was sent to the westward to examine the coast in that direction. The last parties were provided with fifteen days' provisions, and instructed to encircle the island if possible; for we felt pretty certain of its insular character since making our observations from Herald Island.

Their instructions included general orders concerning a close look out for cairns, and observations of currents and tides, as well as the collection of all scientific data possible. Captain Berry's party included Dr. Jones, the chief surgeon, and four men. These were Frank Melms, who had considerable experience in Arctic land journeys, having been a member of Lieutenant Schwatka's expedition to King William's Land in 1878, '79, '80; Oluff Petersen and Thomas Loudon, both old man-of-war's men, transferred from the *Pensacola* three days before we left San Francisco. Dominick, the colored steward, also went along, under the impression that he was going to the North Pole, and inspired with a laudable idea of discovering what kind of a pole it is that he has heard so much about. The vessel was left in charge of Master Charles F. Putnam, who was also intrusted with the magnetic observations, assisted by Ensign George M. Stoney, to whom was assigned the task of surveying the harbor and adjacent coast lines. These officers were especially fitted for their duties by similar work performed by them while connected with the United States Coast Survey, which they merely quitted to join this expedition.

The whole of Friday and the following day, until half past three o'clock, were consumed in fitting out the expeditions, and all was bustle and excitement on board the *Rodgers*. Three cheers were given by those remaining on board as each boat left the ship's side and started upon their separate routes, to experience unknown hardships and perils in their several undertakings.

After the expeditions departed there were mustered nineteen souls on board, including the two Tchouktchis and a Kamtchadal from Petropaulovski, who has become quite attached to the service, and wants to go to the United States when the *Rodgers* returns home. The next day was Sunday, the 28th of August, and one of the most delightful days ever experienced in this land of storms. The sun shone brightly, and no wind disturbed the surface of the water. Advantage was taken of the weather to erect a tent on the adjacent beach for an observatory, and the magnetic dip was ascertained by Putnam, while Stoney established a base line of three miles for his survey of the coast. This is not all that was accomplished, for in the mean time the latitude and longitude of the harbor were determined, a photograph was made of the ship in her present position, and Hodgson, the Pay Yeoman, went up the ice pack in a three-holed skin canoe, assisted by "Liverpool" and "Cockney," and killed ten walruses. He started to tow four of them to the ship, but they proved too heavy, and one after another was dropped, until only one remained. In the mean time a thick fog settled upon the water, and, fearing the walrus hunters might get lost, Mr. Tracey, the carpenter, was sent out with a crew in the dingey to look for them, while the fog-horn was kept sounding at intervals of five minutes until half-past ten o'clock, when they all returned, the walrus in tow making a heavy pull for them. A line was made fast to the animal's head, and it taxed the muscle of every one on board, officers and men, to hoist it over the bulwarks, even with the assistance of ropes and pulleys. It was a medium-sized cow-walrus, and weighed about twelve hundred pounds. It was a valuable acquisition as dog food, and "Liverpool" and "Cockney" skinned and cut it up with evident delight, occasionally regaling themselves with choice morsels of what to them was the daintiest of food, the raw and bloody meat. The civilized diet of the forecastle had begun to lose its attraction, and their stomachs craved the gorging of meat which this walrus made possible, and their spirits were as cheerful with the prospect as their bodies were bloody with the work. The next day two more walruses were killed and brought aboard, and we had a supply of meat for our fifty dogs to last for some time. Our fine weather was about exhausted by this time, and the third day after the excursionists left a storm set in from the north, and we had an opportunity of noting its effect upon the ice. The pack which had been to the eastward off Cape Hawaii was seen to be in motion, and though the wind was blowing off shore, in a few hours the open water that had confronted us was filled with a seething mass of loose ice, huge hummocks rubbing and grinding together with an ominous sound. The sea beat heavily on the outside of the sand spit, behind which we were securely sheltered, and we had reason for congratulation that so much of our work had been done in the bright days after entering harbor.

During our entire stay, which lasted for nineteen days, we had no other such opportunity. It was surprising to see the ice moving constantly to the westward along the shore, when the natural supposition would be that the wind would blow it off. Sometimes when we went to bed we would see pack ice filling the sea as far as the eye could reach, and the next morning when we went on deck would behold a vast expanse of open water, with merely here and there a cake of large ice floating on the surface; and quite as often did we find the solid pack on awakening where the night before scarcely any was to be seen. These rapid changes are most confusing to the mariner, and have given rise to the theory often mentioned by the whalers who frequent these waters, that the ice sinks and rises in obedience to as yet some unknown law of nature.

As the result of their observations the officers remaining with the ship found the magnetic dip to be 79° 15′, and the variation 19° 49′. The directive force of the magnet was found to be very weak and at times erratic.

CHAPTER VII.

ROUND THE ISLAND.

On Board U. S. S. *Rodgers*, Wrangel Island,
Sept. 12th, 1881.

VERY little could be done in the matter of observations for the next few days, but in the meantime we had the excitement of a bear chase to relieve the monotony. About six o'clock on Saturday, the 3d of September, we were about to sit down to dinner when two white objects were seen on the main-land near the shore, which the glass showed to be a she-bear and her cub. In a short time the dingey was lowered, and two of the officers jumped in, armed with rifles, and were rowed ashore against a strong gale, so that in the interval the bears had gained the advantage of forcing a stern chase upon the hunters. When the boat struck the beach all jumped ashore and started in pursuit, headed by Mr. Tracey, the carpenter, who, though drenched to the skin in effecting a landing, abated not his energy in the chase. After going several miles with little prospect of coming up with the game, all returned to the ship except the carpenter, who pointed ahead and shouting "Excelsior!" kept up the pursuit. Success attended his efforts, as he deserved, and he returned at ten o'clock at night after travelling about ten miles and killing both bears.

At eleven o'clock the same night a voice from the sand-spit hailed the ship, and was recognized through the howling of the gale as that of Captain Berry, who had just returned from his inland journey. He was accompanied by one of the men, and said the rest of the party were following more slowly, their feet having suffered from the rough ground over which the journey had to be made, and rendered them unable to keep up. He had come on ahead to send a boat to the head of the bay in which the harbor was situated, and thus save them about four miles of hard walking. The boat started immediately in charge of Hodgson, the pay yeoman, who is an old sailor and well versed in the management of boats in the Arctic waters. In spite of their efforts it was found impossible to make much headway against the sea and wind, and they pulled to the beach about a mile from the vessel and started to find the wayfarers, who needed their assistance so much. The search was all the more difficult as a severe snowstorm united with the gale to baffle them; but they returned at three o'clock in the morning with Dominick and Petersen, whom they had found asleep on the main-land about five miles from the ship. It was a wild night and well for the worn-out travellers that they were found so soon, or the storm would probably have caused them much suffering before morning. Dominick, the colored steward, was quite exhausted when brought on board, and in answer to where he had been found said, in a dazed way, that he and his companion had lost the seacoast and lay down in the "woods" to sleep. The boat party had seen nothing of Dr. Jones, and much anxiety was felt for him on board; the boat was therefore sent immediately back, and Mr. Stoney took charge of her. After much hard work he succeeded in reaching the head of the bay, where he landed and searched the shores of the main-land for several miles in each direction, though without success. About ten o'clock in the morning a voice was heard from the shore of the main-land, and another boat was lowered at once to go to the relief of the wanderers. The surgeon was found, and said he had not suffered materially from the storm, as Frank Melms had stayed by him and arranged a shelter when he found he could not reach the vessel that night. He said he had profited much by the kind attention of Melms, who was not in the least exhausted, and could easily have reached the ship the night before, but would not leave him while he was able to benefit him by his previous Arctic experience. Morrison and Cahill, two of the machinists, were immediately sent up the beach to recall Stoney's party, who got back to the ship about two o'clock in the afternoon, after a laborious night's work, hungry and tired.

Captain Berry had reached a point near the northwestern coast, where, from a mountain 2,500 feet high by barometric measurement, he was enabled to see open water entirely around the island, except between west and south-southwest, where his view was obstructed by a high range of mountains, which, however, appeared to terminate the land in that direction. He then imagined that Waring had passed the northern side, as the distance was comparatively short and he had started with a fine breeze aiding him, and was now on his way back to the ship by way of the western coast. Not wishing to delay the vessel, as he felt he might do if he delayed his return for further profitless research, he started on his homeward trip at once. The interior was found to be entirely devoid of animal life, and of other plants than those growing near the coast. Two ridges of mountains followed the trend of the northern and southern shores, between which a rolling country existed traversed by small streams evidently fed by the melting snow from the mountains. Minerals and specimens of the flora were gathered, and to this interesting collection was added a fine mammoth tusk, found the first day's march from the ship. A number of other mammoth tusks were found in various stages of preservation by various members of the expedition and those remaining at the harbor. As the Captain and Loudon approached the head of the bay on the night of his return, Loudon saw a bear close by over the crest of a hillock, and, dropping his bundle, poured volley after volley into the carcasses of the animals the carpenter had killed but a short time previously, before discovering that they were already dead. The Captain checked him in his career before he had quite ruined the skins so highly prized by the owner.

Acting Lieutenant H. S. Waring was accompanied on his expedition by Doctor J. D. Castillo, and his crew consisted of Fr. Bruch, coxswain; Frank Berk, Wm. Grace, Julius Huebner, and Owen McCarthy. Of these, Huebner had considerable experience in boating in the ice of the Arctic seas upon several whaling voyages, and his knowledge thus acquired proved useful to the commander of the expedition. Amid the cheers of those remaining, Waring started off toward the east full of hope, and with a breeze that sent him swiftly along under reefed mainsail. That night he reached Cape Hawaii, when the wind died out, and he encamped on the shore; where all enjoyed a good night's rest, and the novelty of the experience of tenting on Wrangel Land with the thermometer at 25° Fahr. After rounding the cape on the following morning he pulled to a small island near the mouth of a creek, where were the skeletons of a whale and a walrus. His attention was attracted by some pieces of wood sticking up in the sand, evidently by intention, and he then noticed footprints leading up to the cliff near by. Following them he came upon a flagstaff, from which dropped what appeared to be a United States flag, and attached to the staff was a bottle containing a copy of the New York *Herald* of March 22d, 1881, and documents of which the following are copies :

Copy.

U. S. REVENUE MARINE,
U. S. STEAMER *Corwin*,
WRANGEL LAND, August 12*th*, 1881.

The United States steamer *Corwin*, Captain C. L. Cooper commanding, visited this land in search of tidings from the United States Exploring steamer *Jeannette*. A cask of provisions will be found on the second cliff to the northward. All well on board.

(No signature).

U. S. REVENUE MARINE,
REVENUE CUTTER *Corwin*,
August 12*th*, 1881.

Landed here this date having previously landed at Herald Island. A "cairn," with information inclosed, may be found on the northeast summit of the island.

The finder is requested to send the contents of this bottle to the New York *Herald*. J. C. ROSSE.

He left copies there in place of the originals, which were brought away and have been transmitted to the Secretary of the Navy with Captain Berry's report. At three o'clock that afternoon he rounded a point marked by a perpendicular column of rock about fifty yards from the point and about one hundred feet high. Here heavy pack ice was encountered, extending as far to the eastward as he could see. Near the shore it was somewhat broken and permitted his advance through a narrow channel, where only short paddles could be used. At a quarter past six o'clock the ice drew so close that he was compelled to haul up on the beach when an opportunity afforded, and encamped for the night. The next day the ice still held him, and, accompanied by Dr. Castillo, he walked to the top of a hill toward the north of his camp, and, after a most tedious and trying struggle, reached the summit, from which his eyes were rewarded by observing the trend of the coast toward the west. This he found to be the extreme northeast cape, and no land could be seen to the northward. Toward the west the land was low near the water and ran out in long, low points, forming deep bays which held the ice packed in dense masses to the shore. The following morning the weather was clear and Herald Island appeared in plain view from the beach, bearing northeast by east (magnetic). By nine o'clock the ice opened sufficiently to allow him to move slowly by the aid of paddles, and after six hours' hard work he succeeded in rounding the cape and making about five miles to the westward. At five o'clock another effort was made to proceed, but, after laboring an hour and a half and narrowly escaping being crushed by two large masses by backing out from between them just as they came together with a force that no boat could have withstood, a narrow lead let them in to the beach. Within five minutes after they landed not a vestige could be seen of the opening by which they had so narrowly escaped. Nothing but a grinding and crunching sea of ice met the view. The day closed with a thick fog and a light wind from the northward, which had brought the pack down upon the shore. The next day opened thick, with a strong northerly wind and flurries of snow. The ice continued densely packed against the shore, giving a dubious chance of moving unless the wind changed. A reconnoisance was made along the beach to the northward and westward, and found the condition of the ice the same as at the camp. September 1st was a gloomy day, and no movement of the ice occurred to indicate their liberation. The ice seemed to be a fixture; the necessity of abandoning the boat and making their way back across the land the only prospect. A not very cheerful one it must be admitted. Waring now determined to wait another day, with the hope of a favorable change, and early in the morning sent a party to the extremity of the point to the westward, a distance of about fifteen miles, from where they could see the land trending to the south and west. The next day was spent in preparing to abandon the boat, which was consequently hauled up on the beach above high-water mark, turned bottom side up, and everything made snug about her, with true sailorly instinct and many deep regrets for the misfortune that left this the only course to pursue. The boat mast was erected on a neighboring hill, and a record deposited indicating the route taken by the retreating crew. A dismal snow-storm was falling when, at five o'clock on the morning of the 3rd instant, they started upon their journey. It was intensely cold and the wind blowing in squalls, while the ice was jammed as far as they could see. Their course was directed toward the eastern coast, where they could find shelter behind the hills and drift wood from which to make a fire and cook some food on reaching camp at night. The travelling with heavy loads upon their backs was intensely disagreeable, while to add to their discomfort the snow changed to rain, which drenched their clothes and increased the weight of their burdens. Lieutenant Waring feared to allow the men to sleep in their wet clothing, and forced the march, only resting for a few hours when the night became too dark to see their way. The route lay over a series of hills that were very fatiguing to men unaccustomed to land journeys, but the prospect of reaching the ship the following day kept them up. As soon as it was sufficiently light to see they started again, with sore and stiffened limbs and feet torn by the sharp stones that covered the ground. At seven A. M. they reached the beach, where a rousing fire was started and a hot breakfast prepared, which put new life into the weary travellers; and through the snow and rain they plodded until reaching the head of the bay, where they were overjoyed to find a boat, which had gone there to bring in the skins of Mr. Tracey's bears from the adjacent coast, and about four miles of walking, which to many had now become most painful, was saved them. An hour later we welcomed them aboard the ship, and they soon forgot their pains while enjoying a hot dinner in comfortable quarters and in relating their adventures to interested auditors.

Almost at the same time that Waring started toward the east with a fair wind Ensign H. J. Hunt pulled away upon his course to the westward. He was accompanied by Passed Assistant Engineer A. V. Zane, and his crew consisted of Arthur Lloyd, coxswain; Jacob Johansen, Frank McShane, Joseph Quirk, and Edward O'Leary. It was hard pulling against the wind that sped his brother officer upon his course, and at nine o'clock, when he encamped for the night, he was not more than about nine miles from the harbor. The oars were brought in requisition the following day, and progress was not very rapid. During the day they saw what looked like a cairn upon the beach, and Hunt landed to examine it. His praiseworthy curiosity came near bringing him into trouble, however, for he found himself, before he was aware of it, within about six feet of a huge polar bear taking a post-prandial siesta. As the ponderous brute raised his head and turned toward the intruder they gazed at each other in a dazed sort of a way for a few minutes, when our active young ensign cut short the interview by facing about and starting for the boat at a speed he never before knew himself to possess, shouting loudly for his rifle. In the meantime the bear arose in a dignified and leisurely manner, and slowly walked toward the sea, when Hunt sent a bullet through him that caused him to turn again for the beach, another shot brought him to the ground, and a third so disabled him that Johansen ran up and gave him the *coup de grâce* with the muzzle of his rifle at the animal's port ear. Hunt then had time to look over the race-course where he had made such good time in going for his rifle, and says that his steps were about seven feet long at the least, and the gravel was scattered in every direction. The monster was skinned, and the tenderloin, liver, heart, and glands removed to the boat to reinforce their larder. The liver they pronounced exceedingly palatable; it formed their chief diet for about ten days, and, notwithstanding that it has invariably been spoken of as poisonous, none of the party have as yet experienced any but pleasurable emotions from partaking of it.

The third day out they rounded the southwest point of the island, and their course lay somewhat east of north. The wind was strong, and carried away their main boom. Plenty of ice was encountered the next day, and though working hard they only succeeded in making about four miles upon their course by paddling and hauling. Next day they could only proceed by towing along shore and cutting a way through the ice, and were finally compelled to tie up in lee of a large piece of ice, and bail out. They had finally, however, accomplished about four miles after a hard day's work. Day after day this labor was repeated until they reached the northern point of the island, where they encountered a succession of sand-spits running toward the north and east beyond the main-land, with miles of open water between, which proved to be only shallow lagoons, where they constantly grounded, and extricated themselves with difficulty. In some instances the spits extended between twenty and twenty-five miles from the land, and the ice was so closely packed that at last they could not force their way through it, and were compelled to turn back, much to their chagrin. On the 5th instant they reached the most northerly point of Wrangel Island, and could distinctly see the Northeast Cape bearing to the southward and westward of their position; but the same heavy pack that brought Waring's party to grief baffled the most strenuous efforts put forth by this energetic young officer to encompass the island. Often while working through the ice he found himself compelled to follow leads that carried him far out from the land, and closing behind him, left no prospect of relief. Sometimes midnight found his men still at their oars or wading through lagoons, sounding in that way for a channel to reach the land or cross the water in the direction of their course. The run home, when reluctantly enforced, was made in five days, during which he had an opportunity to verify and correct, when necessary, the establishment of his positions on the outward course.

The 10th of September, the day assigned for reporting

back, had passed, and the day of grace was drawing to a close, when a little whale-boat was seen beating in from the south and west, and we soon were cheering the returned explorers as they drew alongside. The result of their labor was perfectly satisfactory, as they had reached positions within easy view of each other's furthest points; and though no traces were found that we could identify as of the *Jeannette* or the lost whalers, an accurate survey had been made of this land, and its character ascertained. The necessary scientific data had been collected, and a harbor found for the benefit of ice-belayed mariners that may prove of inestimable value to them.

Though no large game was found upon the island, we found plenty of water fowl, which found their way to our board, among them the most delicious plover to be met with anywhere. They were so handy, too, that we kept them perfectly fresh all the time by only shooting them as needed. The assistant who recorded Mr. Putnam's magnetic observations took his gun ashore with him, and as some oscillations of the suspended magnet gave a rest of five or six minutes, he employed the interval by going out to the beach and shooting the plover for next day's dinner. So with the ducks. They were young, tender, and of fine flavor. No game laws stay the hand of the ambitious hunter on Wrangel Land. He can shoot to his heart's content.

Along the sand-spit, near the *Rodgers'* harbor, as well as the entire coast of Wrangel Island, is strewn with drift wood, among which may often be found utensils of wood made by the natives of the Siberian or American coasts, and some are of very ancient date, as is attested by their venerable appearance. A number of specimens were gathered by members of the expedition as relics. Among them can be recognized portions of vessels and articles of civilized manufacture, but whether keeping the sad tale of wrecks and human suffering, or merely washed from the deck of some passing whaler, it would be difficult to tell. Of this nature was a portion of a large spar similar in circumference to the topsail yard of the *Rodgers*, which lay upon the shore not far from our harbor. There was no mark upon it to reveal its former ownership, and it still lies there the silent custodian of its history.

CHAPTER VIII.

IN THE ICE FIELDS.

ON BOARD U. S. S. *Rodgers*,
Sept. 25th, 1881.

SINCE speaking the whaler *Coral* near Herald Island on the 14th instant, we have been chiefly occupied in cruising around the ice pack to the north-east and north-west of Herald and Wrangel Islands. On our way northward the day after leaving our mail with Captain Coon we again passed his vessel, and saw seven other whalers cruising within an area of about ten miles. We also had the privilege of seeing three of the *Coral's* boats pursue and capture a whale, and afterward our course took us within hailing distance of the ship, when, in response to an inquiry if he could spare us a whale-boat to replace the one abandoned on Wrangel Island, Captain Coon expressed his regret that he was unable so to do, as one of his boats had just been "stove" by the whale then in tow. He wished us good luck in our work, and, filling away, we were soon beyond reach of communication.

That same night we reached the ice and lay-to for daylight. But with the sun came a thick fog and snowstorm, during which we ran into a pocket in the ice pack, and had an opportunity of seeing of what stuff this pack consists. It was indeed a very different looking mass from that which surrounded Wrangel Island, where it was old, dirty, and rotten, while in the north it was in high cakes of solid, clear ice and beautiful in its mantle of newly fallen snow. Here were but few small pieces through which a strong vessel might force its way. It was not difficult to see that it did not require many of these large fields to combine and hold a vessel powerless until a few degrees lower temperature locked it still faster in the pack. We then turned about and threaded our way into the open water, which we reached toward evening, and "hove-to" until morning.

The next day we again reached the ice about noon, and entered a lead through which we made our way slowly until we brought up about six o'clock against an impenetrable mass, and Captain Berry descended from the "crow's-nest" at the mast-head, where he always takes his station while working through the ice. His hair and beard were covered with frost, and the entire rigging was enveloped in the same feathery material; making it at once a thing of beauty to the beholder, but a subject of misery to the poor sailors, who had to handle these ice-clad ropes. Scarcely a breath of wind could be felt, and a temperature of seven degrees below the freezing point was quite favorable under the circumstances for the formation of new ice. Fortunately the sky was overcast, and the temperature fell only one degree lower during the night, or our chances of escape when further progress was found to be barred would have been materially lessened. During the night we tied up to a large piece of field ice, about the size of City Hall Park in New York, in a polynia, or open water hole, to which we had succeeded in making our way before it got too dark to continue our contest with the ice. By midnight, however, the open space was entirely filled by the pressure of the ice from the southward, and when we started at half past two the following morning our exit was only effected by putting the bow of the ship between two large cakes of ice and starting the engine forward at its full power. After continuing this sort of goose step for about an hour we succeeded in forcing the cakes sufficiently apart to allow the vessel to squeeze herself between them, and a little while later she was fortunate enough to reach a lead that brought her without further difficulty to the open sea. The work of forcing the cakes apart was materially increased by the new ice that had formed during the night to about an inch in thickness and cemented the large cakes together. During our progress through the leads after entering the pack on the afternoon of the 17th, new ice of but about a quarter of an inch in thickness was constantly met with, and had rather a suggestive appearance, though opposing no impediment to our advance. It only needed a strong southerly wind during that night to have closed the fifteen miles of ice through which we had passed, so that our escape before the winter set in would have been at least improbable. This would have been a matter of serious annoyance, as it would have effectually tied our hands against a further prosecution of the search for the *Jeannette* until released, which would not be before next summer, if released at all.

During the 18th and 19th we steamed along the southern edge of the pack, and examined all openings for a lead that would let us advance further toward the north, but met the heavy pack ice again, extending far toward the south in about 171° 30′ west longitude. Up the western edge of this pack we steamed until we were headed off by the solid ice, and at ten o'clock on the morning of the 19th reached our highest latitude, 73° 44′ north, which is, so far as known, the highest yet attained in this sea, though not a very great advance toward the pole.

The weather has not been sufficiently clear while in the highest latitudes to see land if at a great distance, and so far we have been unable to confirm the reports of land seen to the northward of Wrangel Island. We have steamed right over the so-called "Blevin Mountains" of Wrangel Land, and where "extensive land with high peaks" is marked on the charts, without impediment. We left the northern coast of Wrangel Island, and sailed in a northwesterly direction to 73° 28' north latitude, and 179° 52' east longitude, and found the water deepening as we advanced. At this point we found ourselves in a large pocket in the ice, and steamed for ten miles through newly-formed mushy ice, which was made in spite of a heavy sea that kept it in constant motion. On the edges of the ice pack the ice was crunching and grinding, and the sound emitted could be heard at a great distance. The temperature of the air here was 23° Fahr., and we invariably found it several degrees colder at the bottom of these deep pockets than in the open sea. Large numbers of walruses were seen in the water, and sunning themselves on the edges of the larger floe pieces.

Observations with the deep-sea lead, which have been made hourly since we entered this sea, seem to indicate receding from, rather than approach to, land as we go north, as the water continually deepens as we advance, until, at our highest point, 73° 44' north latitude, 171° 48' west longitude, we found eighty-two fathoms. The character of the bottom was very irregular, sometimes hard, at others black sand, and in many places blue mud, which it was at the deepest sounding.

After cruising along the pack so far without discovering any traces of sledge parties from the *Jeannette*, and our further progress being cut off, we steamed toward Herald Island to anchor there for the purpose of making observations upon the current reported to flow in a northwesterly direction. Just after the ship's course was changed so as to head out of the pocket through which we had been advancing toward the north, a large polar bear was seen swimming toward the ship, and the bulwarks of the vessel at once bristled with riflemen armed to resist an attack. The carpenter, already distinguished as having slain two polar bears in single combat, opened fire and missed, but followed up his first bullet with two others which struck the advancing enemy in the head, and caused him to beat a hasty retreat. Then commenced a running fire from the quarter deck, but though badly wounded in four different places the bear kept on swimming rapidly for the ice, when turning his devoted head around to take another look at the ship, a bullet went crashing into his brain, and he ceased to move. The ship steamed closely alongside, and a rope was fastened to his hind leg, and when hoisted on board he was weighed and turned the beam at eleven hundred pounds.

The weather grew thicker as night approached, and a strong wind prevailed while we held our course toward Herald Island. During the night we passed in view of the lights of some of the whalers, who were still holding their position near where we had left them when going toward the north. As the fog continued we dropped anchor in fifteen fathoms of water at half-past two o'clock on the afternoon of the 20th. During the following twenty-four hours the observations of the current were continued, which indicate a tidal current setting toward the northwest as the water is deepening, and toward the southeast when shoaling, while at high and low water there was no current perceptible. The measurements were made at the surface, and at a depth of ten fathoms.

Toward the night of the 21st the fog cleared somewhat and we got under way, steaming toward the southward and westward, and early next morning found ourselves near Captain Hooper's cairn on Wrangel Island. The weather gradually became clearer and we headed for the north side of the island, where we were fortunate in finding the ice loose enough to admit our approach close to the land, and Mr. Waring went ashore with a boat and succeeded in recovering the whale-boat and all the articles abandoned on his return to the ship, after being headed off by the ice on his previous attempt to circumnavigate the island. We then took our course in a northerly direction and found considerable open water, with the ice pack toward the west.

The reports of lands seen at a distance in these waters should be made with great circumspection, where clouds and fog banks are constantly appearing on the horizon and are so very deceiving. One clear-headed seaman, who has been cruising in these waters for many years in command of a whaler, has grown quite sceptical concerning such reports, and in a recent conversation expressed his doubts of the existence of land north of Point Barrow, as reported by the master of another whaling bark in the year 1875. "It was probably a fog bank," said the veteran whaler, "reported by the man in the crow's-nest."

"On the contrary," was the reply, "all hands on board at the time saw it."

"In that case I am *sure* it was a fog bank, or it would not have been seen from the deck. High land might have been seen from the mast-head a great way off and not from the deck."

"Did you know that there is a dangerous reef extending about two miles southwest of Herald Island?" the same skipper was asked.

"Oh, yes," he replied; "we all know it" (referring to the whaling captains); "and there is a bad shoal recently formed near Point Barrow, where there is only from one to two fathoms of water, and would bring a ship up."

"Well, why don't you report such things," he was asked, "so that they can be put on the charts?"

"Because no notice would be taken of it if we did. They would merely say 'that's only another old whaler's yarn.' We all know these things, and that's enough for us. If others want to know anything about it let them come and find out for themselves. That's our idea of the matter, though we are always ready to give the result of our experience to any who desire it."

And there is a good deal of truth in what the old sailor said.

CAMP AT EETEETLAN.

CHAPTER IX.

EETEETLAN.

CAMP "HUNT," EETEETLAN, N. S.,
November 15, 1881.

ON the 8th of October a small party was landed from the *Rodgers* on the island of Eeteetlan, about twenty-five miles west of Cape Serdze Kamen, on the Siberian coast, the purpose of which was to form a base of supplies for sledge journeys during the winter and spring following, and to serve as a haven for any survivors of the *Jeannette* or missing whalers who might have reached the Siberian coast during the preceding summer or fall. A severe gale, that prevailed for several days previous to the arrival of the *Rodgers* at this point, had caused a surf upon the sandy shore of the main-land that prevented the landing of the party and stores there, but Captain Berry decided to place them upon the island, where a good beach and lee-shore made the landing feasible. A great many advantages that the main-land presented had therefore to be abandoned, such as the constant presence and assistance of the Tchouktchis and a plentiful supply of fresh water, of which the island is almost entirely devoid. Thereby we were subjected to the crowding of our quarters throughout the entire day by such visitors as came in boats or sledges, and had no other place in which to assemble than the little house, that was small enough even for those for whom it was intended. During the three days required to land the stores the carpenter had erected a house 12 by 16 feet, with a sloping roof, from 8 to 10 feet high. The walls were double—that is, were boarded on the inside as well as the outside, with the intention of filling in with grass, but there was none on the island, and sufficient could not be secured on the mainland, while there were white men to look at and furnish the day's amusement for the lazy Tchouktchis. The roof was single, and the cracks and joints were covered with battens to keep out the rain, but failed to accomplish so desirable a purpose. An old piece of canvas that was thrown over the roof and battened down was an improvement, but then it began to get cold and turf was piled on the roof to keep out the frost. Instead of frost, however, the weather grew milder and the rain fell almost constantly, so instead of pure rain water we had mud until the snow fell, when we were again comfortable.

The shore party comprised Master Charles F. Putnam, Surgeon I. D. Jones, the writer, and three sailors—

Frank Melms, Oluf Petersen, and Constantine Tatarenoff—the Kamtchadal dog-driver from Petropaulovski, whose name had been condensed into "Peter" by his mess-mates on board the ship, and indeed few knew he had any other name. On one side of the little room, which constituted the house, were erected three bunks for the men, and on the other side two beds accommodated the commander and surgeon, while I constructed an annex of pemmican boxes and bread cans with a roof and floor of boards, obtained by breaking up boxes containing canned goods. "Peter," who could not read English, selected a nice board from a pemmican box for the door-sill, but it needed not the legend "For Dogs Only" to convince me that my apartment was scarcely better than a kennel. The roof leaked, of course, but a judicious arrangement of India rubber coats made sleep possible. The wind whistled through the interstices between the boxes, but chinking, and a lining of reindeer skins, ultimately secured the next thing to perfect bliss. The lining of reindeer skins was not an original idea, but borrowed from the natives, whose winter homes are thus contrived. They are not nomadic like the Esquimaux, who are obliged to move from the haunts of the reindeer to the sea shore, where they find the walrus and the seal; but have their homes and villages where they dwell throughout the year. The Tchouktchis are divided into two classes, the reindeer tribes, or "Chowchoos," and the walrus hunters, or "Iowans." "Tchouktchis," or "Chookchees," is a name they do not understand or recognize, but seems to be the name given by the Russians indiscriminately to both classes, and I presume is a corruption of "Chow-choo," derived from the fact that the reindeer people who live inland were the first whom the Russians encountered when they entered the country. The inland and shore people are in constant communication, and exchange the reindeer skins and meat for seal and walrus blubber and skins, thus rendering the constant change of habitation customary with the Esquimaux unnecessary. Their houses are large, dome-like tents of walrus skins, in summer, and reindeer skins in winter, sewn together, and drawn tightly over a wooden framework. They vary in size from about twelve to forty feet in diameter, and are usually about twelve feet high in the centre. This tent is called a *Yaránger* or *Yárat*, and forms a shelter from the wind and rain. Within it is erected the sleeping room or *Yorónger*, which is square or oblong in shape, and made of reindeer skins sewn together, and held up by a framework of wood. This is perfectly impervious to the wind, and entirely devoid of ventilation. An open lamp containing seal oil with moss for wick burns there throughout the day, and produces a temperature reeking with foul odors, and varying from eighty to one hundred and ten degrees, even in the coldest weather. Within this apartment the men wear nothing but their trousers, and the women nothing at all save a narrow breech-cloth of seal skin, which makes them appear as if about to engage in the ballet of the "Black Crook," were it not that they are usually ill-shapen, and always filthy with dirt. It would be impossible, with decency, to describe their habits, or explain how their very efforts toward cleanliness make them all the more disgusting. It requires considerable habitude or terrible experience in the open air to find any degree of comfort in such abodes. The Augean stables, or the stump-tail cow sheds, appear like paradise in comparison. And yet these people are often intelligent in appearance, and many of them possess a quiet dignity of bearing that would become a Senator.

They are generally honest, and their vices, such as they have, are derived from intercourse with the white race. As is usual with savages, the women are the slaves of their husbands, and have all the heavy and disagreeable work to perform; the hunting and general out-door exercise being the manly portion. With all their varied duties of a more robust character they find time to sew, and many of them evince wonderful skill with the needle and great taste in ornamentation. The reindeer skins, which are the usual material of their clothing in winter and summer, are of a better quality than those of the wild reindeer, which furnish the clothing of the Esquimaux. The flesh side of the skin is scraped in the usual manner, and is afterward stained with a red clay, found near Serdze Kamen, which gives their clothing a more pleasing appearance and preserves their cleanliness for a longer period. The costume of the men consists of a shirt of soft reindeer skin, that from the fawn or doe preferred, and is worn with the fur inside. In cold weather a coat of heavier skin is worn over this. Both are made to reach nearly to the knee, and are the same length in front and behind. They are made quite full and the sleeves large, except near the wrist. This arrangement of the sleeve allows the hand and arm to be withdrawn inside the clothing with great facility and rapidity, and there are times when speed is felt to be a matter of great concern. Thus, in cold weather they warm their hands and perform other little offices of personal comfort quite common with uncleanly people, as well as with monkeys. A belt of sealskin or cloth, and as ornamental as the taste or means of the owner will admit, is worn to keep the wind from intruding beneath their clothing ; a precaution never used by the Esquimaux except in the coldest weather, and then only when the wind is blowing. Their coats are without hoods, but are cut low and have a piece of long-haired fur around the throat, usually of fox, wolf or dog skin. The skirts and wrists are also trimmed with the same fur. A close-fitting cap is worn when out of doors, tied under the chin, and this also is trimmed with heavy fur during the winter. I have seen many such caps with fur from six to eight inches long surrounding the face, and when of white wolf or dog skin it gives the wearers a peculiar and saint-like appearance, scarcely consistent with their savage nature. When travelling in the coldest weather a large coat is sometimes worn over all, and this generally has a hood attached, which also is trimmed with heavy fur to shield the face from the wind, and to protect this from the wet snow a thin over-coat is worn, made of reindeer skin without the hair, and tanned as soft as chamois. Often, and preferably, their rain-coat is of calico or white cotton stuff, procured from the traders, and the more brilliant the better. We had one piece of six-penny calico, with red and yellow peacocks, whose spread tails presented every known color and tint. It was not stinted as to size either, for the diameter of the tail was only limited by the width of the cloth. This was the favorite pattern with the natives, and when one could get a coat with two peacock tails on the back and two on the breast his happiness was supreme.

Indeed, I found one of these coats at Nishne Kolymsk, more than 2,000 versts from our house on Eeteetlan, and could not fail to recognize it. It adorned the person of a reindeer chief, and I knew he gave the Iowan from whom he obtained it a most fabulous price. In the spring, when they hunt the seal that sleep upon the ice, the Iowans prefer an outside coat of white cloth, and in summer they wear a waterproof coat made of the thin membrane from the intestines of the seal. These are often ornamented with little tufts of feathers, and are quite pretty as well as useful in protecting their reindeer clothing from the rain or surf. The trousers of the men are made to fit tight to the leg and extend to the ankle, where there is a drawing string to close them tightly over the stockings. The inside trousers are of fawn skin and the outside pair are made of skin from the leg of the reindeer, except in the coldest weather, when sometimes the heavier skin is worn while travelling. They are very short in the waist, and though there is a drawing-string there also it is a continual mystery as well as a run of good luck that they are kept up at all. In summer, and when there is open water, they wear boots of seal skin, which vary in length from half way up the calf of the leg to the crotch. In winter the boots are of reindeer legs and shod with the large seal skin until the coldest weather, when soles of bear or reindeer skin, with the fur on, are substituted. These boots are generally short, reaching far enough to be held tightly by the drawing-string at the bottom of the trousers' leg. Sometimes, however, they are long enough to tie just below the knee. In winter also a scarf or comforter is worn made of squirrels' tails, and requiring, I should imagine, the sacrifice of about five or six hundred animals for each comforter. The dress is, however, picturesque and comfortable, and much more agreeable to wear and to look at than that of the Esquimaux.

The dress of the women is very different from that of the men. The coat and trousers are in one piece. The trousers are very wide and the sleeves almost as wide, while at the same time long enough to reach beyond the hand and greatly interfere with perfect freedom in the use of the hands. Consequently, whenever at work anywhere else than at home they drop the dress from off the shoulders and arms, and thus gain the desired freedom for the hands. In cold weather, when travelling, they wear an outside coat with a hood, a very cumbersome and ungainly but comfortable article of dress. Their boots are like the men's longer ones, and meet the trousers at the knee, with long stockings of reindeer skin inside. Some of the women take great pains with their boots and decorate them with intricate needle-work. It is the only ornamented part of their costume. Beads they are very fond of, but only wear them strung around the neck and under one arm. I have seen some belles with strings of beads around their necks that must have been a load to carry, and though constantly in the way as they bend to their work, they rather enjoy the discomfort, as one of the concessions due to the mandates of fashion. The beads are also sometimes entwined with their hair and draped around their shoulders in a still more tantalizing manner, for when caught by any object it not only arrests their movement but pulls their hair besides. Many of the men wear beads for earrings, and such as indulge in this fashion have ears that clearly betoken its inconvenience. The lobe of the ear is sliced in numerous places, and the later holes have to seek a place for themselves higher and higher, and yet they cling to these long strings of beads as if they really improved their personal appearance. Some of the men also wear bracelets and armlets of seal skin, and in fact so do some of the younger women, and some have in addition a band of the same material around the neck and dangling down the breast, while some have this band extended around the body; with the women this necklace is of use, as to it is attached a small bag of seal skin about the size of a quarter of a dollar. Nearly all the men smoke and a few chew tobacco; while, on the contrary, few of the women smoke but all chew, and this little bag is used to carry the daily chew in when not in the mouth, for economy demands that a chew of tobacco shall do its full duty. It is only discarded when a hydraulic press would fail to extract from it anything like tobacco juice. The same system of economy induces the men to mix finely chopped shavings of wood or bark with their smoking tobacco, and their pipes are the smallest known. Even then they fill the bowl with reindeer hair before putting in the tobacco, and when lighted they continue to inhale the smoke without breathing until the tobacco is exhausted. In the mean time the face and neck swell, the veins are distended, the eyes shed tears, and when human nature can stand it no longer they burst into a violent fit of coughing and spitting, which lasts for several minutes. It is of no use speaking to a man from the moment the light is applied to the tobacco until the coughing spell is over. While he is enjoying his pipe he can attend to nothing else. If you were to tell him that a mine beneath his feet was about to explode it would make no difference to him—present comfort cannot be sacrificed to secure future bliss. I saw one Tchouktchi who used snuff. But this blasé man of the world had lived near the Russian settlement at Nishne Kolymsk, and indulged in other vices, such as the use of a fork in eating walrus meat and a spoon made of the horn of the mountain sheep to eat blubber and chopped grass. He was altogether too refined for the society in which he lived.

The house at Eeteetlan was built upon the only beach the island presented, and upon the only spot on that beach which the natives said was not washed by the waves during a violent gale. But before the sea was frozen we saw many anxious hours when the water came to the very foundation and threatened to undermine us. We built a breakwater of stones about two feet from the house and felt easier after that, though it was broken by the waves in several places and the intervening space between it and the house was often filled with water that dashed over it. It was not until the sea was finally frozen between the island and the main-land, and the waves thus stilled, that we felt perfectly secure. That was a happy night. Storm after storm had annoyed us, and twice we had stood watch by turns at night; not that danger threatened our lives, but our comfort. We needed the house to protect us and our stores during the winter, and it is hard to turn out in an Arctic storm to save your property. A storm was raging that night when the sea was sealed, and we had been watching the action of the waves as they washed the pudge of soft ice in from the sea toward the land. For several days the shore of the main-land had been girt with ice, and we could see natives walking upon it with snow shoes. The ice extended from the land in a point toward a point of the island nearest the land. At last the pudge reached this point, and assisted by a snow-storm that was raging at the time, in a few hours closed in the little bays on either side of the point. We were seated in the house at the time and were made aware of the closing of the sea by the sudden cessation of the noise of the waves upon the beach, and going out doors were gratified to find our expectations realized. No more night watches. Our house was safe until spring at any rate. The very next day four natives came over to us on snow-shoes, and the day following many came on snow-shoes and sledges. Communication with the main-land, which had been closed for about two weeks, was again opened, and the natives at least were happy if we were not. But we were glad to see them, and always found it pleasant to have a few around for the sake of companionship. We were only annoyed when the house was filled so that it would be impossible to move without wedging your way through them. And this was the usual state of affairs whenever they could reach us. They were good-natured, though; and when Frank wanted room to cook dinner we would simply invite them to go home and call again when they had leisure. This he called "firing them out;" and when they went it was often only to the outside of the building to flatten their noses against the window and cut off all the daylight, those who had not eligible places at the window being contented with the report from those there of the progress of events inside. This was our daily life at Eeteetlan.

They would bring us walrus tusks and skins to trade, and could not understand why we did not want the things that were so much sought for by the vessels of commerce that came to East Cape and the adjacent coast. Some would bring reindeer meat, which was always acceptable; some would fetch water from the main-land, or, later in the season, ice; and some brought nothing but eyes to gaze all day in admiration or astonishment upon the white strangers with hair on their faces. All this we had to endure day after day during day-time, and our only real enjoyment was during the evening, after dinner, when the table was cleared and our commander would string his guitar and sing sweet little Spanish love songs or some familiar air, when we could join in the chorus. In a small party like ours strict man-of-war discipline was not necessary, and our amusements were often intended for the entertainment or instruction of the men rather than for our own edification. "Peter," our Kamtchadal dog-driver, was taken in hand by Putnam, and got as far in the rudiments of an English education as D-O-G, dog, and C-A-T, cat, while the Doctor and I played "Pinafore" with the other two men. Or perhaps bésique or chess engaged the attention of some during the evening. Sometimes all games and pursuits were abandoned and a general discussion substituted upon subjects of interest to us, or matters we knew nothing about. Our life here, though monotonous, has not been as disagreeable as might be supposed. To be sure there were disagreeable features connected with it, but we knew we did not come here entirely for pleasure. Occasionally, as a great favor, some native was allowed to remain with us over night, and such indulgences were highly appreciated. They knew there was a cup of tea about half-past nine or ten, with a biscuit and bit of cheese, or some sardines, or perhaps a piece of the Doctor's elegant Christmas cake. These little frivolities of the white strangers were highly esteemed by their savage guests, and the habits of the foreigners often imitated. Thce ame of Christian cultivation, however, was only reached by one old reindeer chief, who after dinner leaned back in his chair and demanded the Doctor's napkin, the napkin that was to last the rest of the voyage. This old chief sang for us that evening, accompanying himself upon Putnam's guitar. It was a monotonous melody, and the words, which were the same throughout and oft repeated, were "I—payk—e—com—up," but I never could find out what they meant, or if they meant anything at all.

After the snow fell and the ice bridge was formed, the natives came to us on sledges, and I had an opportunity of examining some vehicles that are a marvel of lightness and strength. Only one or two persons ride on a sled at a time, and the dogs always go at full speed. These little sledges would bound over the rough ice between our camp and the shore, and I at first would expect to see them dashed to pieces at any moment, but they seemed to be made of whale-bone. During the daytime our house is often surrounded with sledges of various sizes, and it looks as if there was a fair in progress. I have counted as many as twenty sleds at one time, with from three to fourteen dogs each at the house; and all the people who came with them, besides those who came on foot, feel that they have a claim to enter our only apartment and be entertained for the day. They would come sometimes long before daylight and before we were awake, and wait outside in the cold perhaps for hours before admitted. They are a patient race of beggars, and if they do not get everything they see it is not because they neglected to ask for it.

CHAPTER X.

LOSS OF THE RODGERS.

CAMP "HUNT," EETEETLAN, N. S.,
December 31, 1881.

DURING the latter part of the month of November I paid a visit to a neighboring tribe of reindeer Tchouktchis to get a supply of meat for our table. Their camp was only about forty miles distant, but the days were very short and the dogs very lazy, so we had to sleep on the snow one night. The next day there was a violent gale accompanied by snow right in our faces, but my guide conducted the sleds with unerring skill across that waste of snow, without a single landmark that I could distinguish, right to the tents of the Tchouktchis we were seeking. When we first saw the tents, though on a level plain, they were not 150 yards distant, so violent was the storm. I found their tents exactly like those of the Iowans; but it was here that I slept in one of these houses for the first time, and I felt as if I would certainly be suffocated by the heat and foul air. The only way I could secure enough comfort to sleep at all was by putting my head outside the front curtain of reindeer skin. My body was sufficiently warm inside the *yorónger* without any other covering. Thus it was we all slept, our heads in one tent and our bodies in another. This method is subject to one objection, as I have frequently found. This outside tent, or *yaránger*, is the shelter for all the dogs, and it is no rare thing to be awakened during the night by a sense of unusual cold and find some affectionate dog licking your face or poking his cold nose along your breast in his effort to gain admission to the interior apartment. I procured a fine young reindeer and returned to the coast to find the gale of the previous day had broken out the ice between our island home and the main-land. I met Putnam at Tay-up-kine, the native village on the shore nearest our house. He was having his dogs harnessed for a trip to Wankaramen, about 150 miles northwest, to deposit provisions to be used by our sledging parties in the spring. He had crossed the open water to the shore-ice the day before in native canoes, and brought his sleds and eighteen dogs with him. Petersen accompanied him on this trip, which occupied ten days. I waited to see them off and then went to the edge of the shore-ice to embark for the island, but the young ice and pudge were so thick that the heavily laden skin-boat could make no progress. An hour and a half's hard work had not advanced us more than three times the boat's length from the shore-ice, and we had to return, which took us two hours more. The next day we made another attempt, but could only get about 150 yards from the shore-ice by using the skin-boat as a bridge from one cake to another, and hauling it over to be again launched upon the pudge. So strong was this young ice that the boat would not sink into it until nearly the whole load was in. Then it did not break, but just gave way like thick mush. Again we were compelled to return, and I made up my mind to await the freezing over of the channel, which I thought would not be long, as the wind was on shore, and kept driving the cakes and pudge upon the point where the bridge was first formed. The next day it was snowing so that we could not see the island, but it looked as if the ice continued to the point; so several of the natives started, with snow-shoes upon their feet and snow-canes in their hands, to try the passage. These snow-canes were a great novelty to me, and are worthy of a description for the ingenuity of their construction. They are made of wood, and a little longer than an ordinary walking-stick. They are generally pointed with a ferule of walrus ivory, and about two inches from the point is a hoop about six or eight inches in diameter fastened to the cane by radii of sealskin thongs. This hoop and network of seal-skin thongs present a broad surface to the snow, and will sustain considerable weight upon soft snow or pudge. The natives always wear their snow-shoes and carry their snow-canes when hunting seal along the edge of the ice or placing their seal nets in the water. It is astonishing what treacherous places they can walk upon when thus equipped. I have seen them walking in the most unconcerned manner upon thin pudge ice which was rolling in long continuous swells from the waves, which had not yet ceased their motion beneath. Here I may state, that I have travelled over ice that had frozen solid, and still preserved this undulating surface, though all motion had ceased for weeks. It must have been a sudden lowering of the temperature that fixed the ice before the water had recovered its level surface. About three quarters of an hour after the advance guard had started it was announced to me that they had reached the island, and that the crossing was all right. So a number of natives were going over, and would take me on a sledge, as I was not accustomed to travelling in snow-shoes. Three sledges started, and about twenty natives followed on foot. The sled I rode upon broke through as soon as it struck the pudge, and I was waist deep in water and slush in a moment, but by lying down and changing my position by rolling around I kept from sinking until they pushed the sledge back that had preceded me, and by holding on to it and paddling with my feet I managed to reach a cake of ice where most of the natives stood. They then put me on another sled, and one man followed pushing, when the dogs were floundering and could not pull me up on to the next cake. In this way, by pulling and pushing from one cake to another, we managed to reach the island in about an hour and a half of as disagreeable travelling as I ever experienced. The natives, on their snow-shoes, could stand with impunity where I sank with the sledge.

Putnam returned a week afterwards, and had some disagreeable experience in a gale of wind and snow while crossing Peelkan Bay, which is called Koliutchin Bay on the charts. He was obliged to spend the night on the ice in that gale, or *poorga*, by which name such storms are known and dreaded in Siberia. It is impossible for animals to proceed in the face of such storms, and there is nothing to be done but wait until they subside sufficiently to admit of advancing. Upon broad plains, such as the *tundras*, or marshes, there is as much danger sometimes in halting as in going ahead, for in a very short time the snow will envelope the whole party and bury them beneath it. Such storms have at times overtaken the post chaises *en route* from one station to another, and after such storms it has been the custom to send out gangs of laborers with some one who is well acquainted with the surface of the country. He may, perhaps, point to a hillock, and say, "I never saw that before," and the laborers are set to work throwing aside the snow, and often have they exhumed a stage coach with its horses and occupants, perhaps all dead or nearly so. As a general rule, however, the natives and residents near the *tundras* know pretty well the indications of the approach of a *poorga* and will not venture to cross until the weather is settled. In other places, where coast lines or wood country present landmarks that can be depended upon, they do not feel the need of so much caution, as the worst to be dreaded is, perhaps, the horrible discomforts of such a storm. During the *poorga* on Peelkan Bay, Putnam froze his wrist, and Petersen the tips of all his fingers. They were but slight frost bites, and, though very sore for awhile, are not to be regarded in this climate. Petersen said he didn't mind freezing the tips of his fingers particularly, except that it prevented him from playing the piano. I think Putnam rather enjoyed it, as it gave the Doctor something to do.

Within a few days after his return from this trip Putnam started for St. Lawrence Bay to visit the vessel, and make arrangements for the spring sledge journey to Nishne Kolymsk to ascertain if the *Jeannette* had been heard of anywhere along the coast. When he reached the village of Chayootoe, two days' journey from the winter harbor of the *Rodgers*, he was startled by the information received from natives, recently from St. Lawrence Bay, that the ship had been destroyed by fire, and only a small amount of provisions saved. They said that no lives had been lost, and that the officers and men were living with the natives in their huts and eating rotten walrus meat. There seemed no doubt of the fact, though the natives could only give the date by the weather, but by this means we fixed the fire on December 1st, and it actually occurred only the day before. As he felt certain of the accuracy of his information, Putnam returned at once to our house for provisions to carry to our shipwrecked comrades, and on the 27th of December started again for St. Lawrencce Bay, with four large sledges beside his own, and as much bread, coffee, sugar, pemmican and canned meat as they could carry. He also took some reading matter, and about a hundred pounds of tobacco and cigarettes, which was about half of what we had. On the 3d of January Captain Berry arrived at Eeteetlan, and confirmed the sad news of the loss of his vessel with nearly all her stores, and ordered me to proceed at once to Nishne Kolymsk, and from there to the nearest telegraph station in Siberia, to forward to the Secretary of the Navy a despatch announcing the loss of the vessel, and then to proceed to Washington, through Siberia and Europe, with his full written report of the disaster. It was a long journey, and one fraught with discomfort if not with danger, but under the circumstances the only thing to be done.

It was nearly nine o'clock on the morning of November 30th when smoke was seen issuing from the fore-hold of the *Rodgers*, then in winter harbor in St. Lawrence Bay, and all the terrors of a fire on shipboard confronted the crew of that doomed vessel. Every man on board took his post with alacrity, but without confusion, and awaited the commands of his superior officer. The hatches were battened down, and streams of water were poured into the hold from the deck force-pump, manned by the crew, and from the steam-pump, worked by the donkey-boiler, under which fires were continually kept up to heat the ship. When the fore-hold was partially opened to admit

THE BURNING OF THE RODGERS.

the streams of water so much smoke escaped that the men at the nozzles had to be constantly relieved, and the fireman was driven from his post in the donkey-boiler room. The door of the donkey-boiler room was then closed and a hole made in the deck above the room, and thus the fires were kept up. It was some time before the main boilers could be used, for the connections had been broken to prevent the pipes freezing, but as soon as they were made fires were started, and by the time there was sufficient steam to be of use the donkey-boiler room had to be abandoned on account of the smoke, and the fires were hauled from under that boiler. In the meantime the Babcock fire extinguishers were discharged through auger holes made through the deck, but did not seem to affect the fire. The head-light oil and powder were then taken on deck, where they could be thrown overboard or placed in the boats as might become necessary, and the vessel brought stern to the wind to keep the fire from spreading aft. Now the smoke began to enter the coal-bunkers and main fire-room, and efforts were made to get out provisions and skin clothing, which were in the after part of the ship, but already so much smoke and carbonic-acid gas had collected in the store-rooms that it was impossible for the men to work there. There seemed but one resort now, and that was to cut the steam-pipe and fill the hold with steam. This seemed for a time to subdue the fire, and the hopes of those on board were raised with the prospect; but the hose melted and the smoke became so dense in the main boiler-room that it was impossible for the firemen to remain longer at their posts. All efforts now had to be directed toward saving the crew, for it was apparent that the ship was lost beyond hope. Such sails as were still bent were spread, and an effort made to run the vessel ashore, for the bay was filled with young ice and pudge, through which it was impossible to force a boat, even its own length, from the ship, and yet not sufficiently strong to bear the weight of a man. It seemed as if fate was against the ill-starred vessel, for the wind, which had been blowing strong during the morning, when it increased the danger, now that a strong breeze was desirable to force the ship through the ice, died out completely and the vessel scarcely moved through the water. What motion she had was directed by the tide and ice, for she would not mind her helm, and drifted into the channel between Lutke Island and a low spit running out from the main-land, where she grounded in shallow water, and again hopes were entertained that something might yet be saved. These hopes, however, were of short duration, for the smoke rendered it impossible to reach the valve that closed the out-board delivery from the engine and by which means the hold could be filled with water, and thus the fires extinguished while the vessel would be held firmly aground. But, with three or four heavy bumps, she passed on over the bar into the deep water of the outer harbor. While passing the low spit which juts out from the main-land, an attempt was made to get a line on shore by means of a light skin canoe, and after one or two failures, which occasioned the most anxious delays, a small line was landed and thus a stouter cable hauled on shore and made fast to a piece of driftwood which was frozen into the beach. By this line it was attempted to warp the five boats ashore, but they made slow progress, and it became necessary to abandon the two rear boats, and their crews were put into the others after the line had been cut clear from the vessel. They were subsequently hauled ashore by the line and all connection with the doomed vessel was severed. It was not midnight when the last boat left the side of the ship, and though but about five hundred yards from the beach it was two o'clock of December 1st before they reached the shore. Before that, however, they saw the flames break out through the fore hatch, and envelope the entire ship, and as if the deserted vessel was making one last despairing appeal for assistance, a sky-rocket went whizzing into the firmament from amidst the flames, and two rifles, or shot guns, which it had been impossible to save from the steerage, discharged their volleys over the grave of the *Rodgers*. Presently the wind changed its direction to the southeast and drove the vessel back directly for the beach, to the most intense gratification of the ship-wrecked crew; but, to their utter chagrin, her course was again changed by the ice and she passed into the channel well up into the harbor, where she was last seen on the morning of December 2d, still burning, and where she subsequently sank. All were too much fatigued to attempt the construction of a shelter, but slept in the open air. The following morning, the wind having shifted during the night to the northward, the ice was seen to have left the shore, and the boats were launched and headed for the native village of Nunámo, near the cape of that name, but the ice again closing in, they were forced to return and again haul the boats ashore. Another night was passed here in a violent snow-storm, with no other shelter than could be provided by the boats with their sails and canvas. It happened that two native Tchouktchis were on board the vessel at the time of the disaster and landed with the crew. As soon as they reached the land they set out for their homes, and, on the morning of December 2d, returned to the ship-wrecked party with other natives and all the sleds of the village. A most cordial invitation was extended to Captain Berry to bring his people to their village, and live with them until relief should arrive from the United States. No offer of assistance could have been more well meant or timely, and Captain Berry very gratefully accepted the hospitality of these generous savages, leaving Ensign H. J. Hunt with a party in charge of the boats and stores until a few days later, when sufficient open water appeared to permit their removal also to the village.

"ONE-EYED RILEY."

Other villages soon requested permission to be of assistance, and asked for their quota of men to take care of, and soon the crew were scattered throughout all the villages that surround the bay. Both the dogs on board the *Rodgers* perished with the vessel, one of them a queer little animal nick-named "One-eyed Riley," who had been a great pet with the sailors.

The grief of the natives when they saw the ship burning, and knew the condition of the ice, was no doubt genuine. The old chief of the village which was the first to offer shelter to the people of the *Rodgers* wrung his hands and cried, "Ship cook 'em, no good. Too many men cook 'em, no go shore." Almost all the men near East Cape speak a little English, and some quite well. One man whom I met on board the steam whale-ship *Belvidere*, a Tchouktchi from Plover Bay, talks English as well as if he had been born in the United States and lived there all his life. He had been for fourteen years before the mast on American ships, and thus had visited nearly every known land. I have no doubt he has the reputation at home of being a big liar, because he tells the truth about the white men's country and about animals that look like little men and have feet like hands and long tails. The natives who visit us at our house on Eeteetlan are never tired of listening to anecdotes about monkeys and parrots, the birds that talk, and I had to translate the parrot language into Tchouktchi for their benefit. This gave more force to the anecdotes, though it made it all the more difficult for the narrator, with only a limited knowledge of the language at his command.

An incident transpired about this time at St. Lawrence Bay that tends to show that in some instances the bread that is cast upon the waters will return even before the many days are up. Shortly after the ship entered the harbor, an old Tchouktchi, named Owingeleen, was out in his canoe hunting walrus when he was caught by a gale and detained on Lutke Island for a week. There were with him at the time a number of men, women and children, and they could neither reach the land nor the ship. They had no food, and Captain Berry, when he noticed their desperate condition and saw them running up and down the beach looking for the disgusting little kelp-fish to stay their hungry stomachs, felt a sympathy for them, and slacked a boat ashore to the edge of the surf, where he threw overboard a keg containing bread, molasses, and canned meat, which washed ashore and was picked up by the natives. Two days afterward the storm abated somewhat, and the old man came aboard to return thanks for the timely gift, and when the bay froze over he would bring some reindeer meat. The incident was forgotten until after the ship was burnt, when the old man made his appearance with reindeer meat and tallow, and said the white men had been good to him. "Now cook 'em ship," he wanted to do something, and took two men to his own house, while recommending the others to the kind offices of his people.

CHAPTER XI.

PROSPECTS OF RELIEF.

CAMP HUNT, EETEETLAN, N. S.,
Jan. 1*st*, 1882.

CAPTAIN BERRY is at a loss to account for the origin of the fire, as the place where it first made its appearance was stored with materials that are not considered subject to spontaneous combustion. He thinks that it may have occurred from the charring of the deck underneath the donkey boiler. The steam pipes for heating the ship all pass between decks except the waste pipe, which returns through the hold, but before reaching that the steam has made the round of the ship and is comparatively cool. The men lost everything except what they had with them at the time when the fire broke out, as the smoke filled the forecastle almost immediately, and when they had once left it they were unable to return. The officers lost nearly all their clothing, and indeed such of their wardrobe as was saved and not required for immediate use was distributed among the men who most needed it. Captain Berry says that all behaved in the most exemplary manner, but has mentioned to the Secretary of the Navy, Master-at-Arms Wm. F. Morgan as especially deserving of credit for his conspicuous gallantry and determination in maintaining his position at the nozzle of the hose in the smoking hold, until dragged out by the rope around his waist more dead than alive. Several times this was repeated, until the Captain forbade his re-entering the hold. This order, however, was unnecessary, for already he was stretched upon the deck, nearly suffocated, and it was more than two weeks before he had recovered his strength so as to be able to walk around unassisted.

Captain Berry expects to be able to engage one of the vessels of the whaling fleet among the first to enter Behring Strait this spring, to take him to St. Michael's in Alaska, where he will await the arrival of the Alaska Commercial Company's steamer *St. Paul*, and engage passage for his people upon her to San Francisco, should no vessel be sent to his relief from the Pacific fleet. He also recommends that any vessel that may be sent to his relief shall bring some presents as rewards for the kind savages who have taken him, with his officers and men, into their houses and fed them through the entire winter. It matters not that their homes are a trifle worse than the meanest shanties in civilized communities, they are their only homes and the welcome was genuine and well meant. Should the gifts come before the party leaves Behring Strait the Captain can see that the presents reach the individuals most deserving. It would cost but a trifle to reward them handsomely. What they want is ship's bread, molasses, tea, sugar, Henry rifles, and cartridges, powder, bullets, lead, caps, shot, knives, axes, saws, and carpenter's tools in general, needles, thimbles, calico, beads, tobacco, pipes, match-rope, matches, pots, kettles, pans, tin cups, chopping-knives, and under-clothing. It would not cost five thousand dollars to make them the happiest savages on the eastern continent, and teach them that it is nothing lost to care for white people who need assistance. There is no doubt but that the Russian Government will decorate with gold medals those who have been most conspicuous in kindness to our people, but, at the same time, it would not be out of place for some recognition to come from the people most interested in those who have received the benefit. It may not seem like much of a gift to feed a hungry man on rotten walrus meat, but there are sometimes occasions in the life of a sailor when even a meal of so disgusting a character as that may prove a great blessing. I remember, before leaving the ship for this island, that I was occasionally tempted, when passing a quarter of beef that hung in the rigging, to cut off a slice of the cold raw meat and eat it. One of my comrades among the officers bantered me about it one day and asked if I did not do it to "show off." He could not realize that anyone could like raw meat. I told him that he might be thankful if, before he got home again, he would not be glad to get anything as good as that to eat. Since the loss of the ship his only food has been the rotten walrus meat of the natives, and he has sent me word here that he remembers what I said, and that he has seen the day alluded to. There is another officer, who had been brought up in Paris and accustomed to the indulgence of a taste educated in that city of supreme cookery, whose stomach revolted at the idea of raw meat, and yet he knew how efficacious it is considered in averting scurvy. He often in the wardroom announced his intention during the winter of forcing himself to eat a certain quantity of raw meat as an anti-scorbutic, and said he intended to select the best portions of reindeer meat and make it into pills, which he would throw down his throat and compel himself to swallow. Poor fellow, he is faring worse than that now, and has no chance or desire to make pills of his food. It is no trifling matter in his case, either, for it was a long time before he could bring himself to eat this food at all, and only then when he was actually starved into it. He has grown thin and weak, and Captain Berry has felt great anxiety for him. Most of the officers and men submitted as gracefully as possible to the force of circumstances, and are in good health and spirits. The want of tobacco is keenly felt by those accustomed to its use, and the lack of a sufficient supply of skin clothing has made it necessary for some to confine themselves to the houses more than is healthful. Captain Berry has, however, succeeded in securing nearly enough to clothe all his people, and on his return to St. Lawrence Bay will take an additional supply from this station.

There was another officer with a dainty appetite, who had grown stout on good things, and often at the mess table in the ward room of the *Rodgers* would send his untasted food out to be given to "the poor," who would gladly number himself with that host now. He has lost a great deal of that graceful rotundity of person that previously distinguished him, for it was a long time before he could eat what was set before him. But youth, a cheerful disposition and sound health have come to his relief and given him an appetite that does more than spice to make his food palatable to him. It will require a long season, however, at the restaurants of San Francisco before the clothes he left there will fit him.

The following letter from one of the officers on the ship at the time of the disaster, which was written to the chief surgeon, who is with the party at this island, and which was not intended for publication, gives a graphic account of the condition of affairs there.

NORTH HEAD, *December 24th,* 1881.

MY DEAR DOCTOR :

To be in the fashion, I will begin by wishing you all a Merry Christmas and a Happy New Year. As the Captain will give you a full detail of the disaster, I'll merely confine myself to a bird's-eye view of the affair, and our present pitiable condition. The fire was in the fore-hold, and, in spite of all our efforts to extinguish it, kept gaining upon us until two P.M., when we had to abandon the ship. All hands were hard at work all day. I myself kept passing buckets of water for a good long while, and then turned to, and, with Stoney and two men, removed all the coal-oil from the sail room, which, being in the immediate vicinity of the fire, got very hot, and consequently little fitted for so dangerous a substance as coal-oil. The dispensary was thick with smoke all day, and when the fire alarm was given I opened it and threw all the whiskey and alcohol overboard. I was kept pretty busy all day between the fire and the sick. We had several accidents, all of which were cases of asphyxia. Morgan, especially, was very ill, and has not quite recovered yet. When he was taken out of the fore-hold he presented all the signs of asphyxia, the breathing being very difficult. We had to employ Sylvester's method for artificial respiration, which proved very successful indeed. Among the other patients were Stoney, Grace and Loudon. The wardroom was full of smoke all day and also of carbonic-acid gas, generated by the burning coal, and the result was fifteen men suffering with acute cephalalgy. All that could be done to save the ship, and all that ingenuity could suggest, was tried, but all to no purpose. Everybody was cool and attended faithfully to his share of the work. No provisions or clothing could be got at, and we lost most of our things. I, for my part, only saved two suits of under-clothing, a pair of trousers, and four plugs of tobacco, for I had no time to attend to my own things, busy as I was with my patients and trying to see them safely stowed in their respective boats. In consequence of this I could save nothing belonging to the medical department except the journal and the atmospheric reports up to date. Orders had also been issued that the boats were to be loaded only with whatever provisions and trade articles we could find about the deck. I hated to see all the instruments and the microscope go, but it could not be helped. The ice was very thick around the ship and had we not succeeded in getting a line ashore with the skin boat some lives might have been lost, for we could not make any headway and the flames were spreading aft, and if we had attempted to reach the beach over the ice we would have broken through and would have been immediately frozen, for we had to spend the night ashore shivering with cold and harassed by hunger, as we had had nothing to eat all day. The subsequent day we made an attempt to reach the village of North Head, about five miles up the coast, but a southerly wind sprang up and choked the bay with ice, so that our boats were utterly helpless. We landed again and built a tent with the boats and their sails, where we spent an uncomfortable night, especially the Captain and I, for we were right under a part of the canvas which, weighed down by the falling snow, formed a percolater through which the water kept constantly dropping upon us. The next morning after that uncomfortable night the natives came down with their sledges to take us to their village. I had the sick comfortably fixed, keeping Morgan on the sleigh I was attached to. To give you an idea of our weakness I need only say that it took us nearly eight hours to reach the village, distant only about four and a half miles. This is not surprising if you take into consideration that we had had scarcely any food and no water for two days. Hunt and his boat's crew were left on the beach to take care of the things that could not be taken on the sleighs. Three days later we all returned to the beach to bring the boats around. A harder and colder work I never undertook, and my right foot was pretty badly frost-bitten. I at first went to the house of a reckless native called "Sam," and for the first week had nothing but rotten walrus. On inquiry I found that the grub was better in the other houses, so I unceremoniously moved into the Captain's house, where the grub is a little better and seldom rotten. But *pour comble de malheur,* our host is suffering from a disease which, though latent now, may break out at any time, as it did last winter, according to his own account, and make it still more unpleasant for us in such confined quarters. Life here is of course very monotonous, and twenty out of the twenty-four hours we spend upon our backs. We all crave for something to do, and especially for something to eat. For my part, I am always hungry. I spend the day craving for something or other, and several times I have dreamed that I was in a good restaurant enjoying a good dinner, when I would be suddenly awakened by our hostess to feast on seal or walrus meat. We saved two half barrels of beans, two tins of coffee, two half barrels of sugar and five of flour, and now and then we indulge in the luxury of a plate of bean soup. To-morrow, in order to celebrate Christmas with proper dignity, we are to have some bean soup besides a cup of coffee. Just think of it! I am impatient for the day to arrive. I have no Christmas presents to send to any of you, but I want one from each. From you I want a four-ounce bottle of molasses; from "Put" a buttered biscuit (half an inch of butter on each half of the biscuit), and from Gilder, two pounds of smoking tobacco, for I don't know what I should do if I were to be without it. Smoking helps to kill the time so much. Remind the Captain to bring down some Tobasco sauce, and some salt and pepper. It is useless to describe the horrible life we are living here, for you will all have a taste of it in April when you come down to meet the whaler.

My best love to all. Your sincere
C.

The winter has been, so far, an exceedingly mild one, but whether unusually so for this coast I have at present no data for ascertaining. The lowest temperature recorded up to date, January 7th, was on the 18th and 19th of December, when the thermometer recorded $-35°$ F.

December 29th it rose to 13°F., with a wind from the east and south to southwest. The natives say it is always milder at this part of the coast than even a few miles to the east or west, and it was not difficult to recognize a considerably lower temperature upon the main-land close by than upon the island, though we had no opportunity of making a test with the thermometer. A very faithful record of the temperature and condition .of the atmosphere has been kept by Frank Melms, one of the party at this island, which will prove very interesting as a portion of the meteorological history of the Arctic.

The position of the island was established by numerous observations of the stars before the weather became too cold to use the necessary instruments, and ascertained to be 67° 03′ north latitude and 172° 45′ west longitude. Among the natives I found two of Lieutenant Hovgaard's visiting cards, on which he had written the date and position of the *Vega* when frozen in, October, 1878, and gave the position, as ascertained by observations with an ice horizon, as 67° 05′ north latitude and 173° 15′ west longitude. The position of the *Vega* during that winter was often pointed out to me by the natives, and agrees most satisfactorily with our observations, for I should estimate her location as about eighteen miles west of Eeteetlan and a little further off shore.

CHAPTER XII.

THE FATE OF PUTNAM.

ANOTHER disaster which befell the crew of the *Rodgers* happened after my departure, and was related to me by Captain Berry at Yakoutsk. When the vessel went into winter quarters it was the intention of Lieutenant Berry to build a small house on shore immediately, and transfer thither a large part of his stores. The weather continued so unfavorable, however, that he had been unable to land material, otherwise there would have been an ample supply of provisions on the beach. Ten days before the fire Mr. Hunt started, with a team of nine dogs, up the coast, with the intention of visiting the officers at the Wood House on Eeteetlan Island, which was about one hundred and fifty miles distant, but owing to the severe storms he was compelled to turn back, arriving at St. Lawrence Bay two days before the fire. The next day Hunt went aboard the ship, leaving his team on the beach, and these were the only dogs saved, some having died and some being lost with the ship. Their condition would not have been quite so deplorable if plenty of dogs had been saved. During that first night on shore they tried to get the rest and sleep so much needed, but the temperature was so low that occasionally they were obliged to get up and run to keep up the circulation. At first it was undecided whether to try and reach St. Michael's in the boats, go to Eeteetlan or remain with the natives at North Head. On consideration it was seen that the journey to St. Michael's was impossible, for the distance is nearly four hundred miles, and the ice would render their boats useless. The Wood House was also out of the question, because provisions for only six men had been left there, and thirty extra men would soon consume them, and leave all in a worse predicament. Besides, they had no way of conveyance, and would have to walk the distance—about one hundred and fifty miles—a very fatiguing journey when the snow is upon the ground. They did not know whether or not the natives would prove friendly, having had but little communication with them since their arrival in the bay.

It was decided to cast their lot with the natives, and next morning the boats were launched (the ice having blown a short distance from shore during the night) and headed for the village at North Head. The ice soon closed in, compelling Lieutenant Berry to haul the boats up on the beach; and a camp was formed with upturned boats, sails and tents, and all made themselves as comfortable as possible during the violent snowstorm which had set in. Half a pound of pemmican each and some bread was served out for the day's fare. Some natives came to the camp in sledges and invited the shipwrecked people to their village. The offer was gratefully accepted, and when the storm abated each crew (the ship's company was divided into boat's crews, with an officer in charge of each) made its way as best it could to the village, about seven miles distant, where they arrived after a hard day's tramp through snow from two to three feet deep. One boat's crew was left in charge of the provisions and boats at the camp. This trip was the most fatiguing of any attempted during the winter, the men being insufficiently clothed and rendered unfit for travel by their recent exertions at the fire.

When the village was reached the crew was divided, two men being assigned to each house or hut; and here they got their first introduction to walrus and blubber. In four or five days the storm ceased, and a party was sent down for the boats and provisions. The ice had been broken up and driven off shore, so the boats were launched and stowed and sailed round to North Head. It was intensely cold, making the trip anything but agreeable. The boats were hauled up for the winter. The first thing was to trade. Lieutenant Berry at once began to trade with the natives for clothing, and he soon had the men comfortably clad. The provisions saved from the ship were kept in reserve, every one being compelled to live on the native food. In three days the supply of meat in the village began to run short, and it became evident to Lieutenant Berry that his crew would have to be divided. Natives from other villages had kindly invited some to come and spend the winter with them, so the crew was divided into three parties. Mr. Zane was placed in charge of one party, and went to the village at South Head; Mr. Hunt, with his party, took up his abode in a settlement a short distance up the bay; Mr. Waring and Mr. Stoney remained with the rest at North Head.

As soon as we who were left on the Island had become established, Mr. Putnam set up a tide gauge and took a series of observations to definitely determine the position of the island, which was found to be, as I said, 172° 45' E. L. and latitude 67° 3' north. He was on his way down the coast with the intention of visiting the ship to report progress when he heard at Inchuan, twenty-five miles west of East Cape, of the burning of the ship. He immediately started back for the Wood House, hired four natives and all the teams he could, loaded the sleds with provisions and started for St. Lawrence Bay. On all the sleds were stowed five boxes of bread, about one thousand pounds of pemmican and a few small stores. In the meantime Lieutenant Berry turned over the command of everything at the bay to Master Waring, and, in company with one native, had started for the Wood House, taking the one surviving team of dogs. At Inchuan he met Mr. Putnam, and gave him orders to continue his trip and to bring Mr. Hunt and Mr. Zane back with him. Early in January Mr. Putnam and his three natives arrived at their destination. He remained several days after delivering the provisions to allow his dogs to recuperate.

On January 10, the weather being fine, they left the North Head for the Wood House, Mr. Putnam driving his own team and Mr. Hunt riding on the sled with him, Dr. Castillo riding with Ehr Ehren—the principal native of the party—and Mr. Zane riding with another native. Dr. Castillo was going up for the trip only, and had made arrangements with a native at St. Lawrence Bay to bring him back. They had not proceeded far when Putnam's sled broke down, and, although repaired by his men, Hunt was obliged to ride with the third native. It is hard to say whether this little accident caused the loss of Putnam or the safety of Hunt. Toward noon the sky became overcast. A wind sprang up from the northward and soon increased to a terrific gale, filling the air so thickly with snow that it became impossible to see the route, and consequently the natives lost their way. They kept on, however, making the dogs face the gale, until six P. M., when the natives deemed it expedient to camp where they were for the night. It was absolutely necessary to come to a halt, because it would have been death to the dogs to compel them to face the gale longer. The air was so thick with the drifting snow that the lead dogs could not be seen by the drivers. This was a night of most intense suffering, sometimes sitting on the sleds to try to get a little sleep, and then compelled to move about to get warm. The thermometer registered — 30° Fahrenheit, and they were obliged to remain in this temperature, without even protection from the winds, from six o'clock in the evening until eight next morning. In the morning it moderated a little, and they decided to return to St. Lawrence Bay and wait until the weather became more suitable for travelling. The storm increased in violence all the time, but as the wind was now behind they had no trouble, and the bay was reached in safety. There being no dog food at North Head it became necessary to go to the south side. The bay was crossed, arriving on the southern shore about one and a half miles from the village of Nutapinwin, their destination. All the heavy gales during this season of the year were from the northward and westward. Just before getting to the village it was necessary to make a sharp turn to the right and go in the teeth of the gale for about two hundred yards. The order in which the sleds were proceeding was, Castillo and Ehr Ehren, Putnam, Zane and Notung and Hunt and a native, who were some distance behind. Proceeded along well until they made the turn to face the gale, when Putnam, not having the ability to control dogs so well as the natives (it is difficult to force the dogs to go to windward in a severe storm), or probably not knowing of the abrupt deviation from his course, as he could not see the other sleds turn, probably kept straight on. Zane, being familiar with the locality, recognized some landmarks when near the village, but Putnam could not recognize the marks, as this was his first visit to the place.

About this time Zane overtook Putnam, and when their sleds were abreast remarked, "Well, Put, it seems that we are all right after all." Putnam answered, "I hope so." They were the last words he was ever heard to utter, and that was the last seen of him. His sled fell a little behind. The natives made the turn with some difficulty, but Putnam missed it, partly owing to his being unable to see them. It is thought that as the wind was quartering he was sitting on his sled back to the wind, which, being very strong, gradually edged his sled out of the track toward the ice, which was but a short distance off. However, he got on the ice, and the supposition is that after going some distance out he became aware of his mistake, and not being able to see which way to go, and his shouts not being heard in such a violent gale, he camped, deciding to wait for clear weather, and also knowing that a search would be made for him as soon as he was missed. On reaching the village, in about five minutes after speaking with Putnam, Mr. Zane went immediately into a house, as he was almost frozen. It was soon discovered that Putnam was missing, and, thinking that he had made some mistake, a native started down to the beach to look for him, and when Hunt came along on his sled he found Notung (the native) yelling with all his might, but, thinking this noise was to guide him, kept on to the village. Here he ascertained that it was Putnam he was seeking. Hunt went in and inquired of Zane if Putnam had arrived; this was the first intimation Zane had of the unfortunate occurrence. Both then started for the beach to assist in the search; they were both now thorougly alarmed, for they could appreciate the danger of being lost in such a storm. They offered every inducement, entreated, and ordered the natives to hitch up the dogs and hunt for the unfortunate man; but they would neither hitch up their dogs nor allow them to use their own dogs, saying that the gale was too heavy, they could not see, and that probably next day would be fine and then all would go out and hunt. All threats proving unavailing, nothing could be done but to wait for the morrow. The gale was increasing in violence every moment. After going down to the beach it was impossible to get back to the houses, the wind blew so strong in the face. During the night the heavy wind detached the ice from shore and carried it to sea. Next morning, at daylight, they again went on the search. Hunt and Zane started along the beach, and natives taking various other directions to look for him. The wind had gone down some, but it was still blowing so hard as to make travelling very difficult. The morning was clear, however, and a considerable distance could be seen. Hunt and Zane gazed on the place which the night before had been one sheet of ice, and saw that it was now clear water, with no ice in sight. They walked along the beach about a mile, until they came to a bluff which they knew it would have been impossible to pass on a sled, and satisfied themselves that he was not on the beach. It was almost certain that he had camped on the ice and been carried to sea with it. The only chance for his safety seemed to be that the wind would spring up from the southward and drive the ice in shore, or that it would become calm and allow new ice to form between the old and the shore, so that the unfortunate man could walk over it.

The next day Hunt and Zane, with three natives, started

for North Head to notify Waring of the sad accident; Castillo was left at South Head to look after Putnam if he should come ashore. After crossing the bay they met Waring and told him of the calamity. He told them to proceed to the Wood House in obedience to the orders of Lieutenant Berry, and he would immediately set out on a search along the coast for Putnam. The Wood House was reached on the 19th, where they found Lieutenant Berry busy in making preparations for a sledge journey along the coast to the westward, expecting Putnam to accompany him. When Waring heard of the accident he was on his way to South Head to get some walrus meat, provisions at his village being scarce; he gave the charge of everything at North Head to Stoney, and went on to search to the southward. At half-past two that afternoon (19th) he received a note from Cahill, one of the crew stationed at South Head, stating that Putnam had been seen on the morning of the 13th on an ice-floe about three miles from shore. The natives would not launch their skin-boats on account of the intervening thin ice (which is even worse on the boats than heavy ice), though every effort was made by Cahill, who offered large rewards, to induce them to do so. Late in the afternoon of the following day word was received that Putnam had been seen from a village six miles south of South Head, on the ice eight miles from shore, and that the natives were making preparations to rescue him. Waring pushed on to the village, reached it that night through a heavy wind and snow storm, blowing hard off shore. It was here ascertained that on the preceding day an attempt had been made by four men of the *Rodgers'* crew, assisted by two natives, to rescue Putnam; but after proceeding nearly three miles they were forced to return, the boat having been cut through in so many places that they were barely able to keep her afloat until shore was reached. Another severe off-shore storm was now raging, and the unfortunate man was lost sight of. The natives were confident that the ice-floe would be driven inside of a point some distance down the coast, and preparations were immediately made to go down to the point as soon as the weather would permit. Now there was trouble in procuring dogs to travel, because the natives at both North and South Head were afraid, on account of some previous difficulty with the natives at Indian Point, to go down the coast or to allow their dogs to go, saying they would be killed. At last, however, a team was scraped up from four villages, ranging over a space of thirty or forty miles. It was the 17th before another start could be made; it opened stormy but soon moderated, and the search continued with one native and a team of eight dogs. The coast was skirted to the sixth settlement, about thirty miles, but no news was heard; the off-shore wind had driven the heavy ice to sea. The next day, not being able to get dogs to continue the journey, Waring was compelled to return to the village next to South Head.

Natives were now despatched along the coast offering great rewards for the rescue of Putnam, or for his body if he were dead. Another heavy gale set in, making travelling impossible. On the 22d a southeast gale brought the ice in shore again, but it was found that the sea had crushed it up into small pieces, no heavy floes being anywhere in sight. Men from down the coast brought no news. The case appeared almost hopeless now, as all of the floes must have broken up during the five days' gale. The ice was not more than five or six feet thick and had much slush and snow on it, and could not possibly have withstood so continuous a storm. Waring retraced his steps and reached North Head at dark on the 24th, but returned to South Head the next day. On the 26th he received a rumor that some dogs had come on shore from the ice. For two days he was prevented by storms from proceeding; but on the 29th, though intensely cold, he started down the coast to identify the dogs. He arrived at Lauren, thirty miles down the coast, in the evening, and found three of Putnam's dogs there. Several dogs came ashore, but the natives could catch only three. The natives said that all came ashore without harness. Whether the dogs really came ashore without harness or whether the natives, fearing the dogs would be claimed and taken from them, told this story to make Waring think they did not belong to Putnam is not known; but the dogs were positively recognized as belonging to the team Putnam drove on that fatal day. Rumors of Putnam's having been seen were constantly coming in, and after being weather-bound for three days Waring, on the 2d of February, started down the coast to verify them. He kept steadily on, searching the whole coast minutely from South Head to Plover Bay. He communicated with several natives who spoke good English, and they were satisfied that Putnam had never come near the shore.

At Engwort (sixty miles from South Head) another dog, with a pistol shot wound in his neck, came on shore ten days previously and was recognized as belonging to Putnam's team. This dog—as, indeed, all were—was very thin and emaciated, covered with ice and had every appearance of having been long in the water. Putnam had probably shot this dog, intending to use it for food, but it had succeeded in escaping. In all six dogs, out of a team of nine, came ashore. At Marcus Bay and Plover

Bay letters were left for the whalers, informing them of the condition of the wrecked crew and urging them to hasten to their assistance. Mr. Waring was more than a month on this trip, getting back on the 18th of February, and did not return until he was fully satisfied that there were no hopes of Putnam's safety.

Under Mr. Stoney's supervision a thorough search of the coast was made to the northward as far as East Cape, but to no purpose. Most of the gales had been from the northwest and the ice could not have drifted up there though there is quite a strong current setting to the northward through Behring Strait.

It is known that Putnam was not dead the third day after being lost, and how much longer he survived can only be conjectured. All this time the temperature was from 20 to 40 degrees below zero, and he had no protection from the piercing winds. True, he was very warmly clad. He probably killed one or more of his dogs for food; he surely did not die of starvation. The floe that he was on doubtless broke into fragments during one of the gales and he was drowned. It would not seem so awful if he had perished in a shorter time, at least it would be some consolation to know that his sufferings were not so prolonged. Some spoke of there being a possibility of his having drifted down to St. Lawrence Island thus being saved; but the officers spoke some natives from the island while on their way down in the *Corwin*, and they knew nothing of the accident. Thus the last hopes of his shipmates were destroyed. The natives gave all the assistance in their power to aid in the search. News of the loss was known all along the coast and men were placed on the lookout within two days after it occurred.

CHAPTER XIII.

ACROSS SIBERIA.

Sradnia Kolymsk, N. S.
March 8th, 1882.

THE sun was above the horizon less than two hours a day at the time I left Eeteetlan for the Kolyma River on my way to the telegraph station in Eastern Siberia, whither I was sent to carry the news of the disaster. This gave very short days and very long nights, which is one of the inconveniences of winter journeys within the Arctic circle. To be sure, it is not so difficult to follow a coast line or travel over a road well known to the driver even in the dark as to travel over unknown territory, but still it has its disadvantages, and these are increased to a near-sighted man, who at night might nearly as well be blind. While upon a sled which is under the guidance of another person, he can nerve himself to submit blindly and confidently to his driver; but even this is trying when the road is so rough as to require all his strength to maintain his position upon the sled. The natives here also have a very inconvenient habit of starting long before daylight, even when they have only a short distance to go and could easily accomplish it by daylight. They will do this also when daylight is followed by a bright moon and the mornings are dark. They have no idea of time, and often mistake the northern light for approaching sunrise. There seems to be some one up and moving around in camp at any hour of the day or night, and you may hear him in the outer tent, when the following conversation ensues between him and some occupant:

The occupant shouts "*May?*" to which there comes a responsive grunt; then the occupant "*Yáytee?*" Another grunt. "*Nerar tóoree?*" Another grunt. "*Elgeró?*" "*E-e-e*," which means yes, and all may be liberally translated as "Hallo," "Is that you?" "Are there two of you?" meaning are you alone, and then, "Is daylight coming?" "Yes." I never knew them to reply "no" to this question under any circumstances, and I believe they say "yes" with a mental reservation that it is a long way off, but will probably come in the course of time. I have gone out sometimes two hours after such a conversation, and not the slightest trace of dawn was discernible, nor would there be for hours afterward. Such things are annoying to one who would like to arrange the hours of travel and departing upon a more reasonable schedule, but it will never do to break in upon the time-honored customs of these people, for you will involve yourself in greater difficulties thereby than by submitting.

The day of Captain Berry's arrival at Eeteetlan there also came from Nishne Kolymsk a Russian named "Wanker," who agreed to take me to that city for the sum of fifty roubles. I did not like the fellow's appearance. His eyes were too close together, and then he had a general hang-dog look that would give him away in the company of saints. I knew he was a liar, because he said he could read, and when I handed him a letter in the Russian language from the Russian Consul in San Francisco he read it all through with the deepest interest and most intense satisfaction depicted upon his countenance, occasionally smiling over some official pleasantry of the Consul's, or stumbling over a particularly hard word, and all the time held the letter upside down. I righted it once, but he immediately turned it again, with a look as much as to say, "I always prefer to read my letters that way." He then returned the letter after having carefully inspected the black border and the watermark on the paper, and said it was "All right;" an opinion for which I was duly grateful. He could talk fluently with Constantine though, and advised me to take him along to drive my dogs and as an interpreter. The interpreting was all well enough as far as they were concerned, and the only difficulty was in understanding Constantine or making him understand me. He was not a youth gifted with much understanding in any language, but at the same time he was of some benefit to me.

As an instructor of the Russian language he proved a total failure. Knowing I had to be for several months among the Russians, I thought that by gaining the start by a few words before I came plump into their country I would acquire an advantage, so I asked Constantine what the Russians said for "yes." "They say 'yes,'" he replied. This was easy enough to remember, so I went to the next word. "What do they say for 'no?'" I asked. "Why, they say 'no.'" This seemed a most remarkable coincidence, but certainly convenient, and I went on to something harder. "What does a Russian man say when he is hungry and wants something to eat?" "Oh, sir, he says he wants something to eat." Now, this was a little more than I could stand, and I immediately took a recess. I saw that the poor fellow had no idea how he spoke what little English he knew. He did not translate it from one language to the other, but had merely learned as a parrot would learn, only with greater fluency, for he seemed to have the well-known facility of the Russians in acquiring foreign languages, having in two months and a half on ship-board learned sufficient to be of considerable use there, as well as to our party on shore. *En route* he drove my sled, but we went very slowly, for the dogs I had were hastily bought after I had made up my mind to this trip, and proved a sorry lot. I found that the natives had not invariably picked out their best dogs to sell me, but, on the contrary, had chosen the poorest always, and when I happened to get a good dog it was because the one from whom I bought it had no poor ones in his lot.

Constantine always examined the dogs as an expert, and had a way of running his hand along the dog's backbone, and if it did not cut his finger he pronounced it a fine dog. He always asked if the dog had been trained as a leader, and seemed to have a most insatiable appetite for leaders. I don't know what dogs he expected to pull the sled in case he got all the leaders he wanted. He was a most faithful loser of articles belonging to his team, and I had to buy nearly a complete set of harness for him, as well as a brake and a whip at every village where we stopped. But when he came to me at one village to buy a whip, after I had just bought him one, not half an hour previously, I closed the market for whips. He said he might lose the first one and then the second would come handy. The second night of our journey we halted at the village of Ynedlin, near which the *Vega* wintered in 1878-9. We were entertained at the house of the chief, the largest house I had yet seen. The sleeping portion was about 30 feet long by 12 wide, and 7 feet high. Here was plenty of room and fresh air. It was here that Wanker promised to meet me the night of my arrival, and hurry me on to Nishne Kolymsk without any delay *en route*, merely expressing his fear that I could not stand the cold and rapid travelling. I was forced to remain at this house four nights, partially detained by stormy weather, and with the hope that Wanker might forget himself, and actually keep his appointment within a day or two. It was fortunate for me that the house was such a pleasant one, since I had to remain there so long. I had an opportunity now to witness their mode of life more closely than ever before, and it was here that I saw for the first time many of those disgusting customs that became so familiar to me afterward. They had plenty of walrus meat, and also of reindeer meat, and we lived well according to Tchouktchi ideas.

No matter how early you may awaken in the morning you will always find the mistress of the household already up—that is, her position changed from reclining to sitting, and as soon as she observes that you are really awake she hands you a few small pieces of meat; not much, only an ounce or two perhaps, but it steadies your nerves till breakfast time—that is, until the others wake up. Then she goes into the adjoining apartment, which is merely an enclosure to keep the dogs away from the household stores, and after fifteen or twenty minutes of pounding and chopping returns with the breakfast. A large flat wooden tray is placed on the floor, and the landlady, dropping off her clothes, takes her position at one end, a position inelegantly but accurately described as "squatting." The family and their guests gather around the board on either side, lying flat on their stomachs, with their heads toward the breakfast and their feet out, so that a bird's-eye view of the table and guests would look something like an immense beetle. The first course is some frozen weeds mixed with seal oil and eaten with small portions of fresh blubber, which the lady of the house cuts with a large chopping-knife. The approved method of eating this food is to take a piece of the blubber and place it somewhere on the pile of weeds and then press as much as you can gather between your thumb and the three adjoining fingers into a mass, which will, if you are lucky, stick together until you get it into your mouth. The man with the biggest thumb has the best chance here. One poor fellow whom I saw further up the coast who had lost his right hand and the thumb of his left had to be fed by his wife. The next course is walrus meat. This is also cut up by the presiding lady and is served with no stinting hand. At this portion of the meal the one who can swallow the largest piece without chewing has the advantage, and the only way to get even with him is to keep one piece in your mouth and two in your hand all the time. After this joint has been thoroughly discussed there comes a large piece of walrus hide, which has a small portion of blubber attached to it and the hair still on the outside. When the meat is rotten the hair can be easily scraped off, but otherwise it is eaten with the rest of the hide. This hide is about an inch thick and very tough, so that it is absolutely impossible to chew it, or, rather, to affect it by chewing. Even the dogs will chew perhaps for half a day upon a small piece of walrus hide hanging from a bag of meat, and fail to detach it. This is, therefore, cut into very small slices by the hostess and finishes the meal. It is really the most palatable dish of the meal, and furnishes something for the stomach to act upon, that generally occupies its attention till the following meal; but it is astonishing how easily a meat diet is digested and how soon one's appetite returns after having gorged at such a meal.

When forced to lie over on account of storms or some notion of Wanker's, and with nothing to do and nothing to read, it seemed to me that all I did was to lie on my back and watch for indications of the next meal. It was all there was to break the monotony, unless my pipe needed cleaning. This was always a welcome task, for by due carefulness I could generally make it last for half a day. There are usually two meals a day in a well provided Tchouktchi household—the breakfast just described and dinner, which comes on late in the evening. The dinner is almost identical in form with the breakfast, except that there is most always some hot cooked meat that follows the course of walrus hide. Sometimes the second course at breakfast or dinner may be frozen seal or reindeer meat, but the first and third courses are invariable, unless changed by force of circumstances beyond the control of the householder. Beside these two meals there is always a similar service to any guest who may arrive during the day from a distance, and all present share his luncheon with him, and not infrequently beat him out, unless he watches closely and keeps himself well provided. I speak feelingly of this matter, for often have I had a luncheon put before me, and devoured by those who had, perhaps, but just finished a meal, while I politely lingered so as not to appear too ravenous. I got over such trifling finally, and could take my place at the board with full confidence that I would get at least my share of what was going.

The evening, after dinner, is often devoted to games. They do not play chess or billiards; but we used to see who could walk the farthest on his hands, with his body

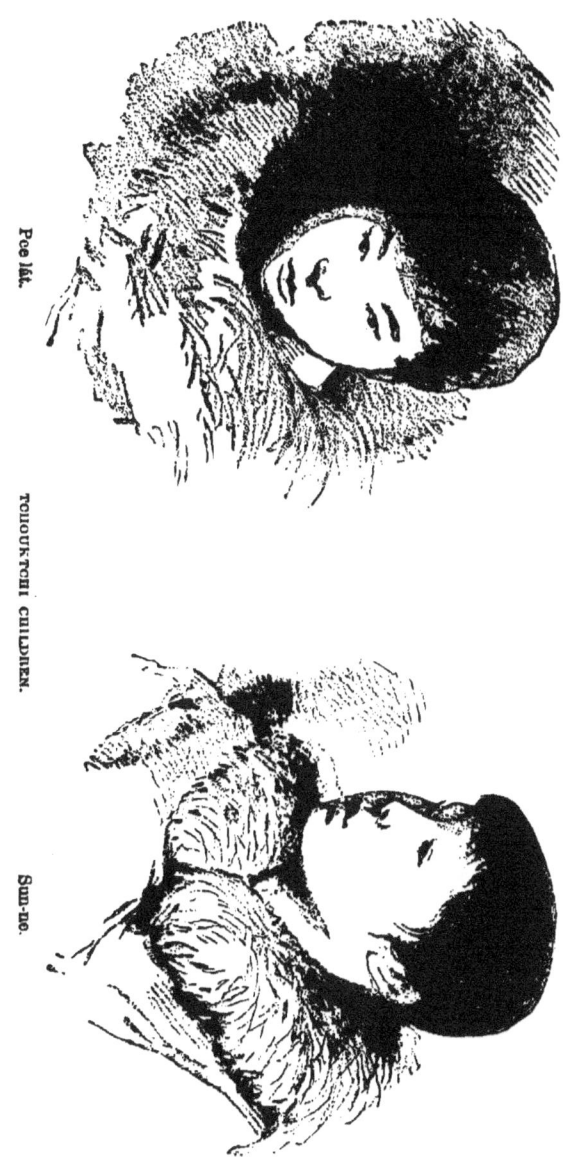

TCHOUKTCHI CHILDREN.

held horizontally from the hips, or upon his knees, while his feet were held in his hands behind him. Or perhaps the lights were extinguished, and some one played upon the drum, or *yarar*, and sang or chanted a most lugubrious melody, or would pass *crescendo* from an almost imperceptible sound into the loudest noise possible, accompanying the drum with a howl like a bear at bay, the most frightful noise he could make; and it did sound prodigious in the dark. During this time the landlord would occasionally shout *Ay-hék, ay-hék*, which seemed to inspire the drummer to renewed exertion. The drum is a wooden hoop, over which is tightly drawn a thin membrane from the skin of the reindeer. It has a handle on one side, and is beaten with a small bit of whalebone. This drumming never ceases from the moment the lights are out until the concert is over, which is generally after about two hours and a half. We had a concert the first night at Ynedlin, and during the performance I heard Constantine breathing heavily and gasping, and occasionally breaking out into groans and tears. This attracted the attention of the performer, who stopped and asked if he was sick. He groaned a "yes," and I thought I would have to resort to my medical stores, consisting of pills and bandages, but I did not know which to use, for upon inquiry it transpired that he had only a broken heart. He wanted to return to Tay-up-kine, the village near Eeteetlan, where was an old woman, named At-túng-er, who had grown-up children and grandchildren, and with whom he, a lad of nineteen years, had fallen in love. When asked what he was grieving for, he said "At-túnger," and after that I felt relieved, for I did not believe he would die of his broken heart.

During the entire journey this same scene was repeated

every time the *yarar* was brought out, and as soon as the lights were restored he appeared just as cheerful as if nothing disagreeable had ever occurred to him. I believe he was frightened, for the noise was at times most fiendish and harrowing, and it was at these portions of the music that he was most affected. It was the best assurance the player could have of the effectiveness of his performance. There were two girls about fifteen years of age in this household, one the daughter of my host and the other some relation, but I could never make out exactly what. The old man often tried to explain it to me by using the fingers of one hand, which he named, and showed that Tay-tin-cón-ne was the same relation to his daughter Mám-mak that his thumb was to his middle finger. But there is where I always fell out. I never could satisfy myself as to the kinship of his fingers. Occasionally during the day or evening these girls used to dance, taking their places side by side as if on the stage for a double clog, and, accompanying themselves with guttural sounds that it is impossible to describe, executed in unison fantastic contortions and gyrations somewhat similar to the Indians of North America. Their costume was the usual evening dress of the country, and consisted simply of a string of beads around the neck and a narrow breech-cloth of seal skin. This was an accomplishment I found had been acquired by all the children along the coast, and such entertainments were not rare.

The 13th of January I moved to the next village, starting in the dark at three o'clock in the morning, and arriving at our destination before noon. There were two other sleds beside mine, which belonged to a man from Ónman, who had with him his wife and son, a young man of about twenty-two years, with yellow hair and light hazel eyes, the first blond I had seen with these people. I afterwards saw another, a woman, at Enmukki, but they are very rare occurrences. The Ónman man entered the house at this place, and after some conversation with the occupants came out and told me we would have to go on to Ónman, which would take all night, as they had no dog food here. They gave us a luncheon of walrus meat, and I concluded to stay, preferring that my dogs should rest without food than work without. I thought, too, that I could get dog food by paying well for it, and after the others had left found I was not mistaken—that it was only a ruse common with these people when they want to get rid of undesirable guests. But I guess the Ónman people made the same discovery, for in half an hour they returned and stayed with us all night. Here, too, I had to wait four days, looking for Wanker or clear weather. These houses along the coast are all so many hotels for the accommodation of those travelling to and fro. At East Cape are certain articles which they can procure by trading, and at Nishne Kolymsk are others, so that they go from one end of the line to the other, a distance of about 1,500 miles, as they are compelled to follow the coast in all its tortuous windings. At East Cape they can get Henry rifles and cartridges, as well as American knives, tobacco and calico; while at Nishne Kolymsk they get Circassian tobacco, a cheap but very strong article, brass smoking pipes, bear spears, and such articles. The stock at East Cape is left by the American whalers, who have their agents among the natives there, and that at Nishne Kolymsk is in the hands of the Russian traders, who, during the latter part of the month of February, hold a fair near there on the river Anui, pronounced Ar-noo-ée. The natives pay nothing for their entertainment or for feeding their dogs, but they expect much from any white strangers who may happen to pass their way. If the native traveller has tobacco or beads, and his host wants some, he gives it to him ; but that is not paying for his board and lodging. He would do the same if he received nothing in return. While at Péelkan, the second station, at the mouth of the bay of that name, I saw many natives who were returning from a trip to East Cape. They told me that Wanker did not intend to come along for some time yet, that he was trading along the coast. This was discouraging, and I determined to proceed to Koliutchin village as soon as possible, and get along as well as I could.

CHAPTER XIV.

ON THE ROAD.

Sradnia Kolymsk, N. S.,
March 9th, 1882.

THERE were places on the road, beyond Wankaramen especially, where a guide was almost a necessity, unless short trips were made in the daylight only and when the coast line could be unmistakably distinguished. I knew I could easily find people going from one village to another until I reached Wankaramen, but from there to North Cape was a long stretch without villages, and it required two or three sleeps upon the snow to reach the village at North Cape, or Dairkíjpean, as the natives call it. It would not be easy to find company there. There was, however, an old man who came to Péelkan on his way back to his house at Wankaramen who said he would take me on from there. He wanted me to give him some biscuit to eat, as his teeth were not equal to the contest with frozen walrus meat; and when he showed me the teeth I agreed with him. On the right side of his upper jaw the teeth were perfect to the middle front tooth, and the lower jaw had the same arrangement on the left side of his mouth, so that when it was closed they fit perfectly and shut up like a pair of scissors; but it must have been perplexing when there was anything to be chewed. It was a long journey across the mouth of the bay to Kolintchin Island, and my dogs were not equal to the emergency, so when night came on I halted and built a snow house. The natives who had started with us reached the village that night, and were much alarmed for our safety when they found we did not get in during the night. Their anxiety was increased when the following day brought a snow-storm, which shut out the island from view, and left us as they supposed without anything to guide us. When we started in the morning I cautioned Constantine to keep faithfully in the tracks of the sleds that preceded us, as they were but faintly discernible under the falling snow. He told me his leader was a good one, and knew how to keep the road. For awhile I trusted to the dog's instinct, but when I found the wind upon my back instead of nearly directly in front of me, as it should have been, I began to doubt it, and asked Constantine where Koliutchin Island was. He pointed straight ahead, as I expected, but I had taken the bearing of the island by my pocket compass when we halted the night before, and on again regarding it I showed my driver that we were going almost exactly in the opposite direction.

I then took charge of the course myself, and after about an hour heard the barking and quarrelling of dogs in a team. I could not see them, but I shouted, and soon two sleds came up that had been sent out to look for us. The drivers were glad to have found us, and said they had been worried all night, thinking we were wandering around on the ice. I told them, however, that we were comfortably housed and that I knew where Koliutchin was, at the same time pointing in the proper direction. Then I showed them my compass, and as the island happened to be just magnetic north of us it appeared all the more wonderful to them. They imagined that it always pointed in the direction you wanted to go. While at Koliutchin Wanker came up, being only eleven days behind, but I felt greatly relieved when I saw him. We subsequently moved to Wankaramen, and proceeded on our journey with greater celerity than before, but not fast enough to satisfy one who felt so entirely dependent upon one man, and he thoroughly unreliable and bad. All along the route the natives, when an opportunity offered, cautioned me against him and said he meant no good by me. They begged me to return to Eeteetlan, and offered to take me there. The only thing that I was afraid of was that Wanker would get up in the night and run off with his team, leaving me high and dry on the beach. But I kept a close watch on him all the time.

In the daytime the natives would have warned me if he attempted to leave, and at night I always slept in the same house with him and would awaken at the slightest noise. During the journey I never trusted myself beyond pistol shot of his sled, and I think he knew I was watching him. At first he used to take advantage of my lack of knowledge of the Tchouktchi language to say things for the entertainment of the savages at my expense, and one day shouted at me in a most disrespectful manner. Then I spoke to him in good sound English. He did not understand what I said, but he knew what I meant, and, assuring me that he only wanted to tie my shoe-string, was ever afterward more considerate in his manner toward me. From Wankaramen to North Cape the weather was intensely cold, and the whole party, native and white, for there were three natives' sleds with us, suffered from frost-bites, though not of a serious nature. We found plenty of drift-wood at several points along the coast, and halted to make tea and cook some meat. This I found took the raw edge off of the cold, and made travelling and sleeping without shelter much more endurable. From North Cape to Oogárkin there were villages at intervals of from five to thirty miles. From Oogárkin to Erktréen, a native village of nineteen houses, near Cape Shelagskoi, there were no houses, and we slept three nights on the snow. Drift-wood was plentiful, and in ordinary weather camping out would not have been as disagreeable as might be supposed. We found several people at Enmatý, near Oogárkin, who were on their way to Nishne Kolymsk, and on the morning of February 8th eight sleds, drawn by ninety-three dogs, started. It was a brilliant sight, or would have been if you could have seen it; but the start was at four o'clock in the morning, about three hours and a half before daylight. Some of the sleds had gaudy calico storm-coats thrown over them, and the harness of several teams was trimmed with red. One man had several small bells attached to his harness, but I never heard a sound from them, and doubt if they had tongues. I believe they were dumb bells and intended solely for ornament.

It was a pleasant day at first, but during the afternoon a storm of wind and snow sprang up from the direction of our line of march, and when we halted at night it was blowing a gale, a genuine *poorga*, which continued throughout the night and the following day. When I lay down to sleep I sought shelter behind a sled, but soon had to leave it, because I found myself nearly suffocated by the weight of snow on top of me. Then I noticed that the natives, more wise than I, had lain down on the crest of the hill and were free from snow. Travelling the next day was simply torture, but it would be equally bad to sit still out of doors, so we kept on. The night was a pleasant one and we slept well. The next halt was upon the rocky coast not a great distance from Shelagskoi, and a huge cavern in the face of the cliff afforded small protection from the wind, but made a most picturesque camping place. The following day we reached Erktréen about two o'clock, and right glad we were to get there, for a frightful *poorga* was raging and the dogs could scarcely make any headway against it. There were plenty of houses here and but little food. In fact, in the house where I slept we fed the occupants, instead of eating their provisions. The next stretch was a long one, and we slept four nights in the snow. We had expected to reprovision our sleds at Erktréen, and were much disappointed at finding so little food. We were, therefore, on short rations, and as a consequence very cold, for nothing seems to defy the north wind like a full stomach. The natives were all very kind to me. They knew that Wanker was not helping me any more than he should, so they each had something for "Kelley," as is my Tchouktchi name. I believe I fared better than any one else in the party. About noon-time of the third day out we reached Rowchooan, as it is called by the Tchouktchis, or Bassarika, by which name it is known to the Russians.

Here is a deserted village of five log houses, which at one time constituted a village of Russian trappers. Here we found a large quantity of bear meat and dried fish for dog food which they had *cachéd* on their way down the coast, and, taking a good supply upon our sleds, we gorged like genuine savages that night, and slept soundly and warm. As night approached on the day following we were near the native village of D'lardlówran, the Barranno of the Russians. Three of the sleds halted on the beach at dark, while the sled to which I was attached and two others started to make a short cut across land to the village. One of the natives with us lives at that place and was anxious to get home after an absence of two months and a half. But without landmarks on the bare waste of snow, and no coast line to guide us, even he had to give up the search though less than three miles from home, and we lay down in the snow to wait for daylight. But before dawn came the worst *poorga* I ever encountered, and when we started in the morning we could see less distance ahead than when we halted in the dark. It was a terrible struggle, that little march of about two miles and a half. The wind blew directly in our faces and drove the sharp particles of hard frozen snow against the eye-balls and cheeks, so that it was impossible to look to windward for more than a hasty glance. The dogs could not face the storm and lay down in the harness, so that we had to go ahead and drag them along, while we waded painfully through snow nearly waist deep. One sled was soon left behind, while Wile-dóte, the native of the neighboring village, and Wanker and I floundered on through the storm.

At last we reached a hillside swept by the wind, and found sled-tracks which Wile-dóte recognized as the right trail, and we trotted along merrily until the sleds were caught by the wind and swept over a precipice. I saw Wile-dóte and his team disappear over the edge of the cliff into a cloud of whirling snow, and knew that in a second we must go too. I could do nothing but close my eyes and set my teeth when I felt myself in the air and falling, I knew not where. Fortunately it was a fall of but about twenty feet to a snow bank, down which the dogs, the sled and I rolled to the bottom, while I saw

Wanker, who had been sitting on the other side of the sled with his back to the cliff, shot over my head and reach the bottom first. I knew no one had been hurt, for the snow was very soft and we were almost buried by the drift before we could regain our feet, and I could not help laughing at the ridiculous figure poor Wanker cut as he passed over my head, rolled up in a little ball, and desperately grasping his brake. He looked like a witch riding on her broomstick. Wile-dóte's sled was broken, and, falling on his leg, caused a slight but not very painful contusion. We then began to look around to find some way out of this pit, but found it surrounded by a high wall of rock and snow, except one narrow drift that led again to the top of the hill. We plunged along as well as we could, but could only make a few yards' advance at a time, for the dogs had to be dragged along by main force. Time and time again we were compelled to throw ourselves down in the snow and rest for ten or fifteen minutes before making further exertion. Once again we were blown off the hill, but this time into a valley, which Wile-dóte recognized as the road to the village, not more than half a mile away.

We now moved along more rapidly and soon found the coast, and a short turn to the right brought us directly into the houses before we could see them. Several times during the morning I had to remove from my face a perfect mould or mask of frozen snow half an inch thick, and my nose, cheeks, chin and forehead were badly frozen. My companions fared no better. Three of Wile-dóte's dogs perished during the storm, and I found upon looking at my watch, after entering the house, that we had been more than seven hours upon the road. The other sled got in toward night, but the three that halted on the beach did not overtake us until the second day after we left D'lard-lówran. At this village we found four Russians from Nishne Kolymsk, who were much interested in the recital of our adventures during the morning. The next morning we again set out upon our journey, three of the Russians accompanying us. Wanker put me on the sled of one of these people, and right glad was I of the change, for now I felt sure that I would reach my destination. This man looked like an honest and an intelligent man, though he could not read, and said so. That night we halted at a deserted hut half filled with snow, but it was a sufficient shelter from a *poorga* that was raging at the time, and ever so much better than sleeping out of doors. Indeed, it was cheerful and cosey, with a fire blazing in the middle of the hut and a little of the smoke escaping through a hole in the roof, but most of it pervading the apartment. The tea-kettle hung over the flame, and a large pot of reindeer meat was cooking on one side of the fire, while we ate frozen fish which my new driver pulled from among the rafters. While we waited for tea my new Russian friends sang a pretty little chorus, and I slept dreaming of home and feeling more at home than I had for weeks.

I had at last reached the borders of civilization, and had no longer to crawl at night into the huts of the savages, and yet I could not forget how often I had been so glad to crawl into those same dirty hovels to escape from storms and hunger.

The next day we reached quite a large deserted village, and Wanker here told me that the next day we would reach his house and that there we would have to wait for Constantine, who was four days behind us, the sled he was with and one other having been separated from us during a *poorga* the first day out from Erktréen. I felt no uneasiness about him, for there was a Tchouktchi and a Russian with him who would take good care of him, and I knew they had plenty of food. In fact, it was the heavy load of food that caused them to fall behind. I told Wanker that I would rather go on to Nishne Kolymsk, as there was a great deal I wanted to attend to which I could do before Constantine arrived. But Wanker would not listen to it, and insisted that I should remain at his house. I poured my complaint into the ear of my driver that day, and, though he understood little of what I said, he did seize the main point, which was that I stayed at Wanker's against my will and preferred to go to Nishne Kolymsk. He said "*Da, da,*" and meant "yes," and here our conversation ended. He delivered me at Wanker's that night and departed early next morning. I failed to shake Wanker's determination during the day, but was equally determined to wait but one day longer, though he said the only people in Nishne who could read were away and would not be there for more than a week. This seemed likely and I began to waver, but the day following my good friend came early with a stranger, and I felt certain that my hour of deliverance was near at hand. And, sure enough, the stranger read my letter from the Consul, and told me I should go along with him. Wanker got very red in the face, and submitted with bad grace to an arrangement that I was certain did not please him. But I saw that the quiet stranger had some power and could enforce his will. Glad enough was I to go away, and with such a kind and considerate conductor, but I was overpowered when I found a covered sled in waiting to take me like a prince in triumph to my destination. It was a bitter cold day, and I was pleased when we halted at a village half-way to the town to get some hot tea, and, as usual, with it frozen fish.

Here the whole village had turned out to receive me, and the men stood in line with their heads bared and bowing as I passed them into the house. There was a friendly crowd here, also, but, though of my own race, I could only talk with them in the language of the savages, and our conversation was consequently limited to my very meagre knowledge of the Tchouktchi tongue, for they all seemed perfectly familiar with it and to speak it and their own language with equal fluency. My new friend took me to his house and did everything in his power to entertain me, and assist in carrying out my plans. I found that he was a Cossack, and acting commander during the absence of that official in Sradnia Kolymsk. I managed to make myself understood, and he told me that at Sradnia I would find some one who spoke French, and that he would send me to that place with a Cossack, who would take me in three or four days, while alone I would be a week or ten days *en route*. After Constantine arrived, and I finished my business at Nishne, I started for Sradnia Kolymsk with my Cossack guide, and bade good-by to some of the kindest people I ever met. All seemed equally anxious to do something for me, and my landlord, who had delivered me out of the hands of the Philistines, seemed really sad at parting. I had been at his house four days, and during that time he had devoted himself entirely to me, trying to make amends for the ill-conduct of my travelling companion, Wanker, who, by the bye, had told the Russians we met at D'lardlówran that he had brought me to the Kolyma because I was big and strong, and he was going to keep me at his house until the winter was past, and then I would be a good hand to catch fish for him. But my engagements did not permit of my remaining until the fishing season arrived. At Nishne Kolymsk I first heard of the loss of the *Jeannette*, and that some of her people had survived; but, though I could get along surprisingly well with the common every-

SRADNIA KOLYMSK.

day affairs, considering that I could not speak the language of these people, I got a very distorted account of the *Jeannette* affair. This was partially owing to my being unable to understand them, and partially because they had not heard a correct account of the mournful occurrence.

CHAPTER XV.

MIDDLE KOLYMSK.

SRADNIA KOLYMSK, N. S.,
March 11th, 1882.

I REACHED Sradnia Kolymsk on Sunday the 5th of March, and was met in the street by a fine-looking old gentleman in a handsome uniform, who addressed me in French, and, informing me that he was the Préfet de Police for the district, invited me to his house. It sounded most delightfully to hear once more a familiar Christian language, and not to be compelled to converse with intelligent people in the language of the savage. At this house I met also M. Kotcheroffski, formerly Préfet of the District of Werchojansk, but who had just arrived to relieve my host, M. de Varowa, as the latter informed me, at the same time stating that he would start for Yakoutsk in a few days, and extending me an invitation to accompany him. I gladly accepted his offer, knowing that thus I could travel faster than if alone, and more than make up the time lost in waiting. In the meantime he offered to send a special courier to Yakoutsk with my despatches, which would gain five days on the fastest journey I could make. This offer I also accepted, and at once set to work preparing my papers for the courier. At Sradnia Kolymsk, as at Nishne, I met with nothing but kindness. All seemed anxious to aid the unfortunate mariners who were thrown upon these ice-bound shores.

SIBERIAN LANDSCAPE.

Sradnia, or Middle Kolymsk, is a Russian settlement of about 500 inhabitants, including Russians, Yakouts, and a few Tchouktchis. The houses are all built of hewn logs, are but one story high, and the windows are glazed with blocks of transparent ice. Some of the houses have windows of glass, but these are always much broken and mended, so that seen from the outside they look like the stained-glass windows of a church. The most conspicuous building there, as in all the little Russian towns, is the church edifice, which is of Oriental architecture, with a dome surmounted by a cross and exceedingly florid in its style of architecture. Adjoining the church, and within the same enclosure, is a small wooden tower surrounded by a block-house, which was built by the first settlers of Sradnia as a means of defence against the savage Yakouts and Tchouktchis. This town is irregularly built and extends over a considerable area of ground, the Government buildings being situated about a mile from the centre. By Government buildings is meant merely the storehouses for grain and bread and for the skins which are received for taxes. These buildings are of logs, with great heavy doors and padlocks about the size of an ordinary valise, while the key is a load of itself. I should imagine that a Keeper of the Imperial Keys, if there is such an office in Russia, would have to be a man trained in athletic exercises from his youth up to accept of such an appointment. When a door there is locked it is locked, and there is no mistaking the fact.

I paid a visit to the storehouses while in Sradnia to witness the process of turning over the property to the new Préfet or Ispravnik, as he is termed, but it was a very uninteresting process and the weather so intensely cold that I did not stay long. A gang of laborers, not in their shirt sleeves, as I had been accustomed to seeing them at home, but heavily clad in skin clothing, were running around with bundles on their shoulders, and dumping them upon one of the platforms of a pair of immense balance scales, such as I thought had long since become obsolete. The beam was suspended in the middle, and had platforms a yard square, hung by the corners to either end of the beam. On one side were piled bundles of skins or grain in cowskin bags, and on the other were heaped up big iron weights, about the size of a 100 lb. shell, with handles. It looked as if the articles to be weighed were exactly counterbalanced by the proper amount of iron weights, and then they guessed how much iron there was. When I thought of a city weigher in New York having to manœuvre such an outfit as this, it occurred to me that the position would be no sinecure. I saw another curious balance here. A sort of combination of the beam with the steel-yard, used for weighing small articles. It has a scoop suspended from one end of a graduated steel rod, in which is placed the article to be weighed. On the other end of the rod is a fixed weight, and the balance is obtained by sliding the rod along the ring that holds it in suspension. I had been used to seeing the weight moved, and it was a novelty to see the whole beam sliding along instead. The rod is round and graduated on many parts of its circumference, so that by moving the weight and turning the rod its limit of usefulness is extended or diminished.

Pacing up and down near the scales with a gun upon his shoulder was a Cossack, who looked strangely, bundled up in furs and under arms. Near the beam stood the new Ispravnik, wrapped up so that nothing could be seen of him except his eyes. I did not blame him for bundling up as much as possible, as I don't remember ever having felt the cold more keenly than during the first three days I was in Sradnia, and M. de Varowa, the retiring Ispravnik, told me that he had never known it to be so cold during his sojourn there as at this time, and that indeed the whole winter, that is the months of January and February, had been regarded by the inhabitants of the town as most unusual. Unfortunately there is no thermometer in any of those towns north and east of Yakoutsk, where observations of the weather would be so interesting. I have no doubt that the thermometer would have marked an unusally low temperature on the 5th, 6th, 7th, and 8th of February by the English calendar in Northeastern Siberia. There was not a breath of wind stirring and the sky was cloudless, all the conditions being favorable for cold weather. On the 9th of February the sky was overcast and there was a very great rise in the temperature, and on the 10th we had a snow-storm. The dwellings in Sradnia, as well as throughout that part of Siberia, consist usually of three rooms, and are heated by an open fireplace built of poles, which extend up through the roof and form a low chimney. The poles are covered with mud to protect them

COSSACK FORT.

from the flames, and the wood is stood on end in the fireplace, resting against the back. There is an almost unlimited supply of wood in the country, and it is of an excellent quality for fuel, as well as for all the purposes

YAKOUT FISHERMEN.

of building. It is easily cut and split, and makes a brilliant flame, and an abundance of glowing coals. On this same fireplace the cooking for the establishment is carried on, apparently with equal skill, by the men and women. The culinary arrangements are, however, of the simplest character, the staples of food being fish, rye bread and tea.

All the lakes and rivers abound with most excellent fish, and the poorer classes eat nothing else. My observations here have led me to doubt the brain-producing character of a fish diet, or else that the fish here are of the right sort for that purpose. I can, however, attest the excellent quality of the fish, especially raw and frozen. In that case the skin is stripped off and long slices cut longitudinally from the fish, and eaten with or without salt, as the taste or means of those who eat may dictate. When eaten thus it is called by the Russians "*struganina*," and by the Yakouts "*tung bullok*." When cooked it is boiled, fried, baked or made into pie or biscuit. Reindeer meat is also eaten by those who can afford it, unless rich enough to eat beef, which they prefer, though why I could never discover, for the meat of the reindeer is much more delicate and tender, and has a peculiarly delicious flavor, probably derived from the fragrant moss that constitutes its food. It is cheap enough to satisfy the most economical housekeeper, a fine fat buck, entire, costing at Nishne Kolymsk only three roubles—that is, a dollar and a half—and at Sradnia five roubles. The meat of the reindeer is always excellent, while the beef is usually coarse grained and tough. At Nishne and Sradnia beef is more expensive than reindeer, at Werchojansk they cost about the same, while at Yakoutsk reindeer meat is the most expensive, and is only exceeded in price by the horse, which is a luxury only to be indulged in by the rich. It is a luxury, I believe, chiefly prized by the Yakouts, though I understand that it is served at the restaurants in Yakoutsk to those who desire it. Breakfast here consists of bread and tea, with perhaps frozen or dried fish, and later in the day meat, soup and tea, and in the evening meat or fish and tea.

It is impossible to imagine what these people would do without tea. It is the universal beverage, and they drink from four to fifteen cups at one meal, sometimes with milk and sometimes with sugar. The sugar is not put into the cup with the tea—it is too precious for that—but a lump is served to each person, and as he sips his tea he nibbles at the lump which is his portion for the meal. It would strike a New Yorker as curious to see the tea brought in upon a waiter, with one plate filled with lumps of sugar and another with lumps of milk or cream, but such is the prevailing Siberian fashion. When I would start out for a journey my provisions would be arranged in bags—one bag for sugar, another for tea, another for milk, and so on. At Sradnia Kolymsk I saw several political exiles—Socialists, nine in all—who are sentenced for various terms. There were also two at Nishne, one a Socialist and the other a Pole who had been implicated in political intrigues inimical to the Imperial Government. His sentence had originally been for twenty-five years at Ahlokminsk, between Yakoutsk and Irkutsk, but one day, in a fit of indignation at the Government, he gave expression to his anger by spitting upon a portrait of his late Imperial Majesty, and was sent to the most distant outpost of the Government in Siberia. I found him a very pleasant old gentleman, of polished manners and education, entirely distinct from the people with whom he is at present thrown; but he has grown gray and aged since he left his home in Warsaw, and says he feels almost equally at home in Siberia. It was rather difficult to talk with him, as he only remembered a few words in French, though he spoke German fluently, but I didn't.

However, by an ingenious intermingling of English, French, German, Russian and Tchouktchi we managed to understand each other passably well.

I visited the Socialists at their houses in Sradnia, and found most of them pretty much the kind of people I had imagined—a sort of intelligent lunatics. But there were exceptions. There were gentlemen whom I could not imagine guilty of an evil thought, and these I found were held in high esteem by the officers of the Government who have them under their charge. They were all interested in the American stranger, and seemed to imagine an affinity between my countrymen and the Socialists. They were much surprised when I told them that their party was but poorly represented in the United States, and that such as we had were foreigners; that I did not personally know of a single American Socialist.

There was one thing that struck me with considerable force when my course was turned from the northern coast of Siberia into the Kolyma River. The second day of my journey on that river I noticed, as we passed near the shore, first higher grass than I had seen before, then a short growth of bushes, then stunted shrubbery, and afterward two solitary lonely trees standing side by side. In the course of a few miles the trees became more numerous along the banks of the river until I reached Wanker's house, which is situated in a grove of trees thirty or more feet high. I had not expected to see all this climatic change in one day's travel. Before reaching his house we stopped at a log house, or *yarat*, to get some tea. This was the first inhabited house I had seen, and I regarded it with due interest. There was but one room, with the fireplace in the corner, on which was blazing a glorious fire that made my frozen nose glow with the heat. There stood the steaming tea-kettle, and as we entered the lady of the house, attired in a loose robe, not gathered in at the waist but flowing from the shoulders half-way down her leather boot-legs, cut some pieces of reindeer meat from one of two carcasses that leaned against the wall with the skins still covering them, and fried them in a pan over the glowing coals. In the meantime a frozen fish was cut into *struganina* and placed before us with an additional plate of dried fish and some preserved cran-

INTERIOR OF A STAROSTA'S HOUSE.

berries, and afterwards the hot tea, that made the remainder of my journey quite comfortable. While we were partaking of the hospitality of the Russian natives three sledge loads of Tchouktchis arrived, and were similarly entertained. I thought it must be a considerable tax upon the time and hospitality of those who live upon the lines of travel to entertain so many guests, for no one passes these houses without entering, and no one pays anything for his entertainment. All the guests excepting myself, even the Tchouktchis, crossed themselves when they entered the house, as well as before and after eating, and when they left. At Wanker's house the entire family crossed themselves in front of the pictures of saints in one corner and bowed as they muttered their prayers. Wanker, too, went through the same forms; but not, I thought, sufficiently to make up for the time he had lost in the Tchouktchi houses along the coast. He spoke the Tchouktchi language perfectly, so that I felt certain that he was at least a half-breed. He wore their amulets to cure him when he was sick, and was with them a skilful *shaman*, or medicine man. No one could excel him in the performance upon the drum, and yet all these were laid aside at home, and he was apparently as pious as any of his family. I never saw religion so universal as the Greek religion in Siberia.

Not only the Russian inhabitants but the Yakouts, Tungusians, Lamoots and Tchouktchis who reside near the settlements are all equally religious. It seemed to me to be a most convenient religion, for it consisted, as far as I could see, in crossing one's self and bowing before the pictures and in fasting upon a fish diet where there was scarcely anything but fish to eat. The most pious old man I saw among them could scarcely restrain his anger at some infringement of his orders one day until he had finished his prayers. He then turned and opened upon the offending head such a volley of—well, if not oaths, they sounded as if they would have been when translated. It is a beautiful religion, at any rate, and abounds in affectionate salutes. All these forms are particularly dear to the Yakout, and never omitted, at least in the presence of a white man. After prayers every one kisses every one else three times—once on each cheek and once on the mouth. This is universal—men, women and children, servants and masters, soldiers and their commanding officers. It is neither the ecstatic nor paroxysmal kiss, nor yet the Platonic, but simply the kiss of devotion. The entire household join in prayers, all standing before the chromos of saints with metallic rays attached to their heads in the most realistic fashion, and cross themselves and bow in unison, unless some one particularly devout prostrates himself upon the floor and kisses the planks in the fervor of his religious zeal.

It was a beautiful sight to me to see the gray-haired Préfet take the little Nányah by the hand and lead her before the family altar, where they stood side by side at their devotions. When finished she would cross her dear little hands and hold them suppliantly toward her companion while he made the sign of the cross over her and dropped his hard hand upon hers. Then she would raise it to her lips and kiss it. This concluded the devotions. It is a convenient religion for a lazy man, for of the 365 days that compose the year nearly all are saints' days or holidays, and no good Christian would work upon a holy day. Were it not that the fish are so abundant I fear these people would starve to death. I never could make out the exact position occupied by *la petite* Nányah in the household at Sradnia. She seemed to unite the duties of a plaything, a daughter and a servant. I first saw her the day that I arrived at the house of the Préfet. My attention had been attracted by a brilliant costume of the Lamoots, and to show it to better advantage the ever-useful Nányah was called upon as a lay figure. There was neither hesitation nor boldness in her manner. She was simply showing the dress, not herself. She had neither fear of the stranger nor hesitation to accommodate him by wearing this gaudy savage costume. With her it was simply a pleasure to please others. I was told that Nányah was to be our travelling companion to Yakoutsk; that she was affianced to an officer of the regiment stationed there, and this would be the first time she had ever been away from Sradnia Kolymsk. Her parents were dead, and she had no near relative except a brother, a lad of about ten years, who was to follow later in company with the traders on their return to Yakoutsk, when the voyage could be made at less expense. During my sojourn in Sradnia, as well as in Nishne Kolymsk, I was frequently invited to partake of the hospitality of some of the inhabitants. At all such entertainments it seemed to be a principle with the host to insist upon my drinking a glass of *vodka*, that is, diluted alcohol, about every five minutes. At first I thought I must submit myself to the customs of the country and sustain myself as best I could, and the consequence was that when dinner was over I had not the slightest idea whether I had eaten anything or not, but was quite sure that I had drank something. Later I found out that all that was required was that you should sip the liquor, and thus avoid the evil consequences of heavy drinking, and governed my drinking accordingly. I learned that the Russian rule is a glass of *vodka* before dinner, before each plate, during each plate, after each plate, and after dinner —that is all.

CHAPTER XVI.

APPROACHING THE LENA.

"LIKE the breaking up of a hard winter" is an expression frequently used, but I doubt if any one knows what "the breaking up of a hard winter" really is like unless he has had the misfortune to travel in Northern Siberia during the spring time. I thought I had seen hard winters and pretty hard breakings up in the northern portion of North America, but they were nothing like the affair in this country. To get the real thing in all its force and significance you must be near one of the great north flowing rivers of Siberia about the time of the spring floods, when whole districts are covered with water and swift moving ice, and no land is to be seen for miles in any direction, but occasional forests apparently growing right up out of the water. To travel over roads where for hundreds of yards your sled is entirely under water and you only maintain a position upon it by half standing up and clinging to the side pieces until the whole concern is dumped into an unexpected hole—this is what you must expect. You will have to make part of your journey on horseback, perhaps, and over such roads and upon such cattle as can be found nowhere else in the world. I refer now to civilized Siberia, that which is governed by officers appointed by the Czar. East of the district of the Kolyma, which extends but a short distance beyond the river which gives its name to the district and lies in about the 161st meridian east of Greenwich, is savage Siberia, and under no control of the Russian Government. The Tchouktchis have never been conquered. A pitched battle with them was the greatest success ever effected by the Cossacks who occupied the land, though some of them passed through the Tchouktchis' country along the northern coast and by way of Behring Strait to the Anadyr before Behring entered the sea that bears his name. The police district of the Kolyma is, therefore, the first one coming from the East sees of civilization. My experience had been so severe and distressing before I reached Nishne Kolymsk that I felt that when I arrived there my troubles would be ended, and the rest of the journey, though carrying me entirely around the world before reaching New York, would be comparatively comfortable and easy, as it would be over regularly established post roads of the Empire. And perhaps it may have been comparatively easy in a general way, but there were many passages of discomfort that would equal any of my previous experiences. The great advantage I found was the increased rapidity with which I could travel. There is no such thing as comfort in Siberian journeys, except, perhaps, in winter and over the more westerly roads.

I was fortunate in having as a companion on the journey to Werchojansk M. de Varowa, the ex-Chief of Police, or Ispravnik, of the Kolyma district. We were accompanied by the little Nányah and a Cossack, whose services were required to take charge of our baggage and have everything arranged as comfortably as possible when we halted *en route* for meals or tea. This journey was my first experience of post-road travel, and made in such company it would be, of course, as rapid and agreeable as possible. The stations where we were to change animals were upon this route from sixty to two hundred and fifty versts apart. (A verst, it should be remembered, is two-thirds of a mile.) Where the stations are far apart there are intervening houses, sometimes inhabited and sometimes mere shelters for travellers, where wood and ice are found conveniently provided for the purpose of cooking meat or tea. The use of tea on the road is universal in Siberia, except in the savage Tchouktchis' land, where it

INTERIOR OF POVARNNIAH.

is impossible to obtain it; and, though new to me, I soon appreciated the advantages gained by its use. I never approved of the use of alcoholic stimulants in Arctic journeys, and in Northern America preferred the weak bouillon obtained by boiling meat, the only method of cooking known to the Esquimaux.

In Siberia I learned that tea is equally efficacious and much more convenient; for you can halt and boil a pot of water for your tea and be under way again long before frozen meat would be even thoroughly thawed. These intermediate resting places are called *povarnniars* (kitchens), and when inhabited no time is lost in obtaining hot water, for a good fire is always burning in the houses in this thickly wooded country, and where uninhabited it does not take much longer to get the pot boiling. Wood is plentiful and of a superior quality for fuel, light and easily ignited, but requiring almost constant replenishing. The chimney is made of small poles which extend upward through the roof from a raised fireplace, and are plastered with mud to prevent ignition. The wood is split into long, thin pieces, and loosely piled on end against the back of the chimney; the strong draught soon gives you a roaring fire. These *povarnniars* are found usually about thirty or forty versts apart, and were generally very welcome during the winter cold. When travelling rapidly with good reindeer we would not stop at every *povarnniar*, but sometimes omit one or two *en route*. The people whose abodes are used by travellers as *povarnniars* receive no recompense for the inconvenience they experience, but feel, I am told, amply repaid by the opportunity of seeing strangers and hearing any bit of news or gossip that may be afloat in this desolate land. I saw that the Yakouts, who are the station masters upon the roads north of the city of Yakoutsk, are not the most enterprising and active people in the world, and it requires some management to secure the change of animals necessary to your journey. They are arrant cowards and can only be moved by bluster and threats. Kindness secures from them only imposition, while they seem to adore those who abuse and browbeat them. My friend, the Ispravnik, did the wrangling upon this route, much to my relief, and we were seldom delayed at the stations. Upon this, as upon all my journeys in Siberia, except when mounted on horseback or upon a single small dog sled, travel was continued during the night as well as day, and consequently we accomplished the 1,500 versts to Werchojansk in eighteen days. During a portion of the route we had horses for draught animals and at other times reindeer. I much preferred the latter, because so much fleeter and so much more docile. It seemed impossible ever to force the Yakout horses out of a walk until your sled overturned, and then they would run, and it seemed equally impossible to stop them.

REINDEER.

The fifth day after leaving the Kolyma we crossed the divide between that river and the Indigirka, and here, by the roadside, upon the crest of the mountain, stood a cross which marks the dividing line between the police districts of the Kolyma and Werchojansk. Here we halted a few minutes and got out of our sleds while the ex-Ispravnik and *la petite* Nányah took their formal and religious farewell of the district we had just left. At the foot of the cross they stood side by side facing the east, the old man baring his gray head to the wind and snow storm, while they muttered their prayers in unison and crossed themselves, the others in the meanwhile respectfully bareheaded and attentive. The train was drawn up on the road, and the horses embraced the interval to paw away the snow and nibble the frost-killed herbage beneath. The cross was hung with bits of cloth and ribbon and bunches of horsehair, and in some of the many cracks that seamed the venerable structure were copper coins, all gifts from previous travellers, to charm away any prospective evil that might attend so great a change of residence. Each member of the party contributed something to this curious collection—the old man a leaf of tobacco, Nányah a ribbon from her brown tresses, while I tied a few hairs from the tail of each horse in our train to one of the sticks that stood in the snow near the cross and from which waved many similar offerings to the idols of the Yakouts and Siberia. It was to me altogether a strange and interesting spectacle, this weird cross, with its ribbons and horsetails waving in the breeze from the summit of a Siberian mountain; the little group of civilized people clad in furs and surrounded by half savage *yemsheeks*, or drivers; the horses, not more civilized than their masters, gathering their food from beneath the snow like reindeer; the sudden transition from devotion to levity upon the part of my companions as they turned from their prayers to participate in the rites of the savages and decorate the cross of the Christians with the emblems of idolatry—all this was equally new and impressive.

Not many days after leaving this spot we came to the village of Abooie, where we rested at the house of the *gollivar*, or headman of the village. He was a large fine-looking Yakout, with short gray hair and a quiet, dignified demeanor that greatly impressed me. He entertained us very handsomely with frozen fish and frozen cream, and made us exceedingly welcome to his house, which was much larger and cleaner than any Yakout dwelling I had yet seen. Two married sons occupied the same house with their father, and one seemed to have no other occupation than keeping the children, who wanted to look at the strangers, upon the other side of the house. He was, like his father, of colossal stature, but, I am afraid, had a

NICHOLAI CHAGRA'S HOUSE.

bad heart, for several times I saw him push the children very gently away, and at the same time slyly pull their hair until they screamed, when he would most soothingly inquire what was the matter. I felt like braining the brute for his cruelty, but knew that my interest in the poor abused little innocents would neither be understood nor appreciated. When our reindeer were harnessed what was my surprise to see our dignified and venerable host put on his big fur overcoat and go as one of our *yemsheeks*. He was a thoroughly good driver, however, and told me almost to the minute when we would reach each *povarnniar en route* and arrive at the next station. I believe him to be a sly old rascal, though, for I detected him winking at one of the other drivers after our arrival

NICHOLAI CHAGRA.

at the station right in the midst of his devotion to the corner saints. His face still presented the same venerable dignity at the time, and I never was more completely surprised than at that moment. I then thought that his son had inherited some of his father's sly deviltry, which, perhaps, accounted for his mild torture of the innocents.

A few days later we reached the longest station on the road, 250 versts. Here chance would have it that there was not a sufficient supply of reindeer, and we had a fine prospect of being left without transportation in the mountain passes. On reaching the first *povarnniar* the next morning after leaving the station we found some Yakouts with sixty fine, strong reindeer returning from transporting the merchandise of one of the Kolyma traders. As they were going our way it seemed a simple matter to hire them to convey us to the next station, but I found the simplicity was entirely my own, and owing to my lack of knowledge of the Yakout perversity, notwithstanding the liberal recompense tendered by M. de Varowa, backed by a special reward offered by me personally, they said they were only willing to travel fifty versts per day and sleep at night in the *povarnniars*, thus consuming four days in a journey that should have been made in a day and a half. No amount of money or threats would move them, and my companion told me that he would therefore take possession of twelve of the best reindeer and leave them with the headman of the village at the next station, together with a liberal price for their use. As may be imagined the drivers were very much opposed to this arrangement, and this led to considerable loud talk, not a word of which I understood. But when, a moment afterward, I saw the old Ispravnik pommelling one of the Yakouts and the Cossack lasso another who attempted to run away, I thought it was time for action and I asked M. de Varowa what I was to do. He said I need do nothing—that they were all very pleasant and bland now; that the only way to make friends with Yakouts was to beat them; and, sure enough, a few minutes later they all came up, hats in hand, and begged we would take all the reindeer we wanted. They even harnessed them for us themselves and mended one of our sleds that was broken.

At Werchojansk I obtained the first complete history of the landing at the Lena delta of some of the officers and crew of the *Jeannette* during the previous fall, and learned that a search party under Chief Engineer Melville was still engaged looking for the remains of those who

WERCHOJANSK.

had already perished or for anyone that might still be alive. Upon inquiry I ascertained that it was a journey of only from about seven to ten days to where I would find Chief Engineer Melville, and I could find no reason why I should leave the country when so near and not find out something about the search party. I therefore bade "Good-by" to my kind old companion and his little charge, Nányah, and started at midnight for the Lena delta, distant about 1,200 versts. A Cossack was detailed by the acting Ispravnik of Werchojansk to accompany me to look after my baggage, to see that animals were furnished promptly at the stations and also to see that I had tea and cooked meat whenever necessary. He was to be, in fact, a general manager of my affairs as well as half guard and half servant. At this time I did not know a single word of the Russian language, as it had not been necessary to learn it. At Nishne Kolymsk nearly all the Russians spoke the Tchouktchi language, and M. de Varowa spoke French as well as his native tongue, and managed everything *en route*. I was simply a passenger in his train. It was different with me now, as, though my Cossack spoke the Yakout language perfectly, he spoke no other except Russian. This seemed at first a serious drawback, but I was not discouraged, for if I had been able to make long journeys through lands peopled only by savages, whose language I did not understand, I was not afraid that I should fail to make myself understood by civilized people. I had also a polyglot dictionary of the French, Russian, German and English languages, with the French as the initial language; which was rather a drawback, as first I must know the French equivalent for what I desired to explain in Russian. It fortunately happened that my Cossack, besides being unusually intelligent for one of his class in that country, was able to read and write, though by no means a scholar—so, with my dictionary and the universal sign language we got along quite well. Our conversations were never very extended, nor could they be called brilliant; it was quite enough if they were satisfactory. My dictionary was never packed away; it was always placed under my pillow in the sled, and always brought into the *povarnniars* and stations with the cooking utensils. Here we would pore over that book until the meal was ready; I would, if possible, find the word I desired to use and point out the Russian term, Michael carefully marking it with his thumb-nail, while he took it to the fire to see it more plainly, or some polite Yakout stood by us holding a lighted stick for a candle. It was a tedious method of communication, but, before finally parting with Michael, some two months and a half afterward, I was able to make him understand nearly everything I desired or that was necessary. Michael was recommended to me as a very energetic and driving fellow, who would make the Yakouts fly around and have things ready quickly, and so I found him to be. He was the veriest tyrant in the houses of the Yakouts, much to my disgust. He would bluster in, kick over their utensils and order them around as if he were the owner and not they. If any of them dared to come over to the side of the house where I was seated he would drive them back, and never was satisfied with anything they did. The consequence was that they all adored him and were ready to kiss the ground he walked on. His manner was just such as to endear him to the Yakout heart. They can never appreciate kindness, but love to be abused. I never could fully understand their character, but knew them to be arrant cowards. With Michael I managed to travel rapidly when the roads permitted, and at all times as rapidly as possible.

CHAPTER XVII.

THE DIARY OF DE LONG.

LENA DELTA, *April 10th*, 1882.

ON April 2d I was more than two hundred miles from Werchojansk. I reached the station of Yoayaska at nine in the evening, and there found a packet of mail matter which was to be forwarded to Irkutsk. The Cossack said that I might open it, and these are the letters which I read:—

LENA DELTA, *March 24th*, 1882.

Honorable the Secretary of the Navy, Washington, D.C.:

SIR—I have the honor of informing you of my successful search for the party of Lieutenant De Long, with its books, records, &c., &c. After several unsuccessful attempts to follow De Long's track from the northward I tried the retracing of Nindermann's track from the southward, and after visiting every point of land projecting into the great bay at the junction of the Lena branches, from Matvey around from the west to a point bearing E.N.E. and forming one of the banks of the river Kugoasastack, ascending the bank, I found where a large fire had been made, and Nindermann recognized it as the river down which he came. I turned the point to go north, and about one thousand yards from the point I noticed the points of four poles lashed together and projecting two feet out of the snow drift, under the bank. I dropped from the sled, and going up to the poles saw the

THE PLACE WHERE THE BODIES WERE FOUND.

muzzle of a Remington rifle standing eight inches out of
the snow, and the gun strap hitched over the poles.

I set the natives digging out the bank, and Nindermann
and myself commenced to search the bank and high
ground. I walked south, Nindermann walking north. I
had gone about five hundred yards when I saw the camp

FINDING DE LONG.

kettle standing out of the snow, and, close by, three
bodies partially buried in snow. I examined them and
found them to be Lieutenant De Long, Dr. Ambler and
Ah Sam, the cook.

I found De Long's note book alongside of him, a copy
of which please find enclosed, dating from October 1,
when at Usterday, until the end. Under the poles were
found the books, records, &c., and two men. The rest of
the people lie between the place where De Long was found

and the wreck of a flatboat, a distance of five hundred yards. The snow bank will have to be dug out. It has a base of thirty feet and a height of twenty feet, with a natural slope.

The point on which the people lie, although high, is covered with drift-wood, evidence that it is flooded during some seasons of the year. Therefore I will convey the people to a proper place on the bank of the Lena and have them interred. In the meantime I will prosecute the search for the second cutter with all diligence, as the weather may permit. The weather has been so bad we have been able to travel but one day in four, but hope for better weather as spring advances.

I have the honor, sir, to be very respectfully,

G. W. MELVILLE,
Passed Assistant Engineer, United States Navy.

Mr. Melville's first letter was followed by a second:

LENA DELTA, *March 25th*, 1882.

The Honorable Secretary of the Navy, Washington, D. C.:

SIR—The following is the list of dead found to date:

Lieutenant George W. De Long, United States Navy.

Assistant Surgeon James M. Ambler, United States Navy.

Mr. Jerome J. Collins.

Neils Iverson, C. H.

Carl August Gœrtz, seaman.

Adolph Dressler, seaman.

George Washington Boyd, second-class fireman.

Ah Sam, cook.

I have the honor to be, very respectfully,

G. W. MELVILLE,
Passed Assistant Engineer, United States Navy.

And when I had read these letters I turned to the papers which accompanied them and found them to be the diary kept by De Long from October 1st till October 30th, 1881. It was the most horrible tale of agonizing, lingering death. Here is what I read:

"*Saturday, October 1st*—111th day, and a new month. —Called all hands as soon as the cook announced boiling water, and at 6:45 had our breakfast, half a pound of deer meat and tea. Sent Nindermann and Alexia to examine the main river, other men to collect wood. The Doctor resumed the cutting away of poor Ericksen's toes this morning. No doubt it will have to continue until his feet are gone, unless death ensues or we get to some settlement. Only one toe left now. Weather clear, light northeast airs, barometer 30.15 at 6:05. Temperature 18° at 7:30. Nindermann and Alexia were seen to have crossed, and I immediately sent men to carry our load over. Left the following record:

"*Saturday, October 1st*, 1881.—Fourteen of the officers and men of the United States Arctic steamer *Jeannette* reached this hut on Wednesday, September 28th, and, having been forced to wait for the river to freeze over, are proceeding to cross to the west side this A.M. on their journey to reach some settlement on the Lena River. We have two days' provisions, but having been fortunate enough thus far to get game in our pressing needs we have no fear for the future.

"Our party are all well except one man, Ericksen, whose toes have been amputated in consequence of frost bite. Other records will be found in several huts on the east side of this river, along which we have come from the north.

"GEORGE W. DE LONG,
"Lieutenant, U. S. Navy, commanding expedition."

Attached to this was a list of the party.

At 8:30 made the final trip and got our sick man over in safety. From there we proceeded until 11:20, dragging our man on the sled. Halted for dinner—half pound of meat and tea. At 1 went ahead again until 5:05. Actually under way 8:30 to 9:15, 1 to 1:40, 3:35 to 4, 9:30 to 10:20, 1:50 to 2:10, 4:15 to 4:35, 10:30 to 10:20, 2:20 to 2:40, 4:45 to 5:05, 3 to 3:25. At 8 P.M. crawled into our blankets.

Sunday, October 2d.—I think we all slept fairly well until midnight, but from that time forward it was so cold and uncomfortable that sleep was out of the question. At 4:30 we were all out and in front of the fire, daylight just appearing. Ericksen kept talking in his sleep all night and effectually kept those awake who are not already awakened by the cold. Breakfast at 5 A.M.—half pound of meat and tea. Bright, cloudless morning, light northern airs; barometer 30.30 at 5:32; temperature at 6, 35°. At 7 went ahead, following the frozen water whenever we could find it, and at 9:20 I felt quite sure we had gone some distance on the main river. I think our gait was at least two miles an hour and our time under way 2h. 40m. I calculate our forenoon work at least six miles, 7 to 7:35, 10:22 to 10:40, 3:20 to 3:40, 7:45 to 8:05, 10:55 to 11:15, 3:50 to 4:05, 8:15 to 8:30. Dinner camp, 4:15 to 4:20, 8:40 to 8:50, 1 to 1:30. Total, 9:20 to 9:40, 1:40 to 2, 5h. 15m.; 9:50 to 10:12, 2:15 to 2:35 at least, 2:45 to 3.

Two miles an hour distance make good ten to twelve miles, and where are we? I think it the beginning of the Lena River at last. Sogaster has been to us a myth. We saw two old huts at a distance, and this was all; but they were out of our road and the day not half gone.

Kept on the ice all the way, and therefore think we were over water; but the stream was so narrow and so crooked that it never could have been a navigable stream. My chart is simply useless. I must go on plodding to the southward, trusting in God to guide me to some settlement, for I have long since realized that we are powerless to help ourselves. A bright, calm, beautiful day brought sunshine to cheer us up. An icy road and one day's rations yet. Boats frozen, of course, and hauled up. No hut in sight, and we halt on a bluff to spend a cold and comfortless night. Supper—half-pound meat and tea. Built a rousing fire. Built a log bed. Set a watch, two hours each, to keep fire going and get supper. Then we stood by for a second cold and wretched night. There was so much wind we had to put up our tent halves for a screen and sit shivering in our half blankets.

Monday, October 3d, 1881—113th day.—It was so fearfully cold and wretched that I served out tea to all hands, and on this we managed to struggle along until 5 A.M., when we ate our last deer meat and had more tea. Our morning food now consists of four-fourteenths of a pound of pemmican each and a half-starved dog. May God again incline unto our aid! How much farther we have to go before making a shelter or settlement He only knows. Ericksen seems failing. He is weak and powerless, and the moment he closes his eyes talks, mostly in Danish, German and English. No one can sleep, even though our other surroundings permitted. For some cause my watch stopped at 10:45 last night while one of the men on watch had it. I set it as near as I could by guessing, and we must run by that until I can do better. Sun rose yesterday morning at 6:40 by the watch when running all right. 7:05 to 7:40, 7:50 to 8:20, 8:30 to 9, 9:15

to 9:35, 9:50 to 10:10, 10:25 to 10:45, 11. Back, 11:20, 11:30, 11:50, 11:50. Dinner, 35, 30, 30, 20, 20; total, 155 = 2 hours 35 minutes, say 5 miles.

Our half day's work I put, as above, five miles. Some time and distance were lost by crossing the river upon seeing numerous fox traps. A man's track was also seen in the snow, bound south, and we followed it until it crossed the river to the west bank again. Here we were obliged to go back again in our tracks, for the river was open in places and we could not follow the man's track direct. Another of the dozen shoals that infest the river swung us off to the eastward, too, and I hastened to get on the west bank again, reaching there at 11:50 for dinner—our last four-fourteenths of a pound of pemmican. At 1:40 got under way again and made a long spurt until 2:20. While at the other side of the river Alexia said he saw a hut, and during our dinner camp he said he again saw a hut. Under our circumstances my desire was to get to it as speedily as possible. As Alexia points out, it was on the left bank of the river of which we were now on the right side, looking south, but a sand-bank gave us excellent walking for a mile or two until we took to the river and got across it diagonally. Here, at 2:20, I called a halt, and Alexia mounted the bluff to take a look again. He now announced he saw a second hut about one and a quarter miles back from the coast, the other hut being about the same distance south, and on the edge of the bluff. The heavy dragging across the country of a sick man on a sled made me incline to the hut on the shore, since as the distance was about the same we could get over the ice in one-third of the time. Nindermann, who climbed the bluff, saw that the object inland was a hut—was not so confident of the one on the shore. Alexia, however, was quite positive, and, not seeing very well myself, I unfortunately took his eyes as best and ordered an advance along the river to the southward. Away we went, Nindermann and Alexia leading, and had progressed about a mile when plash in I went through the ice up to my shoulders before my knapsack brought me up. While I was crawling out, in went Gœrtz to his neck about fifty yards behind me, and behind him in went Mr. Collins to his waist. Here was a time. The moment we came out of the water we were one sheet of ice, and danger of frost bite was imminent. Along we hobbled, however, until we reached, at 3:45, about the point on which the hut was seen. Here Nindermann climbed the bluff, followed by the Doctor. At first the cry was "All right, come ahead," but no sooner were we well up than Nindermann shouted, "There is no hut here." To my dismay and alarm nothing but a large mound of earth was to be seen, which, from its regular shape and singular position, would seem to have been built artificially for a beacon. So sure was Nindermann that it was a hut, that he went all round it looking for a door, and then climbed on top to look for a hole in the roof. But of no avail. It was nothing but a mound of earth. Sick at heart, I ordered a camp to be made in a hole in the bluff face, and soon before a roaring fire we were drying and burning our clothes while the cold wind ate into our backs.

And now for supper nothing remained but the dog. I therefore ordered him killed and dressed by Iverson, and soon after a stew was made of such parts as could not be carried, of which everybody except the Doctor and myself eagerly partook. To us two it was a nauseating mess, and—but why go on with such a disagreeable subject. I had the remainder weighed, and I am quite sure we had twenty-seven pounds. The animal was fat, and as he had been fed on pemmican presumably clean; but immediately upon halting I sent Alexia off with his gun inland toward the hut to determine whether that was a myth like our present one. He returned about dark, certain that it was a large hut, for he had been inside of it and had found some deer meat scraps and bones. For a moment I was tempted to start everybody for it, but Alexia was by no means sure he could find it in the dark, and if we lost our way we would be worse off than before. We accordingly prepared to make the best of it where we were. We three wet people were burning and steaming before the fire. Collins and Gœrtz had taken some alcohol, but I could not get it down. Cold weather, with a raw northwest wind impossible to avoid or screen, our future was a wretched, dreary night. Ericksen soon became delirious, and his talking was a horrible accompaniment to the wretchedness of our surroundings. Warm we could not get, and getting dry seemed out of the question. Every one seemed dazed and stupefied, and I feared some of us would perish during the night. How cold it was I don't know, as my last thermometer was broken by my many falls upon the ice, but I think it must have been below zero. A watch was set to keep the fire going and we huddled around it, and thus our third night without sleep was passed. If Alexia had not wrapped his sealskin around me and sat alongside of me to keep me warm by the heat of his body I think I should have frozen to death. As it was I steamed and shivered and shook. Ericksen's groans and rambling talk rang out on the night air, and such a dreary, wretched night I hope I shall never again see.

Thursday, October 4th—114th day.—At the first approach of daylight we all began to move around and the cook was set to work making tea. The Doctor now made the unpleasant discovery that Ericksen had got his gloves off during the night, and that now his hands were frozen. Men were at once set at work rubbing them, and by 6 A.M. had so far restored circulation as to risk moving the man. Each one hastily swallowed a cup of tea and got his load in readiness. Ericksen was quite unconscious, and we lashed him on the sled. A southwest gale was blowing, and the sensation of cold was intense. But at 6 A.M. we started, made a forced march of it, and at 8 A.M. had got the sick man and ourselves, thank God, under cover of a hut large enough to hold us. Here we at once made a fire, and, for the first time since Saturday morning last, got warm.

The Doctor at once examined Ericksen, and found him very low indeed. His pulse was very feeble. He was quite unconscious, and under the shock of last night's exposure was sinking very fast. Fears were entertained that he might not last many hours, and I therefore called upon every one to join me in reading the prayers for a sick person before we sought any rest for ourselves. This was done in a quiet and reverent manner, though I fear my broken utterances made but little of the service audible. Then setting a watch we all, except Alexia, lay down to sleep. At 10 A.M. Alexia went off to hunt, but returned at noon wet, having broken through the ice and fallen in the river. At 6 P.M. we roused up, and I considered it necessary to think of some food for my party. Half a pound of dog meat was fried for each person, and a cup of tea given, and that constituted our day's food, but we were so grateful that we were not exposed to the merciless southwest gale that tore around us that we did not mind short rations.

Wednesday, October 5th—115th day.—The cook commences at 7:30 to get tea made from yesterday's tea leaves. Nothing to serve out until evening. Half a pound of dog meat per day is our food until some relief is afforded us. Alexia went off hunting again at 9, and I set the men gathering light sticks enough to make a flooring for the house, for the frozen ground thawing under everybody kept them damp and wet and robbed them of much sleep. Southwest gale continues. Barometer, 30.12 at 2:40. Mortification has set in in Ericksen's leg and he is sinking. Amputation would be of no use, as he would probably die under the operation. He is partially conscious. At 12 Alexia came back, having seen nothing. He crossed the river this time, but unable longer to face the cold gale was obliged to return. I am of the opinion we are on Titary Island, on its eastern side, and about twenty-five miles from Ku Mark Sirka, which I take to be a settlement. This is a last hope for us. Sogaster has long since faded away. The hut in which we are is quite new and clearly not the astronomical station marked on my chart. In fact, the hut is not finished, having no door and no porch. It may be intended for a summer hut, though the numerous fox traps would lead me to suppose that it would occasionally be visited at other times. Upon this last chance and another sun rest all our hopes of escape, for I can see nothing more to be done. As soon as the gale abates I shall send Nindermann and another man to make a forced march to Ku Mark Sirka for relief. At 6 P.M. served out half pound of dog meat and second-hand tea, and then went to sleep.

Thursday, October 6th—116th day.—Called all hands

at 7:30. Had a cup of third-hand tea, with half an ounce of alcohol in it. Everybody very weak. Gale moderating somewhat. Sent Alexia out to hunt. Shall start Nindermann and Noros at noon to make the forced march to Ku Mark Sirka. At 8:45 our messmate Ericksen departed this life. Addressed a few words of cheer and comfort to the men. Alexia came back empty-handed—too much drifting snow. What, in God's name, is going to become of us? Fourteen pounds of dog meat left and twenty-five miles to a possible settlement. As to burying Ericksen, I cannot dig a grave, for the ground is frozen and we have nothing to dig with. There is nothing to do but bury him in the river. Sewed him up in the flaps of the tent and covered him with my flag. Got the men ready, and with half an ounce of alcohol we will try to make out to bury him, but we are all so weak I do not see how we are going to travel. At 12:40 read the burial service and carried our departed shipmate to the river, where a hole having been cut in the ice he was buried, three volleys from our Remingtons being fired over him as a funeral honor. A board was prepared, with this cut on it: "In memory of H. H. Ericksen, October 6, 1881. U. S. S. *Jeannette*." And this will be stuck in the river bank almost over his grave.

His clothing was divided up among his messmates. Iverson has his Bible and a lock of his hair. Supper at 5 P.M., half a pound of dog meat and tea.

Friday, October 7th—117th day.—Breakfast, consisting of our last half pound of dog meat and tea. Our last grain of tea was put in the kettle this morning, and we are now about to undertake our journey of twenty-five miles with some old tea leaves and two quarts of alcohol. However, I trust in God, and I believe that He who has fed us thus far will not suffer us to die of want now. Commenced preparations for departure at 7:10. One Winchester rifle being out of order is, with 161 rounds of ammunition, left behind. We have with us two Remingtons and 243 rounds of ammunition. Left the following record in the hut:

"*Friday, October 7th*, 1881.—The undermentioned officers and men of the late United States steamer *Jeannette* are leaving here this morning to make a forced march to Ku Mark, Sirka, or some other settlement on the Lena River. We reached here Tuesday, October 4, with a disabled comrade, H. H. Ericksen, seaman, who died yesterday morning and was buried in the river at noon.

"His death resulted from frost bite and exhaustion due to consequent exposure.

"The rest of us are well, but have no provisions left, having eaten our last this morning."

Under way by 8:30 and proceeded until 11:20, by which time we had made about three miles. Here we were all pretty well done up, and seemed to be wandering in a labyrinth. A large lump of wood, swept in by an eddy, seemed to be a likely place to get hot water, and I halted the party for dinner—one ounce of alcohol in a pot of tea. Then went ahead and soon struck what seemed like the main river again. Here four of us broke through the ice in trying to cross, and, fearing frost bite, I had a fire built on the west bank to dry us up. Sent Alexia off meanwhile to look for food, directing him not to go far or stay long, but at 1:30 he had not returned nor was he in sight. Light southwest breeze, foggy. Mountains in sight to southward. At 5:30 Alexia returned with one ptarmigan, of which we made soup, and with half an ounce of alcohol had our supper. Then crawled under our blankets for a sleep. Light west breeze, full moon, starlight, not very cold. Alexia saw the river a mile wide with no ice in it.

Saturday, October 8th—118th day.—Called all hands at 5:30. Breakfast, one ounce of alcohol in a pint of hot water.

Doctor's Note.—Alcohol proves of great advantage. Keeps off craving for food, preventing gnawing at stomach, and has kept up the strength of the men, as given—three ounces per day, as estimated, and in accordance with Dr. Ambler's experiments.

Went ahead until 10:30. One ounce alcohol. Half-past six to half-past ten, five miles. Struck big river at 11:30. Ahead again. Snow banks. Met small river; have to turn back. Halt at 5; only made advance one mile more. Hard luck. Snow. South-southeast wind, cold. Camp. But little wood. Half an ounce of alcohol.

Sunday, October 9th—119th day.—All hands at 4:30. One ounce of alcohol. Read divine service. Send Nindermann and Noros ahead for relief. They carry their blankets, one rifle, forty rounds of ammunition and two ounces of alcohol. Orders to keep the west bank of river until they reach a settlement. They started at 7. Cheered them. Under way at 8. Crossed the creek. Broke through the ice. All wet up to knees. Stopped and built fires. Dried clothes. Under way again at 10:30. Lee breaking down. At 1 struck river bank. Halt for dinner; one ounce alcohol. Alexia shot three ptarmigan. Made soup. We are following Nindermann's track, although he is long since out of sight. Under way at 3:30. High bluff. Ice moving rapidly to northward in the river. Halt at 4:40 on coming to wood. Find canal-boat. Lay our heads in it and go to sleep. Half ounce alcohol. Supper.

Monday, October 10*th*—120th day.—Last half ounce of alcohol at 5:30. At 6:30 sent Alexia off to look for ptarmigan. Eat deer-skin scraps. Yesterday morning ate my deer-skin foot nips. Light southeast wind. Air not very cold. Under way at 8. In crossing creek three of us got wet. Built fire and dried out. Ahead again until 11; used up. Built fire; made a drink out of the tea leaves from alcohol bottle. On again at noon. Fresh south-southwest wind. Drifting snow. Very hard going. Lee begging to be left. Some little beach and then long stretches of high bank. Ptarmigan tracks plentiful. Following Nindermann's track. At 3 halted, used up. Crawled into a hole in the bank. Collected wood and built a fire. Alexia away in quest of game. Nothing for supper except a spoonful of glycerine. All hands weak and feeble, but cheerful. God help us!

Tuesday, October 11*th*—121st day.—Southwest gale, with snow. Unable to move. No game. Teaspoonful of glycerine and hot water for food. No more wood in our vicinity.

Wednesday, October 12*th*—122d day.—Breakfast, last spoonful glycerine and hot water. For dinner we had a couple of handsful of Arctic willow in a pot of water, and drank the infusion. Everybody getting weaker and weaker. Hardly strength to get firewood. Southwest gale, with snow.

Thursday, October 13*th* — 123d day. — Willow tea. Strong southwest winds. No news from Nindermann. We are in the hands of God, and unless He relents are lost. We cannot move against the wind, and staying here means starvation. After noon went ahead for a mile, crossing either another river or a wind in the big one. After crossing missed Lee. Went down in a hole in the bank and camped. Sent back for Lee. He had laid down and was waiting to die. All united in saying the Lord's Prayer and Creed. After supper strong gale of wind. Horrible night.

Friday, October 14th—124th day.—Breakfast, willow tea. Dinner, half teaspoonful sweet oil and willow tea. Alexia shot one ptarmigan. Had soup. Southwest wind moderating.

Saturday, October 15th—125th day.—Breakfast, willow tea and two old boots. Conclude to move at sunrise. Alexia broken down ; also Lee. Came to an empty grain raft. Halt and camp. Signs of smoke at twilight to southward.

Sunday, October 16th—126th day.—Alexia broken down. Divine service.

Monday, October 17th—127th day.—Alexia dying. Doctor baptized him. Read prayers for sick. Mr. Collins' birthday, forty years old. About sunset Alexia died. Exhaustion from starvation. Covered him with ensign and laid him in the crib.

Tuesday, October 18th—128th day.—Calm and mild. Snow falling. Buried Alexia in the afternoon. Laid him on the ice of the river and covered him over with slabs of ice.

Wednesday, October 19th—129th day.—Cutting up tent to make foot-gear. Doctor went ahead to find new camp. Shifted by dark.

Thursday, October 20th—130th day.—Bright and sunny, but very cold. Lee and Kaach done up.

Friday, October 21st—131st day.—Kaach was found dead about midnight between the Doctor and myself. Lee died about noon. Read prayers for sick when we found he was going.

Saturday, October 22d—132d day.—Too weak to carry the bodies of Lee and Kaach out on the ice. The Doctor, Collins and myself carried them around the corner out of sight. Then my eyes closed up.

Sunday, October 23d—133d day.—Everybody pretty weak. Slept or rested to-day, and then managed to get enough wood in before dark. Read part of divine service. Suffering in our feet. No foot-gear.

Monday, October 24th—134th day.—A hard night.

Tuesday, October 25th—135th day.

Wednesday, October 26th—136th day.

Thursday, October 27th—137th day.—Iverson broken down.

Friday, October 28th—138th day.—Iverson died during early morning.

Saturday, October 29th—139th day.—Dressler died during the night.

Sunday, October 30th—140th day.—Boyd and Gœrtz died during the night. Mr. Collins dying.

* * * * * * * * * *

There the diary stops. When I had read it I tried to tell the Cossack what it was, but I could not speak. In many passages of the narrative I recognized experiences of my own. For the first time in my life I found it impossible to restrain my emotion before strangers, and buried my face in my hands for ten or fifteen minutes.

MONUMENT HILL.

CHAPTER XVIII.

HOW THE BODIES WERE FOUND.

BOOKOFF, LENA DELTA,
April 24th, 1882.

DURING the next fortnight I gathered supplementary details of the tragedy. On the 16th of March, all preliminaries having been arranged, Chief Engineer Melville's search party started from the temporary depot he had established at Cas Carta to make a thorough and exhaustive search for Captain De Long and his unfortunate companions. The search party as organized consisted of Chief Engineer G. W. Melville, commanding; James H. Bartlett, assistant engineer of the *Jeannette*, and William

Nindermann, who was one of the two sent ahead by Captain De Long to seek the aid they could not reach in a body, and thus escaped the tragic fate that awaited those left behind. Besides those mentioned, the search party comprised Messrs. Greenbek and Bobookoff, interpreters; Kolinkin, a Cossack, and a Russian exile, Yafeem Kapella, general assistant and supervisor of the Yakout dog-drivers and helpers, who were Tomat Constantin, Georgie Nicholai, "Capitan" Inukkenty Shimuloff, Story Nicholai, Vassilli Koolgark and Simeon Illak, with Ivan Portnyagin and his wife, cook and helper.

The search was first from Usterday, following the track of the retreat, until arriving at Matvey. This search resulted in finding nothing new concerning the lost ones, and then Chief Engineer Melville decided to work back upon Nindermann's line of retreat. They started on the 23d of March from Matvey and soon found the wreck of a scow for which they had been looking, as Nindermann felt it would be a surer guide than any other to the remains of his former shipmates. He had passed this wreck when in company with Noros the first day they separated from the main body, and was convinced, judging from the condition in which he had left his companions and the rate of travel they were able to maintain, that they had not advanced far beyond this conspicuous object. And so it proved, for after they had found the wreck they had not hunted along the bank more than about five hundred yards when they came upon the barrel of a rifle, which, with the ends of four poles lashed together, upon which it hung, was protruding from the snowdrift. Three poles had been lashed together to support one end of the ridgepole of the tent, while the other extended back and rested upon the bank.

Two natives were at once set to work digging out the snow on either side of the poles, which here was about eight feet deep, and soon each came upon a body at the same time. Thus Boyd and Gœrtz were found, and Chief Engineer Melville, after directing them to clear away the snow toward the east, ascended the bank, here twenty feet above the level of the ice, to find a place in which he could take a round of angles with his compass. While proceeding in a westerly direction his attention was drawn to a camp kettle about a thousand yards from the boat wreck, and, approaching, he nearly stumbled over a bare hand protruding up out of the snow. Stooping down and removing the snow, which was not over a foot in depth, he found the remains of the unfortunate commander of the expedition, Captain De Long, and within three feet of him lay Dr. Ambler, while "Sam," the Chinese cook, was stretched at their feet. All were partly covered by the half tent which they had brought up with them when their companions no longer needed it, and some pieces of blanket had also been used to secure a little warmth. Near by were the remains of a fire, and in the camp kettle some pieces of Arctic willow, of which they had made tea.

On the ground near him lay Captain De Long's pocket journal, a few extracts from which mournful record I have already sent you. It seemed apparent that he, with the surgeon and "Sam," had died the day of the last entry in this journal; and probably the book had not been returned to his pocket after making that entry, for his pencil was also on the ground near the book. He had ever been particular to make some entry in his journal each day, and when nothing transpired he desired to mention he merely wrote the date and the number of days since the vessel sank and the retreat commenced. Before leaving the tent place to drag their weary, shoeless feet to their last rest they had respectfully covered the face of Mr. Collins, their brother officer, with a cloth. The tent had been pitched in a deep gorge in the river bank. The two boxes of records were found at the tent place, below the bank, and a little further toward the east were the medicine chest and the flag, still upon its staff.

The bodies of Iverson and Dressler were lying side by side just outside of where the half tent shelter had hung from the ridge pole, and that of Mr. Collins was further in rear on the inside of the tent. Lee and Kaach were not discovered for some time ; but by referring to the Captain's journal the searchers found the statement that after they died their bodies were carried "around the corner out of sight" by the three officers, who, with the cook, were now the only survivors, and too weak to bury their fallen comrades. By sounding through the snow toward the west the missing bodies were found in a cleft in the bank near by. None of those found had boots on their feet, but instead had wrapped rags around and tied them on to protect them somewhat from the cold. In their pockets, however, were found the remains of burned skin boots, which showed but too plainly to what strait they had been reduced for food. The hands and clothing of all were burned, and it seemed that in their last despairing effort to gather some warmth they had actually crawled into the fire. Boyd was found lying directly upon the remains of a fire, and his clothing was burned through to the skin, but his body was not scorched.

It was Chief Engieeer Melville's intention to bury the remains upon the bank where they were found, but the natives assured him that in all probability any tomb would be washed away, as when the river broke up in the spring there would be about four feet of water over the entire delta. He therefore had them all removed to the top of a hill of solid rock about three hundred feet high, about forty versts to the southwest, and there constructed a mausoleum of wood from the wreck of the scow near where they were found. First a gigantic cross was hewn out of a solid piece of driftwood and erected on the crest of the hill, and around it was built a box six feet wide, two feet deep and twenty-two feet long, placed exactly in the magnetic meridian. 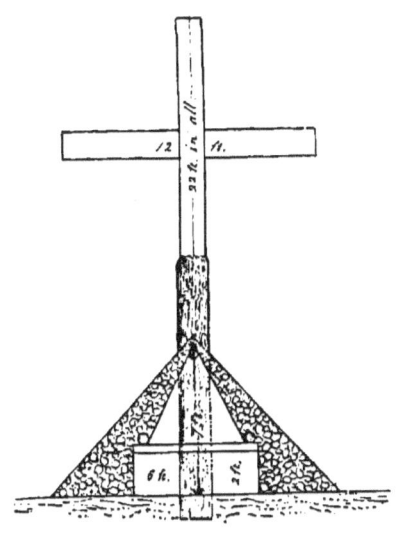 After the bodies had been placed

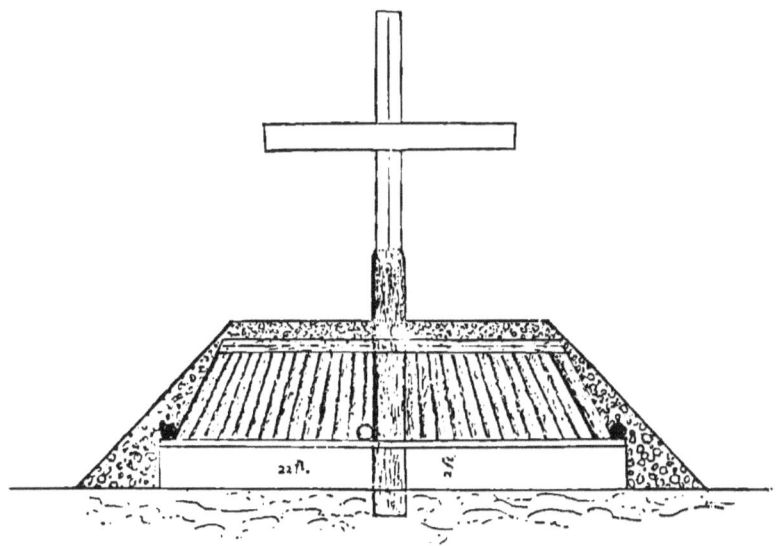

DIAGRAMS OF TOMB.

therein the box was covered with timbers laid side by side and a ridge pole sixteen feet long framed into the cross five feet above the lid of the coffin, the ends supported by timbers having the same inward slant. The cross itself is twenty-two feet high from the surface of the rock, is one foot square, and the cross-beam is twelve feet long by one foot square.

On the cross is engraved the following inscription, cut in by the search party at their house at nights:—

```
                In
             MEMORY
                of
                12
                of
               the
             OFFICERS
               and
               MEN
                of
   THE ARCTIC STEAMER "JEANNETTE,"
        WHO DIED OF STARVATION
     IN LENA DELTA, OCTOBER, 1881.
             Lieutenant
           G. W. DE LONG.
          Dr. J. M. AMBLER.
            J. J. COLLINS.
               W. LEE.
              A. GŒRTZ.
             A. DRESSLER.
            H. ERICKSEN.
             G. W. BOYD.
             N. IVERSON.
              H. KAACH,
               ALEXIA.
               AH SAM.
```

Chief Melville has made arrangements to have the pyramid sodded this spring, under the direction of the commander at Bulun, in case he has finished his search in time to escape before the breaking up of the rivers. The structure is a very creditable affair, and conspicuous from the river at a distance of twenty versts.

When the records and books were found they were immediately closed and no one permitted to examine their contents, with the exception of Captain De Long's pocket journal, and of that only the month of October, in order to serve as a guide in prosecuting their further search. The articles of value and such things as would be of interest to friends of the deceased were also boxed up, and, together with the records and flag, were at once sent to Yakoutsk in charge of Mr. Bobookoff and the Cossack, to be placed in the care of the Governor of the district until the arrival of Chief Melville or instructions from the Navy Department concerning the disposition to be made of them. In the meantime diligent search has been made for the remains of Alexia, which the Captain's journal says were carried out upon the ice abreast of the scow and covered with slabs of ice, but as yet they have not been found.

As soon as the entombment had been completed the search party started on the 10th of April to look for any traces of Lieutenant Chipp's party having reached the delta or adjacent coasts. It would be impossible to make a complete search of the delta, for that is merely an immense sand-bank, cut in every direction by thousands of large and small rivers, many of them navigable, but most of them changing their direction from year to year. A search at this time by so small a party could necessarily only cover the coast line before the sledging season is over, and after that all traces would be removed by the breaking up and overflow of the river. In this last search Chief Melville was to take a westerly course as far as the Olenek River and return by the northwest coast to Cas Carta, while Bartlett and Nindermann started together from Cas Carta and went in company as far to the northeast as Barkin. Here they were to separate, Bartlett taking the eastern coast, while Nindermann returned to Cas Carta by the northern shore.

Neither Bartlett nor Nindermann found any traces of those they were seeking, and at this date Chief Melville

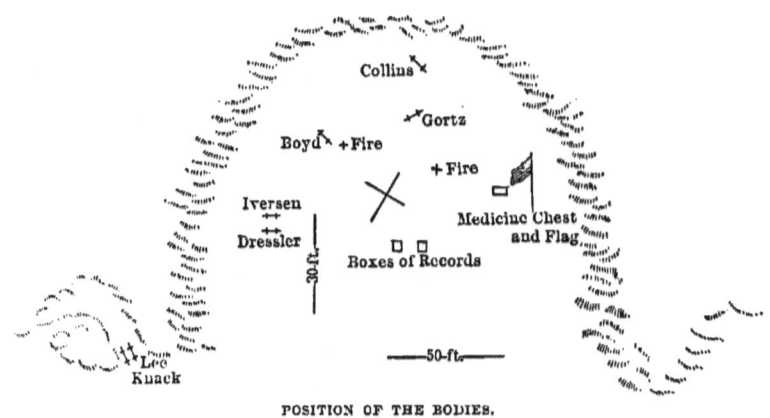

POSITION OF THE BODIES.

has not returned. He was unfortunately delayed three days after the others in starting by circumstances over which he had no control and may have found it a serious inconvenience when the time for sledging was drawing so rapidly to a close. After his return to Cas Carta the entire party will join Bartlett, who is at Germavelok, and from there a search will be made to Cape Borchoya and the bay of that name. If nothing should transpire from these last searches the sad presumption must prevail that Lieutenant Chipp's boat swamped in the gale of September 12 and all on board of her perished.

THE JEANETTE SURVIVORS IN YAKOUTSK. (*From a photograph.*)

Prof. Newcomb. Noros. Wilson. John Sing. Iniguin. Leach.
Lauterbach. Chief Eng. Melville. Lieut. Danenhower.
Bartlett. John Cole. Nindermann. Manzen.

CHAPTER XIX.

THE VOYAGE OF THE JEANNETTE.

IN relating the story of the *Jeannette*, of which conflicting accounts have been given, I prefer to rely on the journal kept by Captain De Long during the voyage, and read by me while travelling up the Lena River, and on the statement made to me by Nindermann and Noros, the two survivors of the Captain's boat. The crew numbered thirty-three all told when the vessel entered the Arctic Ocean. She left San Francisco July 8, 1879; she sank June 13, 1881. She was put into the ice pack within two months of her departure; she was frozen in before the end of November, and she never again came out. The record of the two years in the ice is extremely monotonous. It was only when the *Jeannette's* last moments approached in the summer of 1881 that the interest of the tale begins. At this point it is taken up by the journal of De Long. His notes run as follows:

Saturday, June 11*th* (ship's date *Sunday, June* 12*th*, correct date).—At half-past seven A.M. the ice commenced to close in on the port side, but after advancing a foot or two came to rest. One watch was employed in hauling heavy floe pieces into a small canal on the port bow to close it up and to receive the greater part of the thrust. The ice at ten A.M had advanced toward the port side until these floe pieces had received the thrust, and everything quieted down again. The situation of the ship and her surroundings may be seen from the following rough diagram:—

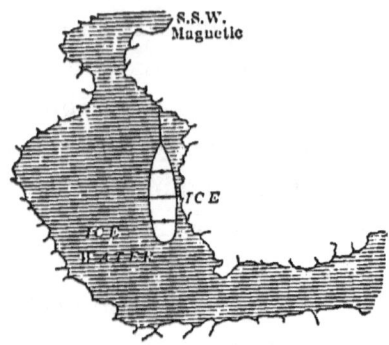

At FOUR P.M. the ice came down in great force all along the port side, jamming the ship hard against the ice on the starboard side of her and causing her to heel 16° to starboard. From the snapping and cracking of her bunker sides and starting in of the starboard ceiling, as well as the opening of the seams of the ceiling to the width of 1¼ inches, it was feared that the ship was about to be seriously endangered, and orders were accordingly given to lower the starboard boats and haul them away from the ship to a safe position on the ice floe. This was done quietly and without confusion. The ice in coming in on the port side also had a movement toward the stern, and this last movement not only raised her port bow, but buried the starboard quarter, and jamming it and the stern against the heavy ice effectually prevented the ship rising to pressure. Mr. Melville, while below in the engine room, saw a break across the ship in the wake of the boilers and engines, showing that so solidly were the stern and starboard quarter held by the ice that the ship was breaking in two from the pressure upward exerted on the port bow of the ship. The starboard side of the ship was also evidently broken, because water was rising rapidly in the starboard coal-bunker. Orders were now given to land half the pemmican in the deck-house and all the bread which was on deck, and the sleds and dogs were likewise carried to a position of safety. At 4:30 there was a lull in the pressure, and it was assumed for the moment that the ice had united under the ship, and being as close together as it could come would occasion us no further injury, and that we might be able to take care of the vessel yet. The ship was heeled 22° to starboard and was raised forward 4' 6", the entire port bow being visible also to a height of 4' 6" from the forefoot. In the early morning we had been able to see through the water down alongside the stem on the starboard side, and we could see that the forefoot was bent to starboard about a foot. This would indicate that the pressure received on the 19th of January, 1880, was from port to starboard, instead of the other way, as we then supposed. But at 5 P.M. the pressure was renewed, and continued with tremendous force, the ship cracking in every part. The spar-deck commenced to buckle up and the starboard side seemed again on the point of coming up. Orders were now given to get out provisions, clothing, bedding, ship's books and papers, and to remove all sick to a place of safety. While engaged in this work another tremendous pressure was received, and at 6 P.M. it was found that the ship was beginning to fill. From this time forward every effort was devoted to getting provisions, &c., on the ice, and it was not desisted from until the water had risen to the spar deck, the ship being heeled to starboard about 30°. The entire starboard side of the spar-deck was submerged, the rail being under water and the water-line reaching to the hatch combings. The starboard side was evidently broken in abreast of the mainmast and the ship was settling fast. Our ensign had been hoisted at the mizzen and every preparation made for abandoning, and at 8 P.M. everybody was ordered to leave the ship. Assembling on the floe we dragged all our boats and provisions clear of bad cracks and prepared to camp down for the night. Took an account of what we had and found the following:

4,950 lbs. pemmican (American).
1,120 lbs. hard bread.
260 gallons alcohol.
100 lbs. cut loaf sugar.
400 lbs. extra crew sugar.
100 lbs. tea.
92¼ lbs. mutton soup.
176 lbs. mutton broth.
150 lbs. Liebig's extract beef.
252 lbs. canned chicken.
144 lbs. canned turkey.
36 lbs. green corn.
12½ lbs. pigs' feet.
32 lbs. tongue.
42 lbs. onions.
18 lbs. pickles.
120 lbs. chocolate.
36 lbs. cocoa.
205 lbs. tobacco.
48 lbs. veal.
44 lbs. ham.
150 lbs. cheese.
210 lbs. ground coffee.
60 lbs. whole coffee.
75 bottles malt extract.
½ bbl. lime juice.
2,000 rounds Remington ammunition.
1 gallon brandy.
3 gallons whiskey.
2 bottles whiskey in lime juice.
7 bottles brandy.
First cutter.
Second cutter.
First whale-boat.
Iron dingy.
McClintock dingy.
6 tents sleeping bags.
33 knapsacks, packed.
5 cooking stoves.
2 boat sleds.
4 McClintock sleds.
2 St. Michael sleds.
2 medicine chests and medicine.

Sunday, June 12*th* (*Monday, June* 13*th*).—At 1 P.M. we were turned out by the ice opening in the midst of our camp. All our gear and belongings were transported to a place of safety, and again piped down at 2 A.M., leaving a man on watch. At 1 A.M. the mizzenmast went by the board, and the ship was so far heeled over that the lower yard-arms were resting on the ice. At 3 A.M. the ship had sunk until her smoke-pipe was nearly awash. At 4 A.M. the *Jeannette* went down. First righting to an even keel she slowly sank. The maintopmast fell by the board to starboard ; then the foretopmast and finally the mainmast near the main-truss. When she finally sank the foremast was all that was standing. At 9 A.M. called all hands and breakfasted, after which we collected all the clothing and arranged it for distribution. Besides the contents of the packed knapsacks and the clothing in wear we find we have the following :

28 woollen overshirts,	20 trousers (cloth),
24 woollen drawers,	8 fur blankets,
27 woollen undershirts,	18 woollen blankets,
24 sack coats,	13 skin parkies,
8 overcoats,	

and they were divided among all hands as required, much of it being in excess. * * * Everybody being bright and cheerful, with plenty to eat and plenty of clothes. Even music is not forgotten. Lauterbach serenaded us to-night with a mouth harmonium. A work tent was set up for my use ; kept the silk flag flying. Temperature about 23° all day. Men visited the wreck ; they found one chair on the ice and some oars and spar planks. Chipp better ; Danenhower lively. At 9:45 P.M. I read divine service.

Monday, June 13*th.*—Called all hands at seven A.M.; breakfast at eight. Turned to at nine, and set to work mounting first and second cutters and whale-boats on their travelling sleds. I have concluded to remain where we are until all our preparations are well made, and then to start properly. We have provisions enough to live upon for some time without impairing our sixty days' allowance for going south. Our sick are progressing favorably, and this delay will also tend to their advantage. Sweetman visited the place where the ship sank, but nothing could be seen but a signal chest floating bottom up. There is much water sky in all directions; the air is very damp and raw. We all slept very well last night, being both warm and comfortable. During the afternoon the boats were mounted on the sleds and got ready for hauling. Between time we shifted the camp to the westward, as we were too near the edge of the floe in case of accident. Chipp's tent was placed to the rear and to windward, so that he might not be kept awake by the "snorers," as was the case last night. Then we moved all our boats to the front of the tents and the provisions to the front of the boats, and had supper in our new location. We had carried out of the ship all the drinking water we had on board, and made it last until Sunday night, but now we are, of course, down to what we can scrape up from the ice. We select the oldest and highest hummocks and scrape off the broken-down crystals when we can find them; but, of course, the sun has not had power enough yet to do any great amount of melting. The snow, or rather ice, is fresh to the taste, but the Doctor, by a nitrate of silver test, finds it much too salty. However, we cannot help ourselves, and with lime juice, which we take daily, must try to avert the danger. Just now we are living royally on good things and not working very hard, and we are in glorious health, except for some occasional traces of the old lead poisoning suspicions. Temperature at eight P.M. 18°, and very damp.

Tuesday, June 14th.—Called all hands at seven, breakfasted and turned to by nine A.M. Then set two men from each tent, under Melville's direction, to get together our sixty days' provisions. The Doctor with one man set to work dividing up (and fortifying) the lime juice among three water breakers. Dunbar, with two men, overhauled and relashed the three McClintock sledges to get them ready for stowage and loading. The balance of the men continue the work of making extra foot-nips, reducing sleeping bags and making such additions to their comfort as are possible. Our sick list is not progressing favorably. Alexia was very sick all night with stomach ache, groaning all the time and vomiting violently. Kuehne is quite sick, and both he and Alexia are laid up in their sleeping bags. Chipp seems brighter. Weather clear, bright and pleasant. Temperature at ten A.M., 10° in the shade; minimum during night, 12°. To the south the openings in the ice are shown by light masses of thin, bright fog sweeping away before the wind. Barometer, 30.37—but I am a little suspicious that my pocket barometer is out of order. At two commenced loading up five sleds with provisions. Divided over 3,960 pounds pemmican and 200 gallons alcohol among the sleds, and then, having our weekly ration bags ready, we switched off to fill them. The daily allowance of tea is one ounce; coffee, two ounces; sugar, two ounces. Sights obtained at six P.M. place us in 153° 58′ 45″—a drift since the 12th of 13½ miles north, 84° west. Thus far we are getting along very well. Everybody is bright and cheerful and our camp has a lively look. The arrangement is as follows :—

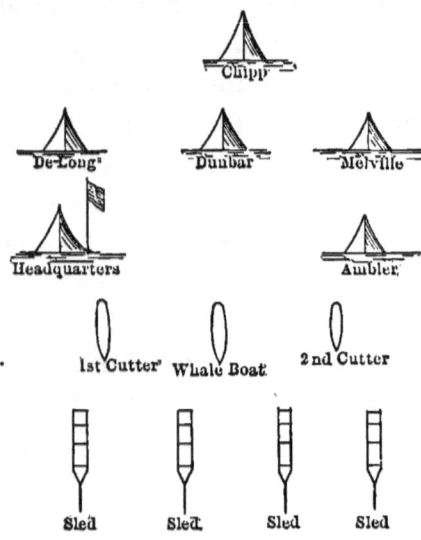

After supper no work was done except putting two rifles apart for each tent—ten in all—which are to be carried in the boats—four in the first cutter, four in the second and two in the whale-boat.

Wednesday, June 15. — Weather dull, gloomy and foggy, but after ten A.M., it cleared away to a bright sunshiny day. The night has been cold (10°). I did not sleep well, having found it impossible to keep my shoulders covered by my sleeping bag, but everybody else seems to be all right and to have slept well. The sick are as follows:—Chipp is better; he says he has slept well and feels bright. Danenhower goes around with his game eye darkened and does a number of things. Alexia has had a bad night and is quite sick this morning. Kuehne still remains shut up in his tent. During the forenoon we were engaged in bagging as much tea, coffee and sugar as possible, and in dividing the weights among our five sleds. This was completed by eleven A.M., and we then set to work to lash and secure the loads. The distribution of weights was as follows:—

	No. 1.	No. 2.	No. 3.	No. 4.	No. 5.
765 pounds pemmican		720	720	720	720
40 gallons alcohol		40	40	40	40
36 pounds Liebig		36	—	—	18
61 pounds C. L. sugar		—	—	—	61
60 pounds X. C. sugar		—	—	—	—
4 bags bread		4	4	4	2
30 pounds ground coffee		30	—	30	—
90 pounds tea		—	—	60	—
10 pounds X. C. sugar		—	—	—	—
1,059		1,318	1,252	1,342	1,325

On the ice yet, 30 pounds roast coffee, 30 pounds ground coffee, 1 bag of bread, which must go in the boats. Still short of sixty days' provisions, viz: 315 pounds pemmican, 43 pounds tea, 55 pounds sugar and 37 pounds coffee. We are, of course, leaving behind us many provisions, as well as our two dingies and one St. Michael's sled. As our progress will necessarily be slow, I am of the opinion that each encampment for a week after our start will be near enough to our present location to enable us to send back a dog sledge each halt to bring forward our supplies for the succeeding twenty-four hours. In this case we shall not break in upon our packed sledges. Dinner at one P.M. Turned to at two P.M. Sleds all lashed, and I notice No. 2 (Chipp's) has a sled flag already mounted with the name "Lizzie." Upon calling Nindermann's attention to our having none he informed me that ours was under way and that he should like to call it "Sylvie," to which I had naturally no objection. Sights to-day place us in latitude 77° 17 north, longitude 153°

42′ 30″ east—a drift since yesterday of three and three-quarter miles, 72° north. Temperature at six P.M., 19°; wind northeast; force 2. During the afternoon I issued the following order:

[ORDER.]

UNITED STATES CUTTER *Jeannette*, IN THE ICE, LATITUDE 77° 17′ NORTH, LONGITUDE 153° 42′ EAST, ARCTIC OCEAN, *June* 15*th*, 1881.

When a start is made to drag our sleds to the southward the clothing allowance for each officer and man will be limited to what he actually wears and the contents of his packed knapsack. Each may dress in skins or not, as he pleases, at the start, but having made his choice he must be ready to abide by it. Extra outside clothing of any kind (except moccasins) cannot be taken. The contents of the packed knapsacks are to be as follows:

2 pairs blanket nips or duffle nips.	1 skull cap.
2 pairs stockings.	1 comforter.
1 pair moccasins.	1 pair snow spectacles.
1 cap.	1 plug tobacco.
2 pairs mittens.	1 pipe.
1 undershirt.	2 rounds ammunition.
1 drawers.	24 wax matches.

Soap, towels, thread and needles at discretion, an extra pair of moccasins, making five in all, with its foot nips, may be carried in the sleeping bag, but nothing else is to be put in the sleeping bag. Each officer will see that the allowance is not exceeded in any particular.

Sled No. 1 stow sleeping bags, tent, knapsacks and mess-gear in first cutter.

Sled No. 2 stow as above in second cutter.
Sled No. 3 stow as above in whale-boat.
Sled No. 4 stow as above in second cutter.
Sled No. 5 stow as above in whale-boat.

If at any time we go in the boats—

Sled crew No. 1 goes in the first cutter.
Sled crew No. 2 goes in the second cutter.
Sled crew No. 3 goes in the whale-boat.
Sled crew No. 4 goes in first cutter.
Surgeon, Mr. Cole, and cabin steward in whale-boat.
Remainder of No. 5 in second cutter.

Further orders or modification of the above will be given as necessary. Very respectfully,

GEORGE W. DE LONG,

Lieutenant United States Navy, Commanding Arctic Expedition.

An almost cloudless sky and in consequence a broiling hot sun shining down on the floe makes us very uncomfortable. We are all terribly sunburned, and our noses, lips and cheeks are all beginning to get sore. Our eyes are all right yet, however.

Thursday, June 16th.—De Long records long streaks of water sky to the southward and southwest. He also permits the men to each take half a blanket in anticipation of cold. At half-past four Mr. Dunbar is sent ahead southward to mark out a good road, and then the Captain issued the following order:

> UNITED STATES CUTTER *Jeannette*, IN THE ICE,
> LATITUDE 77° 18′ NORTH, LONGITUDE 153° 25′
> EAST, ARCTIC OCEAN, *June 16th*, 1881.

We shall start to the southward at six P.M. Friday, June 17 (Saturday, June 18), and our travelling thereafter is to be done between six P.M. and six A.M. The order of advance will be as follows:

First—All hands drag the first cutter and dogs the No. 1 sled.

Second—Starboard watch drag the second cutter, port watch drag No. 4 sled and dogs drag No. 2 sled.

Third—Port watch drag the whale-boat, starboard watch drag No. 3 sled and dogs drag No. 5 sled.

Alexia's three dogs will drag the St. Michael's sled; Kuehne, Charley, Tung Sing and Alexia to report to and accompany Lieutenant Chipp. The daily routine will be as follows:

Call all hands, 4:30 P.M.
Breakfast, 5 P.M.
Break camp, 5:40 P.M.
Under way, 6 P.M.
Halt, 11:30 .P.M
Dinner, midnight.
Pack up, 12:40 A.M.

Under way, 1 A.M.
Halt, pitch camp, 6 A.M.
Lime juice and supper, 6:30 A.M.
Set watch, pipe down, turn in, 7 A.M.
Course, S. by E. ½ E. mag.

As long as it is possible to do so the St. Michael's sled will be sent back each morning to bring up provisions now in this camp in order that we may not have to break in upon our sled stores. But when we do commence upon our loaded provisions the following will be the ration table:

Breakfast.	*Dinner.*	*Supper.*
4 oz. pemmican,	8 oz. pemmican,	4 oz. pemmican,
1 oz. ham,	1 oz. Liebig,	1 oz. tongue,
3 lb. bread,	½ oz. tea,	½ oz. tea,
2 oz. coffee,	2-3 oz. sugar,	2-3 oz. sugar,
2-3 oz. sugar.		¼ lb. bread.

GEORGE W. DE LONG,
etc., etc., etc.

Captain De Long continues: During the afternoon the sleds and boats were each supplied with flags.

The *Jeannette* carries my silk flag.

The second cutter *Hiram* carries flag "Hiram."

The whale boat *Rosey* carries flag "Rosey."

No. 1 sled carries square blue flag "Sylvie," with the motto, "Nil desperandum."

No. 2 carries swallow tail "Lizzie."

No. 3 carries flag ——.

No. 4 carries white flag with red Maltese cross; motto, "In hoc signo vinces."

No. 5 carries flag "Maud;" motto, "Comme je trouve."

Then called all hands to muster and read the foregoing order. We are now, I believe, ready, and will start at six P.M. to-morrow. The St. Michael's sled was loaded, officers divided into watches, and next day (Friday) De Long prepared a record, to be left in a water breaker on the ice, giving a history of the *Jeannette's* cruise, her discoveries of the two islands (Jeannette and Henrietta), etc. After it was written it was carefully sewed in a piece of black rubber and placed in an empty boat breaker, "which, left in the ice, may get somewhere."

CHAPTER XX.

THE RETREAT.

THEN the start was made, and is thus recorded in De Long's journal:

"At 5 P.M. called all hands again, and as soon as possible had supper, or, as it might be called now, breakfast. Broke camp at 5:50 P.M., and though 6 was the time for starting it was 6:20 P.M. before we got under way. All hands started with the first cutter, while the dogs, managed by Anequin, attempted the No. 1 sled. The cutter went easily enough, but No. 1 sled was more than a match for our dogs. Occasionally stopping, we lent a hand to start the sled from a deep rut, and finally, seeing the necessity of more force, I detached six men from the cutter and went back with them to help the No. 1 sled. And to this the origin of our day's trouble may be referred. When I sent Mr. Dunbar ahead yesterday it was to plant flags for our first day's journey, and upon his return I could see but three flags, and supposed there were no more. Melville accordingly dumped the provisions at the third flag as the end of our day's journey. Upon the cutter reaching the third flag Melville wanted to stop, but Dunbar informed him there was a fourth flag beyond, and that that was the end of the first day's journey. Of course I could not be everywhere on a road one and a half miles long, and Melville in his uncertainty about my wishes had to be guided by Dunbar's idea, so that the first cutter, instead of halting by our provisions, was carried on beyond them, to my extreme annoyance when I learned of it. Meanwhile the six men and myself went back to the No. 1 sled, and by almost superhuman exertions got it along a quarter of a mile. We then got the second cutter and the whale-boat along to where we had left No. 1 sled, and while wondering what kept Melville and the men away so long I saw that Chipp (who was ahead) had come to a standstill. Hastening toward him I found that the ice had opened, and that our remaining effects would have to be unloaded and ferried over. Here was a nice fix. Sending back at once for the light dingy, I got Chipp and the hospital sled over and sent him to bring the cutter party back. Time was slipping away, and all that the six men and myself could do, with the assistance of the dogs, was to get the cutter and whale-boat with No. 1 and No. 2 sleds as far along as the ferry. By 10 P.M. the first-cutter party returned, and we at once launched the two remaining boats, hauled them across and got them up on the ice on the other side. To avoid unloading the sleds a road was sought and found higher up, where, by filling in with some large pieces of ice, we managed to get an uncertain way of crossing the opening lead. While so crossing we doubled under the right runner of No. 1 sled, and had to stop lest we should ruin it. No. 2 and No. 5 each broke a runner, the tenons of the uprights breaking short off. And, in fine, by the time we had crossed this lead (12:10 A.M. on Saturday, June 18th) we had three disabled sleds, were already an hour late for our dinner, had our provisions half a mile further on, and the mess gear and sleeping gear of No. 1 sled half a mile further beyond still. However, there was no help for it, so buckling to our two boats we started on, and by

1:30 A.M. had reached the black flag and our provisions. During the advance with the first cutter Lauterbach had doubled up with cramps, Lee frequently was falling down doubled up with cramps, for which he can assign no cause except lead-poison. At 7 we had supper, and at 8 A.M. set the watch and piped down—a weary lot of mortals."

Next day De Long writes: "All hands seem bright and cheerful; none of us are stiff after our hard work, strange to say. The sick are as follows: Chipp, used up about the legs; Alexia better; steward better; Kuehne better. Our experience thus far has not been very encouraging. We have had such terrific roads, such soft and deep snow and such ugly ice openings that our difficulties have been increased. The necessities of the case have led to overloading the sleds, and, though they would have gone well enough on smooth ice, the snow would stop these or any other sleds. Twenty-eight men and twenty-three dogs lying back with all their strength could only start one 1,600-pound sled a few feet each time, and when sliding down a hill she would plunge into a snow-bank, and it was terrible work getting her out. Though the temperature was between twenty and twenty-five we were in our shirt sleeves and perspiring as on a hot summer day. I see very clearly that we must run with lighter loads and go over the same ground oftener. I hoped to be able to advance our boats and provisions on three separate hauls, but I must be satisfied if we now do it in six." Next day, Sunday, most of the provisions from the original camp were brought up and distributed among the sleds, and on Monday the time was occupied in bringing up the remainder, and on Tuesday morning, at eight o'clock, De Long writes, they were only one and a half miles from the first starting place of Friday, the 17th. That night it rained heavily and no advance was made.

De Long writes: "At no time of the year is travelling worse than at present. In the winter or spring months it is, of course, cold and comfortless, but it is, nevertheless, dry. In the autumn or late summer it is favorable, because the melted snow has all drained off the hard ice, and the travelling is excellent. But just now the snow is soft enough to sink into, and progress is almost impossible, and when a rainy day sets in our misery is complete. Even the dogs cower under the boats for shelter like hens, or snuggle up against the tent doors begging for admission. On shore the pattering of the rain on the roof has a pleasant sound to those within, but out here it is far from pleasant. No fires, of course, except for cooking, and no place to dry clothes, and little streams of water trickling down on you from the tent ventilating holes make your own wetness more wet. These halts and long camps have shown me that several of our party have been carrying more than I can permit. It is astonishing how many 'little things that don't weigh anything' have crept in, and it is equally surprising how great is their aggregate weight. I shall have one more clearing out before leaving this camp."

Tuesday, June 21st.—At half-past two A.M. the rain ceased. Sent Mr. Dunbar ahead to make a road where necessary and to place flags. At half-past three A.M. I took a *narta* (sled) and nine dogs, and with Kaach carried forward 450 pounds of pemmican and fifty pounds of Liebig. Mr. Dunbar had cut two roads, one through piled up hummocks and another through a broken ridge. There is an ugly place where the ice has cracked and opened to a foot in width, and if it opens further, requiring bridging or ferrying, we shall again have our hands full. Called all hands at six P.M.; at half-past seven got under way; sent Melville ahead with Nos. 1 and 2 sleds, and two dog sleds and Ericksen and Leach with the other *nartas* to the old camp to bring forward the remainder of the stores. Left the camp pitched and sleeping gear and mess gear convenient to the boats, in the event of our having to dine here. The Doctor, with the sick, remained, of course, with the tents. By half-past eight P.M. Melville and his party and the two advanced dog sleds had come back to camp, having left the first load at the crack in the ice mentioned this morning, it having widened, as I feared it would, during our sleep. By nine the second instalment was sent along, and by half-past nine the camp was broken, and the whole boat, with two more dog loads, under way. Mr. Dunbar and two men remained ahead to try and get a large piece of ice down to bridge the opening. I had instructed Melville, in case Mr. Dunbar had managed to bridge the opening, to get all our traps through the gap, and as he did not return from the first cutter I concluded this was being done. As I was anxious to get forward to see the state of things ahead I sent Ericksen and Leach back with three dogs for the dingy, and placing No. 1's mess gear in the dog sled I started on with three dogs. This brought us to

Wednesday, June 22d.—I had hardly gone a quarter of a mile when I came to an ice opening, and, in spite of my strongest efforts, the dogs scattered across some lumps, capsized the sled, dragged me in and sent all my mess gear flying, having accomplished which and reached the other side themselves they sat down and howled to their hearts' content. Floundering across I managed to collect my scattered property and get safely over and then righted and dragged out the sled. As soon as resistance was removed away went the dogs again. Reaching the ice opening which had occasioned the delay at one A.M. I found Melville afloat and adrift on an ice island, with all the boats and sleds, nothing having been got through the gap. I shouted to him to get dinner and I would get to him later when the dingy came up. But he managed to get a cake of ice dragged to me and I ferried across with my dog team and mess gear. At once we set to work getting floes in place as a bridge and before sitting down to dinner we got two sleds and a lot of dog loads through the gap on to the heavy ice beyond. At half past one we sat down to dinner, and at two Ericksen and Leach arrived with the dingy. At twenty minutes past two A.M., turned to and ran the whale-boat and second cutter through the gap. Then sending Melville back with his party for the first cutter, Ericksen, Leach and myself pushed on two dog teams, with pemmican and bread, as far as the flag. When we got back to the gap the Doctor and the sick were adrift, the ice having opened out during our absence. Dragged cakes of ice down and made a crazy bridge, over which the sick walked, and then we got the medical stores across, and after bridging, dragging, digging and filling in we had everything, first cutter included, through the gap by six A.M., and on the hard ice. Melville had to launch the first cutter and paddle her part of the way, but he got her up in time to take a share in the work of the rear guard. At twenty minutes past seven we had supper, and a more tired and hungry set of mortals could not well be found. We got ready to bag—having come only about half a mile in ten hours' hard work. At nine A.M. piped down. Slept till six P.M., when all hands were called. Sick, so so. Chipp has had a bad night and is much the worse for wear. Alexia is so easily upset by a little stomach ache as to lose his grip altogether. Lauterbach looks as if he were going to attend a funeral any moment and must keep his countenance to the proper point of solemnity. Danenhower's trouble is of course his blindness. Mr. Dunbar begins to wear again, and I have cautioned him to be careful of himself for a few days and not to exhaust all his strength. At fifty-five minutes past eleven P.M. the marked halting place was reached by the sleds—the first time in our experience we were able to get in one half day to the indicated place, have dinner on time and get ready for a new start after dinner. This was because we were on solid ice and had no openings.

Thursday, June 23*d.*—Sat down to dinner at quarter past twelve A.M., and turned to at quarter past one. At half past two the sky cleared and the sun came out brightly, the fog rolling away magically. At seven camp pitched. This is the first really good day's work, and yet I do not think we have made good more than a mile and a half, though working seven hours steadily. To the southward of us the ice is terribly confused, and presents no chance for an advance as yet. But no one can tell what six hours may bring forth, and when we get up again we may see something. Longitude is about 152° east. At half past eight A.M. piped down, and at six P.M. called all hands and breakfasted; at seven sent Mr. Dunbar ahead through the most likely looking part of the rough ice in front of us to try to find a road. At eight started ahead on our day's work, and, to save unnecessary detailed description, I will here mention once for all our manner of procedure. The daily routine and manner of progress marked out on the 16th has had to be abandoned for several reasons, chiefest of which was the impossibility of telling one minute how the ice would be the next in disarranging plans, and next in importance because men *cannot* do this kind of work ten hours each day without breaking down. By and by, perhaps, when our loads are lighter, we may be able to do it, but just now it is out of the question.

Our route having been indicated by several black flags placed after a halt or before a start Mr. Dunbar goes ahead at eight P.M. to make sure that no bridges have become necessary in the meantime. Then right after him goes Melville, with nearly all hands dragging the heavy sleds. No. 1 sled (already christened the *Walrus*) requires all his force, but generally he can start two of the others at one time. Ericksen and Leach run two dog sleds, trip after trip, all day, while I load and occasionally run one myself ahead to mark progress and indicate the route. The loaded sleds being up Melville's party come back for the boats. I then start the Doctor ahead with the sick, to go as far as the heavy sleds have been dragged. I then get the medical sled and run a load up to the same place. By this time the boats are up, cooks are ordered there to get dinner, while Melville and his party drag the sleds ahead another stage. Then, midnight (Friday, June 24), dinner succeeds; at one we turn to, drag the boats where we left the sleds, then along go the Doctor and the sick to that place, then ahead go the sleds again, again the boats, the dog sleds, and finally at half-past five or six A.M. I bring up the rear guard; we prepare for supper, pitch camp and the dog sleds get up with the last load. At seven we sup, at eight pipe down, to be called at six P.M. We therefore haul nine hours a day, sleep and rest ten, meal hours three; the other two hours are occupied in pitching camp, serving out and cooking food, breaking camp and marking the road ahead. There is no work in the world harder than this sledging, and with my two line officers constantly on the sick list I have much on my hands. In Melville I have a strong support, as well as a substitute for them, and as long as he remains as he is, strong and well, I shall get along all right. The Doctor is willing and anxious to pitch in and haul like a seaman, but I consider him more necessary for the sick, and have directed him to remain with and accompany them.

To-day we have done very well, having made one and a quarter miles (estimated) good. The ice opened on us twice, and gave us and the dog sleds some trouble. The heavy sleds had gone on before the ice opened. One dog sled got half overboard, and we had to cut the dogs adrift to save them from being drowned, while two of us held the sleds back. The prospect for our next start is encouraging. We are now on a piece of old ice which seems to extend for several miles yet. To-day has been unusually disagreeable on account of water on the surface of the ice. Frequently the men broke through over their knees, and dragging under these circumstances is hard work. In parts here and there around water has formed, and, though the low temperature freezes it at night, the sun thaws the ice in the middle of the day and we suddenly flounder in. A minute later the water will drain off to the sea. We are still in the dark as to our position. Chipp is very weak, only just strong enough to be able to walk from place to place by easy stages. I am very seriously disturbed about him. Lauterbach was restored to duty yesterday evening. Alexia still sick; unable to do any duty.

Star informs me that he has often come across written papers in our provision packages, and he has brought me this one, which he found yesterday among some coffee :—

This is to express my best wishes for your futherance and success in your great undertaking. Hoping when you peruse these lines you will be thinking of the comfortable homes you left behind you for the purpose of aiding science. If you can make it convenient drop me a line. My address is G. J. K., Post Office box—, New York city.

Saturday, June 25th, found us getting ready for dinner, which we sat down to at one A.M. At midnight I had got a meridian altitude, which to my amazement gave me a latitude of 77° 46′ north. There was no mistake in the observation, and I went over my figures a half dozen times to find any mistake. But each time 77° 46′ was the result. I overhauled my sextant, but that was all right, and my amazement increased. To start in 77° 18′ north, travel south a week, and then find one's self twenty-eight miles further north than the starting point is enough to make one thoughtful and anxious. For a long time I pondered, and for the moment was inclined to attribute the strange result to some extraordinary refraction; but, upon looking back to my rejected Sumner of the 23rd, I found that the intersection gave 77° 46′ and so was more anxious than ever. At half-past four A.M. and half-past seven A.M. I got another Sumner, and this gave me 77° 43′ for a latitude, very rough means of making a skeleton chart accounting in part for the difference from the lower meridian altitude. More anxious than ever I determined to sit up until noon and get the upper meridian altitude before committing myself to plans for the future. At noon I got a meridian altitude and this gave me latitude 77° 42′, and of this at least there is no doubt. My Sumner of this morning was accurate and my midnight observation was out only by the greater refraction of such a low altitude. I therefore accept the situation and shall modify my plans to this extent—instead of making a south course I shall incline more to the southwest, for as the line of our drift is northwest, a southwest course will cross it more rapidly than a south and bring us quicker to the ice edge. * * *

Such a rough country as we have before us requires more careful examination than a short run ahead can give, and I have therefore sent Mr. Dunbar ahead to seek a road out of our difficulty, while I let the camp remain "on their oars." After our hard day's work of yesterday this additional rest is welcome, and if a good road is found we can make a long step this afternoon.

Sunday, June 26th, 1:15 A.M.—Mr. Dunbar returned with bridge-makers and two dog sleds. I pushed ahead. Melville accidentally fell in the water and got wet to his waist, and during the morning's work the *Walrus* (No. 1 sled) fell in, sticking her nose well under the ice. However, she was got out. Though the road generally was better than the day before no less than five bridges had to be built, and consequently when, at half-past six A.M., I halted and pitched camp we had made only half a mile good south-southwest. It has been blistering hot since midnight, though the thermometer marked only twenty-three degrees in the sun. The sky was cloudless. A light south-southwest breeze fanned along, but we all suffered from the heat. Our hands and faces are all swollen and blistered, and my hands are very painful. At half-past seven A.M. had supper; at half-past eight A.M. read divine service, and at nine A.M. piped down.

Monday, June 27th, 1 A.M.—Turned to at five minutes past two A.M., and from this time to seven A.M. we had the hardest time we had had yet. We succeeded in advancing only half a mile further south-southwest, making one and a quarter miles in eleven hours' steady work. Just after leaving our halting place we had an ice opening to cross twenty feet in width, and while we were bridging it it opened twenty feet more. By great effort we succeeded in dragging in three large pieces for bridges, and by herculean efforts got our sleds and boats over, launching the first and second cutters. Beyond this (three-eighths of a mile) we had another ice opening, about sixty feet in width, and to bridge this we had literally to drag an ice island thirty feet thick and hold it in place. Hardly had we done this when the lead widened, and we had to scour around for more huge blocks to serve our purpose. There seems to be a general slackness to the ice and a streaming away without any resistance. It is hardly late enough to find leads of any length, but there are openings enough to give us serious trouble. To work like horses all day for ten or eleven hours and get ahead only a mile is rather discouraging, and the knowledge that we are very likely going three miles north-northwest to every mile we make southwest keeps one anxious. Melville and the Doctor are the only ones to whom I communicated our latitude, and to whom I intend it shall be confined; for no doubt great discouragement, if not entire loss of zeal, would ensue were such a disagreeable bit of news known. I dodge Chipp, Danenhower and Dunbar lest they should ask me questions. Thus far everybody is bright and cheerful, and singing is going on all around. I hope our good health and spirits may long continue. Chipp is improving in health.

Wednesday, June 29th.—Going ahead with the dog sleds and Mr. Dunbar we suddenly came to water, and peering into the fog it seemed as if we had some extensive lead ahead. Going back hurriedly I sent the dingy ahead for an exploration, but, alas! it was fruitless. The favorable lead which we thought we had turned out to be another water opening, seventy-five feet wide, which we had to bridge. By great good fortune a large piece was handy, and by hard hauling Dunbar, Sharwell and I succeeded in getting it in place, and a fortunate closing of the lead a foot or two jammed it in as a solid bridge. Unfortunately openings were occurring in our rear and we had more bridging to do there. Never was there such luck. No sooner do we get our advance across one lead than a new one opens behind it and makes us hang back lest our rear should be caught. By the time we have got a second sled ahead more openings have occurred, and we are in for a time. These openings are always east and west. By no means, seemingly, can we get one north and south, so that we might make something by them, and these east and west lanes meander away to narrow veins between piled up masses, over which there can no road be built, and between which no boat can be got. It is no uncommon thing for us to have four leads to bridge in half a mile, and when we remember that Melville and his party have to make always six and sometimes seven trips the amount of coming and going is fearful to contemplate. Add to this the flying trips of the dog sleds and the moving forward of the sick at a favorable moment, and it is not strange that we dread meeting an ice opening. This very old and hard ice is beyond doubt paleocrystic. I measured one floe and found it thirty-two feet nine inches thick, and where it is not mud stained it is rounded up in hummocks, resembling alabaster. Over this we sledded and dragged well enough, though it was, as the men said, "a rocky road to Dublin." I encountered one piece which was sixteen feet thick, which I am inclined to think was a single growth, for not a line of union of layers could be seen.

Danenhower came to me to-day requesting and urging his being given duty to perform, claiming that he could do a man's work by hauling, &c. Inasmuch as I consider him unfit to perform any duty whatever, and as he would be an impediment and hindrance to anything he attempted on account of his one eye, I refused positively to assign him to any duty whatever until he was discharged from the sick list. Chipp seems to be gaining strength. The temperature has been steady at 30° all day, but it seems much colder. We always get our feet wet early in the morning, and that keeps us uncomfortable until we stop to camp. A thick fog seems to penetrate to our bones all day.

Thursday, June 30th.—Toward midnight we had observed a low line of black cloud in the west, extending from the southwest to the northwest, and it promised a rising fog. By the time we had halted it had spread around in its accustomed way, north and south, and by 1:30 A.M. the sky was entirely overcast, a wet, damp, fog, like fine rain, shutting in everything. The daily recurrence of the phenomenon makes me believe that we are drawing near open water, for I hardly believe that such a fog could arise from ice openings. Daily toward midnight the sun's power wanes and the water begins to give off vapor slowly, which is condensed on being carried by the wind over the cold ice, and is deposited or carried along as fog, &c. Generally speaking, when we turn out, at 6 P.M., the sun is shining brightly, and when we go to bed, at 9 A.M., it is shining again. But between midnight and camping time it is foggy enough. After dinner —1:50 A.M.—we pushed ahead again. By going ahead with Mr. Dunbar I managed to mark out a good, long route of one and a half miles, and terminating in a good, flat floe piece. But it required some little bridging and considerable road-making and managing, and a roundabout road of five miles. However, we accomplished it with no other accident than breaking one St. Michael's sled and springing a crossbar of the first cutter's sled. On top of the old ice we have encountered many pools of water, which seem to me as being the same kind as those mentioned by Captain Nares, and from which the *Alert's* people drank steadily. Seeing some of these pools freeze to-day at 32° I imagined they might be fresh water, but the Doctor tested some with nitrate of silver and found it contained much salt!

Friday, July 1st.—Records good ice road, but that the rain commenced to fall at 6:30 A.M. During the whole of our sleeping time the rain was falling in showers, and when we were called the pattering of the drops could be heard on our tent. Our bags are, of course, wet again, and in some of these, mine and Ericksen's particularly, the feet end is as wet as a sop. Ericksen, Boyd and Kaach turned in with dry foot-gear, and turned out wet to the knees. I managed to get my feet doubled up to a dry place and slept with tolerable comfort for some hours until my bones commenced to ache with the infernal hardness of the ice on which we were lying. Snow would be softer, of course, but the heat from our bodies would soon melt it and we would be lying in a pool of water before long. There is so much snow water all over the ice that we cannot find a place dry enough to make our rubber blanket a sufficient protection. The dinner time is our most uncomfortable part of the twenty-four hours. Our feet and legs are wet in the first half hour of our marching, but as long as we move ahead we do not mind it, but when we halt for dinner our feet get cold and generally remain so until we camp at night and change our foot-gear.

Sunday, July 3d.—It took us until 12:30 A.M. to get all our sleds and boats up to the beginning of smooth ice (*i. e.*, ice with two feet of slush and water over it and holes where you suddenly sink to your knees), and then we halted for dinner. The sun now began to try to force its way through the clouds and fog, and it seemed to grow much colder. To avoid the wind as much as possible the tents were slewed around across the wind, and we huddled under their lee while we ate our dinner. * * * At 9 A.M. read the articles of war and had divine service. At 9:30 piped down. Everybody is bright and cheerful, and apparently (except Chipp and Danenhower) in excellent health. We have abundance of food, good appetites, sleep well, and, as Mr. Cole expresses it, he "seems to get more spring in him every day." My sights place us in 77° 31′, and 151° 41′ east—a change of position since June 25th of thirteen miles south, 30° west. As our distance made by account is twelve miles it would seem that we have had no current against us. But, of course, I cannot tell. We may have been set down that much in three days by our northerly winds, and, therefore, I must accept the position as simply showing where we are, and push on for the edge of the ice.

Monday, July 4th.—At 1:45 A.M. halted for dinner. At 3 sharp set out again, and though some little confusion was imminent because the *Walrus* took the wrong road we avoided all serious delay, and by 6:20 A.M. had advanced everything one mile, making the, to us, unprecedented distance of two and a quarter miles in eight hours and twenty minutes. For the last quarter of a mile our course lay over some beautiful hard ice, parallel to a narrow lead, and we were able to send two sleds ahead at a time, and the second cutter and whale-boat together, making the first cutter our only "all-hands" haul. This reduced the number of trips from seven to four, a great saving, though possible only for short stages, because such work soon exhausted the men's breath. Having been sixteen days under way we have sensibly reduced the amount of our provisions hauled on the dog sleds, and, in consequence, these sleds got home some little time in advance of the boats and heavy sleds. So I have ordered some redistribution of weights. * * * The prospect is not bad. I find we are not consuming our daily ration of one pound of pemmican, nor have we ever done so, and, strange to say, the dogs do not sometimes eat theirs. We all like it amazingly, eating it cold three times a day like cake out of our hands, but yet we seem to have enough on less than a pound. Our greatest comfort morning and evening is Liebig's extract of beef tea. Our daily allowance of one ounce per man is sufficient to give us a pint morning and evening, and I know of no more refreshing and comforting thing up here than this same warm drink. Some tents take the whole ounce at dinner, but we in No. 1 prefer it when we get up and when our day's work is done.

Our flags are flying in honor of the day, though to me

it is a very blue one. Three years ago to-day at Havre the *Jeannette* was christened, and many pleasant things were said and anticipations formed, all of which have gone down with the ship. I did not think then that three years afterward would see us all out on the ice, with nothing accomplished and a story of a lost ship to come back to our well-wishers at home. My duty to those who came with me is to see them safely back and to devote all my mind and strength to that end; my duty to those depending on me for support hereafter impels me to desire that I should return also; but, these two duties apart, I fancy it would have made but little difference if I had gone down with my ship. But as there is nothing done without some good purpose being served I must endeavor to look my misfortune in the face and to learn what its application may be. It will be hard, however, to be known hereafter as a man who undertook a Polar expedition and sunk his ship at the 77th parallel.

Piped down at nine A.M. Called all hands at six P.M. Breakfast at seven P.M. Under way at eight P.M. Three hundred yards from our camp we came to an ice opening 150 feet wide, right in our way. As we are now doubling our fleets—that is, dragging two sleds at a time —such an opening was a serious inconvenience. A small thick floe piece was floating in the middle of the lead, and I hoped to get that pressed into service before any delay could occur. Sending for the dingy I succeeded in getting the lump in tow and ready for a flying bridge ferry while the other boats were coming up. The two cutters and two sleds were then carried across. Everything was got over all right. Soon after we had to make a second ferriage and then a number of bridges before we reached the hard ice which Dunbar and I had visited before our last camp. Ice which was connected then was all open and moving now, and it was not until one A.M. of Tuesday, July 5, that we had everything in sufficient security to sit down to our dinners. The snow was falling quite heavily in large flakes and we rigged up our rubber blankets from the boats' rails to protect us, making our dinner halt look like a small country fair, as some of the men said. I could not help remembering that there were many people under canvas in Hoboken to-day, picnicing, who would like a little of the coolness we were now having, but it seemed to provoke a desire to exchange places with them, and I said nothing more.

CHAPTER XXI.

BENNETT ISLAND.

CAPTAIN DE LONG proceeds: At two A.M. we turned to and went ahead. Ice openings again annoyed us somewhat, but we set to work bridging them. While so doing the whole pack seemed to get alive, and the tossing and tumbling that went on for fifteen minutes was uncomfortble to witness. Large floes which had been held under the others became liberated, and, rising to the surface, floundered around like huge whales. When the floe edges came together large blocks were broken off and reared on end twenty-five and thirty feet high. A mass of rubble coming together raised up an enormous piece until it stood like a monument thirty feet above the surface of the floe. Long thick snouts shoved up above and over even floe pieces like immense snow ploughs, and groans and shrieks came from all directions as these snouts rose and advanced inch by inch. When long floe pieces reared up to thirty feet and toppled backward they broke in large lumps and scattered themselves for yards. And yet we seem to have got out of paleocrystic ice. Our road yesterday and to-day has been over ice that more nearly resembles the pack ice which we entered near Herald Island than anything else, and with occasional exceptions seems to be one season's growth, the thickness varying between seven and ten feet. If this be a correct assumption we may be out of the drifting pack and in the ice clinging to the Liakhoff Islands, in which case I hope many days will not elapse before we get in a lead to some purpose. Chipp is not nearly as strong as he would have us believe. I mentioned yesterday that the Doctor stopped his whiskey to see the effect. Last night (our sleeping time) he ate nothing, had no sleep and was groaning and tumbling around all the time. This we learn from Dunbar, for Chipp asserts he is "first rate," and tells Dunbar to say so when he is asked by the Doctor. Foolishly enough, he wants to be discharged to duty, thinking he is able to work.

Friday, July 8th, has completed one mile of the most disheartening and discouraging day we have yet had. The fresh northwest wind had opened the ice in all directions except the one we wanted and a constant succession of ferriages and bridges fell to our lot. The wind seemed very searching, and finally our customary fog and misty rain set in, making us wet as well as cold. We did not have dinner till two A.M., it taking us six hours to make our last half mile. At three we turned to again, and by seven went into camp. Supper at half-past seven. Barometer 29.58 at 36°; temperature 31°. Piped down at nine A.M. Called all hands at six P.M. Fresh breezes, northwest. Three to five, a very little blue sky and sun. At quarter to eight, snow squall. At eight P.M. got under way.

Saturday, July 9th, we had advanced everything one and a quarter miles and had come to a halt for dinner. Our travelling to-day must make up for our mishaps and delays of yesterday. We can do well enough when the ice holds together; it is only these ugly openings which make us lose ground. Generally speaking one mile made means seven miles travelled by the men. What with coming and going, getting ahead to see the road and going back to see the rear close up, I am three times over the road night and morning, and I know from my own sensations how welcome the camping hour must be to Melville and the men. The northwest wind continued fresh while we were at dinner, and though we cowered under the lee of the boats we were cold and miserable. Our usual fog made things still more uncomfortable, and I think no one was sorry when at ten minutes past one A.M. I gave the order to turn to and go ahead. * * *

Sunday, July 10th.—We encountered considerable needle ice, so called by Parry, and by him attributed to the action of rain drops. In our opinion this is caused by the more rapid driving away of the salt in some places than in others, leaving bunches or tufts of long spikes. A piece of honeycomb cut down through shows the same general formation. Got a fair Sumner this morning, from which I determine our position to be 77° 8' 30", longitude 151° 38"—a change of position since the 30th of 26¾ miles south 30° east. By account we had made about sixteen miles southwest, so this shows how little can be done with any certainty. Keeping on in our course is all that can be accomplished, and, in my opinion, if our longitude be right, a southwesterly course will soonest bring us to the edge of the ice. Supper at half-past seven. Divine service at a quarter to nine. Piped down at nine.

After supper quite a little excitement was created by the cry of land. To the southwest was something which certainly looked like land, but the fog assumes so many deceiving forms that we cannot be sure of anything. The nearest Siberian island is 120 miles from us, and unless we are going to discover new islands I cannot believe that we have seen land to-day. I think we made three and a half miles to day in nine hours and a half's work. Under way at a quarter past eight o'clock P.M. At nine I started forward and met Anequin coming back in haste for a rifle, saying that Mr. Dunbar had seen a bear. Getting to the front I met Mr. Dunbar, who, sure enough, had encountered Bruin, and, like a prudent man, having nothing more dangerous than a boarding pike, took to his heels. While turning a sharp corner he met the bear at thirty yards' distance, and upon retreating was followed in chase for a short spell. The bear then sat down and looked at him, and, while Mr. Dunbar was waiting for a rifle, waited conveniently in the neighborhood, leaving only as Anequin with the weapon came in sight. Clouds to the southwest gave more indications of water than anything else yet seen. Calling Mr. Dunbar's attention to them he expressed his opinion that "such clouds did not hang over ice." Climbing to the top of a hummock, twenty feet above the water level, and examining carefully with a glass I saw unmistakable *land and water*. It now appears that this was the land seen yesterday. At all events it is land sure enough, and water, too. What it may be no one can say, whether newly discovered land or (our longitude being out) some portion of Siberia. It can hardly be any one of the Liakhoff islands. Another pleasant feature is our course (southwest) being a straight line to it. My change from south to southwest may, therefore, be a wise act, resulting in our speedier liberation. Judging by ordinary distances I should say the land is ten to fifteen miles distant, and as I could see quite a large expanse of water, with long stretches of detached ice, it may be that once at the margin of this icefield through which we are now toiling we may have open water to the Siberian coast; thus verifying some part of the statements of Russian explorers. We have exploded so many theories of other people that it will be hard to make us believe that we can have left the ice behind us short of the Arctic Circle. One month ago to-day our ship went down, and I do not see any one the worse for the work that has fallen to us since. That it is hard work there can be no dispute. It is conceded by everybody to be the hardest work they ever had. The drag, drag—the slips and jerks, the sudden bringing up of the hauling belt across the chest are fearfully trying, and the working with pickaxes through floating ice makes every bone ache. * * *

Tuesday, July 12*th.*— * * * Nothing could be seen of the land and water we saw yesterday. The southwest horizon was foggy. Many guillemots were seen, several gulls, an auk, and, strange to say, the Doctor picked up a live butterfly, which I have preserved. This is not a *habitué* of the ice, and was certainly blown from the land by the southeaster of yesterday or by the southwester which followed it. * * * Then follow descriptions of daily journeys over ice, ferriages and hard work. Upon looking to the southwest a land-like appearance was again seen, and several also declared they could see the water.

Thursday, July 14*th.*—De Long continues:—Our men's boot soles are wearing out so rapidly on the sharp ice over which we are travelling that their demands for repairs exceed our supply. I have already authorized the use of the leather from the dingy's oars, and this A.M. I had to have the leather cut off the first cutter's steering oar for patches. This leather will last longer than skin patches, but I hope the time is not far distant when I can have at least this one care and anxiety removed from my mind. * * *

Friday, July 15th.—The land seen again. Our course has been steadily southwest. All things being taken into consideration I assume that we are near land and water. During dinner (twenty minutes of two to twenty minutes past two A.M.) we saw the moon for the first time, I think, in two months. And what was more satisfactory, we saw a seal in a lead near us, and Mr. Collins shot him, while the dingy this time got him before he sunk. Course west and south (true). The seal came in splendidly for food. At a quarter past seven A.M. we sat down in No. 1 tent to a simply delicious supper. After our long diet of pemmican the change alone was a luxury. We did not stand upon our ship ideas of hanging the seal up until the animal heat had disappeared, or keeping it for a few days. The seal was shot at half-past two, skinned at four and eaten at seven, and we feel as if we had dined at Delmonico's. Over seven thirty-thirds of twenty pounds was cut up in small lumps, boiled in water, three and one-half ounces of Liebig added, one pint of bread crumbs; and for a feast I shall long remember it. No. 4 tried to fry their six thirty-thirds, and so very successfully that Melville says it tasted like fried oysters.

Saturday, July 16th.—The weather bright and pleasant. The island showed more plainly than yesterday, but no water could be seen. Mr. Collins shot another seal, which was secured by the dingy, and we have another luxurious supper ahead. Previous to getting sights I had a mishap which was annoying. Going to the top of a hummock to get a look at the land Mr. Dunbar and I had to go out of the road and jump some rather wide openings. Going was all right, but coming back, upon jumping a four-foot opening, the ice broke under me as I jumped, and I went into the water up to my neck. My clothes held me up for a moment, and Mr. Dunbar grabbed me by the head, as he thought, but by the whiskers principally, as I realized, for he nearly took my head off. My knapsack was away to the rear, and I sent Johnson back for it when I reached the dingy. However, I soon got dry clothes, and, thanks to the bright sun, my wet ones were soon drying. By the capsizing of dog sled lost 270 pounds pemmican. * * * The event of the day was the seal, a fine, large, fat one, giving us food and boot grease. Not much less in importance was the appearance of a walrus—the first one seen by us in a very, very long time. Though fired at and hit by Mr. Collins and Nindermann he remained under water finally after many reappearances. The land showed somewhat plainer to-day, but I could see no water. My observations place us in latitude 76° 44′ and longitude east 153° 25′—a change of position since the 10th (six days) of thirty-four miles southeast. As this land bears west and south of west (true), it can hardly be one of the Liakhoff Islands, even if our longitude is a long way out. Supper at a quarter past ten A.M. Our seal was simply delicious. * * *

Chipp was discharged from the sick list and returned to duty. This relieves Melville, who now takes charge of the road and bridge making in place of the Doctor, who now becomes a reserve. At nine P.M. the island is much plainer in sight than ever. I am again in hope that we have made another discovery. Working my longitude over will correct latitude. I find we are in 76° 41′ and 153° 30′ east—a change since the 10th of thirty-seven miles south, 43° east; soundings, twenty-three fathoms. This brings me along to Sunday, July 17th. * * * Mr. Dunbar thinks that in two days we can reach the water, but the land seems as distant as ever. * * * A very curious seal trick came to light by my breaking through the ice. He had two holes leading from the sea, connected by a covered way under the snow and thin crust. I suppose it was to give him a resort in case a bear headed him off. On the ice by the air-hole was a cavity in which the seal had lain and rubbed the shedding hair off his skin.

From this time to Tuesday, the 26th of July, Captain De Long's notes refer at some length to the difficulties of the roads over the ice, the gradual approach to the land, and the more and more confused masses of ice and water which had to be got over. He records the shooting of a seal, a bear and a walrus. There is also mention made of an appearance resembling land to the northward, seen by Mr. Collins and Mr. Chipp, but so uncertain that he did not deem it wise to alter his course to verify its existence.

During the night of July 26th Mr. Collins, who turned out during the night, said we were in front of the valley of the island, and he could see clear water between us and an ice-foot next the land. The solution, I think, is as follows :—

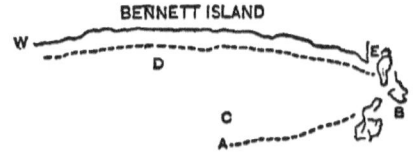

A.—Own position.
E.—East end of south side of island.
W.—West.
B.—Ice rapidly drifting to southwest before the wind.
C.—Water and drift pieces.
D.—Ice-foot or strip of fresh ice.

I think we are far enough under the lee of point E to

escape drifting with the ice pressing down along the island and passing the point E, even if we are not in an eddy so created and then pushed in closer to the land. As nothing can be seen clearly it would be folly to move into a probably endless confusion, and I shall therefore wait until some plan can be safely carried out.

I do not think I shall ever forget yesterday ; such a tissue of difficulty and vexation can be experienced nowhere else. Such a shifting of ice and opening of leads. Hardly had we commenced to move our things along what seemed a fair road than the road broke up. Ice broke under us, ice slid away from us, ice moved to the right when we wanted to go to the left, and *vice versa*, and each instalment of provisions got safely across was considered by me as barely rescued from destruction. And all this time the land not half a mile off was tempting us by its solidity and appealing to our desire for rest by its moss covered hills and slopes. At eight A.M. yesterday, when we concluded to go on and work for twenty-four hours, so many good roads, each leading seemingly directly on shore, presented themselves that I was embarrassed in a choice, but in fifteen minutes they had fallen to pieces and become puzzling mazes of ice and water. There was no question that when I gave it up at six P.M. everybody was used up and could not possibly have gone further. Everybody was wet up to his knees, stiff legs and cramps annoyed us until we had been an hour or two in our bags, and we were too tired, in fact, to get the rest we stood so much in need of. However, we are all right again this morning and none the worse off. Better, off, in fact, for if we had not put in the twenty-four hours in full we would have been out on the heavy drift ice and probably miles away from the land by the time this gale is over (spoken of previously). At noon the fog broke away and showed the land for a few moments. We were exactly as I had supposed and indicated by the sketch on another page. The pressure of the ice on swinging off the easterly point has backed us in toward the bay, and between our floe and the land there is about two miles of water nearly clear of ice. I assumed that against our floe are a number of large blocks and hummocks, offering serious difficulty to any attempt to launch our boats. On the off side of these hummocks the sea is breaking considerably. The wind tears around us in fierce gusts. No. 6 tent has been twice blown down. We will see what the state of affairs is after dinner. Dined at half-past twelve P.M. luxuriously on bear stew. By half past one the land was again in fog, and otherwise the situation was as before. My desire was to go ahead, but prudence told me to wait until the weather moderated. The barometer is still falling, the rain beats down from time to time, and nothing can be seen through the fog. I decide to wait for an improvement, and then I shall push on in the second cutter and try to land some provisions. Soundings in thirteen fathoms; no drift indication. Our ice is evidently jammed tight. Probably at the first chance the loose hummocks now pressing against us will slack off and leave no place to launch our boats, even if our floe piece does not go bodily in toward the land.

During the afternoon the ice scene was constantly changing. At one moment ice seemed to reach from our floe to the land. At another time lanes of water were seen, and once our floe was left as an island, while it would have been possible to launch a boat and reach the shore. I confess I was tempted to try it, but I realized that the whale-boat could carry nothing but her crew safely until her garboards were repaired, and that it would take six or seven trips of the two other boats to carry our effects. Before I could have got our boat in the water, however, ice shoved in between us and the land and we were once more helpless. It seems as if Providence were directing our movements, for the floe upon which we camped last night is the only large piece of ice to be seen; all else is confusion and trouble. Had I gone further or stopped short of this place it is hard to say where we would be now. We are moving west slowly, about a mile or a mile and a half from the land, and are now (seven P.M.) abreast a large glacier, whose broken edge—it may be twenty feet high—we can see with a glass. I have watched carefully all day for a landing place, but not one has shown. The coast is either steep cliff or glacier, and neither is a successful landing place. The barometer is now at a stand, and I think 29.63 at 33 degrees; and though rain is occasionally falling, and the sky is dark and threatening where the fog does not hide it altogether, I am in hopes the weather will improve during the night. Supper, bear stew, at six P.M. Piped down at nine.

Wednesday, July 27th. — Called all hands at six. Breakfast at seven. The wind has veered to east and is dying away. Patiently and hopefully I waited all the forenoon for a clearing, but (one P.M.) the fog still hangs about us impenetrably. The barometer goes up 29.72 at 38 degrees and the temperature 30 degrees. Soundings in sixteen fathoms water, and I am afraid we have drifted down abreast the point west and are too far west to hope for any benefit from the bay in which yesterday we shoaled water to thirteen fathoms. In which case we are now beginning to open the west face of the island. This will be the last forlorn hope for open water in the neighborhood. And yet there is much to be thankful for. Everybody is in excellent health in spite of our terribly hard work. The appetites are something wonderful to think of and our sleep is sound and unbroken. Forty-one days of our march over the frozen sea have had no bad effect. One bear is so nearly consumed that for supper we have only half our usual ration to serve out. (In five meals we have eaten about 250 lbs. of bear meat. The gross weight was probably 450 lbs.) The only trace our marching shows on us is tender feet, and that probably arises from their being so often wet. Wading through ponds would make wet feet if our foot-gear was changed every hour. At six P.M. had supper. At forty-five minutes past six the fog lifted a little and showed us the land seemingly about half a mile off. We have drifted along shore since last evening and have left on our right hand the glacier which we were in front of last night. But ahead of us, and apparently extending into the land, was a very heavy floe of blue ice, and separated from us by a few insignificant openings. Such a chance was not to be lost. All hands were at once turned to, and at fifteen minutes past seven we went ahead with all four sleds, officers dragging also, and then bounced along the boats, and in an hour we had everything on the heavy floe. This we now found to be a mile and a half in width after going over it, and we were still separated from the land by a half mile of broken ice, water lanes, &c. I at once made up my mind that it could not be done to-night and that I had better devote a day to it. The wind had veered to east-southeast, was blowing fresh and rain began to fall steadily, and when, at a quarter to eleven P.M., just inside the blue floe edge, I gave the order to camp, I think I did a very prudent and sensible thing.

Thursday, July 28*th*.—Called all hands at seven, breakfast at eight; windy (east-southeast), foggy and disagreeable. Land in sight at times. We have gone a short distance to westward. Barometer 29.78 at 36 degrees; temperature 29 degrees. Under way at ten minutes to nine A.M. Sent Mr. Dunbar ahead, and after a while we succeeded in crossing the broken ice which had stopped us last night. Here we had a small floe, across which we speeded. The fog now shut in impenetrably, and I feared we were in for a troublesome time. Mr. Dunbar now returned, however, and informed me that after crossing this floe we should find large ice blocks with only two-feet openings, and that the blocks extended to the ice foot or fast ice; and that, moreover, he had climbed up on the ice foot and advanced a hundred yards over it toward the land. This was too good a chance to lose, and away we went. But, though we made all haste and got over our last ferry and across the small floe in splendid time, when we reached the further edge we found everything fallen to pieces, and more water and rapidly moving ice than we could undertake. Much of the moving ice looked like small bergs broken off from a glacier foot, and from the rounded lumps of ice on top and their almost straight edges I am inclined to think they were icebergs. By half-past twelve P.M. we had everything up to the floe edge and halted for dinner. The sun now tried to break through the fog, and I hoped for a clearing, but at half-past one P.M., when we turned to, the fog was as thick as ever. The situation had improved somewhat, for another floe piece had now come along, and a few loose pieces afforded a convenient bridge. Away we went, but the floe piece was a small one and we soon reached its edge. Here was another confusion, but we could make out a larger floe ahead. Everything was embarked on an ice-cake for a ferryboat and a hauling line run to the floe. By great effort we got our piece clear by four P.M. and commenced to haul over.

Suddenly everybody gave a shout, "Look!" Away up over our heads, 2,500 feet, towered the land, and we were swinging past it like a mill stream. Hurriedly sounded in eighteen and a half fathoms. Soon our floe was reached; away we jumped over sleds and boats, and, seeing two or three large cakes nearly together, ran everything rapidly over until we at last stood at the base of the ice foot. It was a narrow squeeze, for the men with the tents and remaining provisions on their shoulders had hard work to run fast enough to get on the last cake before the other cakes were swept away. Now that we were on the last cake our position became critical. We could not get up on the ice foot, for ten feet of water and small lumps intervened, and we were sweeping along by it at the rate of three miles an hour. Our cake was none of the strongest, and in the swirling and running masses and small bergs I feared we would be broken up and separated. It was an anxious moment. The southwest cape of the island was not half a mile away and this was our last chance. Over two weeks of dragging and walking to reach this island seemed about to be thrown away. I soon noticed our cake began to turn around and saw that it might be whirled into a kind of corner against the fast ice, where if it remained long enough a landing might be effected. "Stand by!" was the order now, and with sled ropes in hand we waited the trying moment. Soon our cake caught and *held!*

"Now is the time, Chipp!" I shouted, and away he went. One sled got over on the rough ice foot all right; a second nearly fell overboard; the third did fall overboard, dragging in Cole, and a piece of ice had to be dragged in by sheer force to bridge for the fourth. Then I started the St. Michael's sleds, and they seemed to stick somewhere. Watching our cake closely I saw signs of it giving way. "Away with the boats!" but Nindermann thought he could float the boats below and haul them over. No sooner said than done, and away they went into the water. The men were hurried from the sleds into the boats, and I saw the first cutter just beginning to haul out, when away swept our ice cake, carrying Melville, Iverson, Anequin and myself, with six dogs. Wilson had carried one load of dogs over in the dingy, but he could not get back for the remainder. Chipp was on the ice foot with the boats and I knew he could look out for everything, and I felt pretty certain we had saved everything. For ourselves on the drifting ice cake I had some little anxiety, but one corner of our cake fortunately soon after drifted near a fast berg, and by making a flying trip through the air we escaped in safety.

At last! But though standing still we were not ashore. The ice foot extended out from the land many yards, and was a confused mass of piled-up ice blocks and ridges, honeycombed, cracked and broken and presenting a simply impassable roads for travel with sleds. Glad enough was I to get a solid foothold anywhere, and I gave the order to camp at half-past six P.M. (our first sled having got on the ice foot about five), everything being hauled in as near to the land as possible—say fifty feet from it. Rocks were occasionally slipping down and falling into a little stream of water at the foot of the cliff, the stream being where the thawing of surface ice had left a channel about four feet deep. The face of the cliff was literally alive with dovekies. Supper at half-past seven P.M. At half-past eight P.M. all hands were called to muster, and, led by me, everybody waded or jumped or ferried over to the steep slopes of *débris*, while our colors were displayed. When all had gathered around me I said:

"I have to announce to you that this island, toward which we have been struggling for more than two weeks, is newly discovered land. I, therefore, take possession of it in the name of the President of the United States, and name it 'Bennett Island.' I now call upon you to give three cheers."

And never were three more lusty cheers given. With great kindness three were then given for me. I now change the date to the correct one, and record that at half-past eight P.M., Friday, July 29, I added Bennett Island to American soil. Our landing cape I name "Cape Emma." Piped down at nine P.M. Fresh east wind, thick fog, ice off shore rapidly moving west. The birds kept up a fearful chattering all night, but we slept well in spite of it.

CHAPTER XXII.

NINDERMANN AND NOROS.

FROM Bennett Island to Semenoffski Island the experiences of the retreating party were but a repetition of the scenes since leaving the sunken vessel. I will therefore pass over those incidents of the retreat which occurred after the landing on Bennett Island until the separation of the boats at the mouth of the Lena. Nindermann and Noros, the seamen, who were in the cutter with De Long, here continued the narrative. "On September 12th," says Nindermann, "we were steering south, with a fresh breeze from the northeast; the wind soon increased, and the sea ran quite high; about noon there seemed to be some trouble with the whale-boat; Mr. Melville called out to the Captain that his boat was leaking badly; all three boats were hauled up on the ice, dinner was eaten and the whale-boat was repaired; after dinner the boats were launched and the course laid to the southward; the wind increased and the sea was rising; toward evening it was blowing a gale; a reef was taken in the sail of the first cutter; the sea was continually breaking over the boat and there was great difficulty in keeping her free of water; the whale-boat was on the weather bow and the second cutter on the port quarter, some distance away; Captain De Long signalled to the boats, intending to tell them to keep as near together as possible; the sea was running so high the whale-boat could not slow down so as to come alongside; another reef was taken in the sail by the first cutter, but it had to be shaken out again shortly after that; it was then getting dark, and the whale-boat, being the fastest sailer, was out of sight; the second cutter could be seen astern, but before long she was also out

NINDERMANN AND NOROS.

of sight; the wind and sea still increased, and the first cutter took in water over both sides and the stern; Ericksen was at the tiller, and the boat was running so close before the wind that the sail jibed two or three times and nearly swamped the boat.

Finally the sail jibed again and both mast and sail were

carried away, the boat took in a heavy sea, and with great difficulty the water was gotten out, as she was full up to the thwarts; another sea would have sunk her; as soon as the mast went overboard the boat came around head to the wind; the Captain ordered a drag to be made, using the sail and boat breaker; the drag was put out over the stern, and the boat behaved pretty well for some time until the drag was carried away; another one was then made; a cross was made, using the mast and an oar, weighting it with a heavy pickaxe at the head; about midnight there seemed as if there were two seas running from different directions, making it very choppy and continually breaking into the boat and keeping the men bailing all the time; the next day the wind and sea were high until toward the evening, when the sea began to go down; we were obliged to lay-to that night; the next morning the Captain asked me what I had in the boat with which to make a jury sail; I replied a hammock and an old sleigh cover, and that we could make a sail out of them; Gœrtz and Kaach were then set to work, and as soon as the hammock and sleigh cover were sewed together the mast was stepped, sail set, and the course was laid south-southwest; at noon the sea had gone down a good deal and the wind shifted to the westward; we were still on our course; toward the evening the Captain's hands and feet began to swell, so that he could not write in his journal; he put his feet in a sleeping bag and sat up in the stern of the boat; when night set in the wind had hauled more to the southward; we could not make our course, but were obliged to tack; the Captain gave me orders to stay about four hours on one tack and then go about on the other tack and to call him in case anything should happen; we kept on tacking during the night; the next morning the wind hauled to the north and east so that we could lay our course again; I took soundings and found eight feet of water; about ten o'clock I stood up in the stern sheets and saw on the horizon dark spots that looked like land; this was on the morning of the 15th of September; I told the Captain, but as he was sitting down he could not see it, and at first thought I was mistaken; on standing in a little further we could soon see land while sitting down in the boat; we could see young ice east and west and for some distance toward the land; as there was no lead to be seen through the young ice we ran into it under sail until we got stuck; we then used the oars in breaking the ice ahead of us while we forced the boat through it; we pushed on until we were about three miles off the mouth of the river; the water rapidly shoaled until we had only about two feet of water and soon after our boat grounded.

The entire day was passed in endeavoring to find deep water; at times all hands were in the water pushing the boat along, and great suffering ensued from the cold, wet and fatigue. Toward evening, all hands being pretty well exhausted, the Captain determined to lay alongside the ice till morning; after supper the men got out their sleeping bags, but found them so wet that they could not be used, so each person passed the night as he best could, all suffering extremely from the cold. The next morning the boat was pushed off shore. About ten o'clock the Captain, finding he could make no progress to the westward, put the course to the north and east; the water was very shoal, and the boat continually grounded in the mud. When the men pushed on the oars the boat would be crowded ahead a foot or two, but when the oars were withdrawn for a new purchase the boat would settle back into about her former position; toward afternoon the wind freshened and the shoal water became very choppy, frequently breaking into the boat and keeping all hands drenched to the skin. By this time the boat had been worked away from the young ice about a mile and a half, and, finding no further progress could be made in that direction, the Captain gave orders to return to the ice; two days had been passed in the attempt to reach the land, and during this time the only water to be had was from melting the young ice. After dinner that day the Captain said he could do nothing else, so had concluded to make a landing by wading. I made a raft out of the boat sled upon which to place some of the boat's load for the purpose of lightening her. About three P.M. the Captain gave orders to shove the boat in toward the shore; after going about twenty yards the boat again grounded, and the Captain, seeing no other resource, gave orders for all hands to strip and get overboard; Captain De Long, Dr. Ambler, Ericksen and Boyd were the only ones who stayed in the boat. The sail was set and the men got into the water and took hold of the painter to drag the boat; about fifty yards were made in this way, when the boat again grounded, and the Captain gave orders for every man to take a back load and wade ashore; every one took what he could carry and all started to wade: sometimes the water was only knee deep, at times up to their waists; frequently some one would fall into a mud hole, from which he would be extricated with great difficulty. About a mile from the beach young ice was encountered, through which it was necessary to break their way. At last the boat was made fast and all hands made another trip to the shore, then returned and dragged the boat a little further, but she soon grounded, and the men started ashore with another load; in this way, alternately lightening and dragging the boat toward shore, they managed to get her to the young ice, which was about a mile and a half from the beach; when it was found impossible to get the boat any nearer; the sick people had to get into the water and wade, as it was not possible for any one to carry them through the ice, and with such a soft, slippery bottom. I and another seaman made a final trip to the boat to see if anything had been left, and when we started to return found it so dark we could not see the beach, so had to feel our way back through the young ice. On reaching shore I found a large fire going and the men sitting around trying to dry their clothing.

The events of the next few days being recorded in the last diary kept by De Long Nindermann continues:

On the 6th of October Ericksen's condition left no hope of recovery, and it was feared that he would be unable to move on further. I was alone in the hut and the Captain asked me if I was strong enough to go to Kumak Surka, which he said was only twenty-five miles distant. He thought that I with a companion would be able to make the journey and return to them in four days. He told me that if we failed to find people at Kumak Surka we should then go further to a place called Ajakit, which he said was about forty-five miles further to the south than Kumak Surka. "If you find people," he said, "come back as quickly as possible and bring with you meat enough to feed us until we can get to the place." The Captain asked me which of the men I would take with me on the journey, and I said Noros. He asked me if I would not rather take Iverson, but I said no, Iverson had been complaining of his feet for some days as having given him very much pain. To my selection the Captain then agreed. He said further, "Nindermann, you know that we have nothing to eat and that I can give you nothing with you on your journey; but I will give you your portion of the dog meat." As we talked about these things the Doctor walked up and looked at Ericksen, and exclaimed, "He is dead!" We were all awed. The Captain then said, "Nindermann, now we will all go southward." This was about nine o'clock when Ericksen died. The Captain then asked me where we could find a place to bury him, whereupon I answered that the earth was too hard frozen to dig a grave and that we had no implements with us; we could do nothing else than make a hole in the ice of the river and bury him there. The Captain said yes, it must be so, and then told Noros and Kaach to sew the body up in a portion of the canvas belonging to the tent. At midday we were ready to bury him, the flag was placed over him, and we had a little warm water with alcohol in it for our dinner. When we had drunk that the Captain said: "We will now bury our shipmate." All were very still, and the Captain spoke a few words to us, and when he was finished we took our comrade toward the river, and then made a hole in the ice with a hatchet. The Captain then read the service for the dead, and Ericksen's body was let into the river and was carried away from our eyes by the stream. Three shots were fired over his grave, and then we went back to the hut. The weather was very bad, the wind was very strong and the snow drifted fearfully. We had not much to say one to the other. The Captain told me to go out and see how the weather was, if it was good enough for us to make a further journey. I went out, but the weather was so bad and the snow drifted so strongly that I could scarcely see anything, and I said it would be better to wait till the storm abated, for we could not see where we were going if we started out. I thought the day was just such a day as the one in which we buried Captain Hall. The Captain then said "We will wait till to-morrow." That evening we ate our portion of dog meat. The Captain said, "This is our last meat, but I hope we will soon have some more." Then we all laid down to rest.

On the 7th of October when we awoke the wind was pretty strong and the snow was still drifting. We made preparations to continue our journey. We left in the hut a repeating rifle, some ammunition and a record. We took nothing with us but the records and papers, the Captain's private journal, two rifles and the clothes we wore. I suggested that all the papers should be left there in the hut and that when we found people I would go back and fetch them, whereupon the Captain answered:—"Nindermann, the papers go with me as long as I live." We then left the hut and went in a southerly direction until we came to a large river, which we then thought was the Lena proper, but it was the one that we now call the Duropean. When we left the hut I had forgotten to say we made a short cut across a sand pit, about southeast, then struck a river, went along on the west bank of the river for some distance to the south, then as the river took a turn we had to go southeast again, then struck another small river where there was no water at all, going south for a short time, then going to the east for a short distance, when we struck the Lena, as the Captain supposed it to be at the time. That is the river he was found on. The Captain said, "Nindermann, do you think the ice is strong enough to bear us?" I said, "I will try it." I went a short way on the river when I broke through, but was not very wet. When I looked around me I saw the Captain quite near to me, and he had broken through up to his shoulders. I helped him out and we went back to the bank, made a fire and dried our things. It was then midday and we made some alcohol and warm water to drink.

On Sunday, October 9, after divine service, Captain De Long sent Nindermann and Noros southward, repeating the instructions to Nindermann that he had given him the day before Ericksen's death. Nindermann says: "The Captain gave me a copy of his small chart of the Lena River, saying, 'That is all I can give you on your journey; information about the land or river I cannot give you, for you know as much as I do myself. But go southward with Noros, who is under your command, until you reach Kumak Surka, and if you should not find any one there then go on to Ajakit, which is forty-five miles southward from Kumak Surka, and should you fail to find people there then go on to Bulun, which is twenty-five miles southward from Ajakit, and if there are no people there go southward until you do find people. But I think you will find people at Kumak Surka. If you should shoot reindeer not further away than one or two days' journey from us come back and let us know.' He gave me further the order not to leave the western bank of the stream, because, he said, on the eastern bank I should find neither people nor drift-wood. He told me that he could not give me any written instructions, because if he did the people would not be able to read them, but I should do the best I could and use my own judgment. He gave me strict orders that we should not wade through the water. He then said adieu to us and that as soon as he was ready he would follow in our footsteps as rapidly as possible. Then all gave us three cheers and my comrade and I left them. They were all in good hopes that we would be able soon to bring back assistance. My hopes, however, were not so bright, for I knew that it was very late in the fall, and that in all probability the people had gone away to the south." Noros here said: "We did not follow the river round, but took a straight cut across the land. The mountains were ahead of us and we knew that the river ran near them. It was an island we were on. There was a river (the Duropean) on the other side of it. Nindermann and I reached the river and walked along it about five or six miles. We stopped before noon and had a little alcohol. After that we walked on till we came to a little canoe on the top of the bluff, and perched on the canoe we saw a ptarmigan. Nindermann shot at it with his rifle, and, though he took out some tail feathers, the bird got away. We went down to the beach, where it was easier walking than on the bluff. We walked there about a mile, when we again took to the bluff, principally to look around us and to see if we could see any game. Nindermann happened to get up on the bluff first and exclaimed, 'They are deer—give me the gun.' We could see them; they were not more than half a mile away, but partly to the windward. So Nindermann took off his heavy clothes and lightened himself up and then crawled along in the snow. I gave him the cartridges and said, 'Nindermann, make sure of your game; that may be the saving of the whole of us.' He said, 'I will do my best.' I was almost smoke-blind at the time and could not see very well, but I watched his movements very eagerly. I could make out his progress, and saw him crawling slowly up. There were several deer, perhaps a dozen; two or three were grazing and keeping the lookout, and the others were resting on the ground. Nindermann got to within two or three hundred yards of them, when one of them caught sight or wind of him and gave the alarm to the rest. I saw Nindermann start up, and, seeing the deer making off, he fired three shots at them, hoping to bring down one with a chance shot. But he missed. They all escaped. Nindermann came back much disheartened. 'I could not help it,' he said; 'I could not do any better,' so we had to put up with it. Then we started off again and made another pretty good stretch, till we felt exhausted and determined to seek shelter for the night. The best place we could find was beneath the high bluff, at a place where the earth had fallen away, and here we built a fire, had our alcohol and there spent the night. We did not sleep much it was so cold, and most of our time was occupied in keeping up the fire." (This camping place was near the place where Captain De Long later built his last signal fire—perhaps a mile from the deserted raft.)

"We had to go whichever way the wind blew us, and so we got away to the northwestward somewhere. Anyhow that day's travel took us out of our course so far that it took us nearly two days to get back again to a point opposite to the bluff on which we were when the gale commenced. We pushed on in spite of the wind and the drifting snow and sand. That night we could not find any shelter on the banks, and so we dug a hole in the drift for a shelter. This took us three or four hours to do, as we had nothing to work with except our hands and sheath knives, but at last we managed to dig a hole large enough for the two of us to creep into. After we had got in the hole the wind drifted the snow upon us and soon filled the entrance of our little place, and next morning we had to work a long time before we could get out of the drift again. We got up and started out again; we did not use any of our alcohol to speak of; we were saving it up as much as we could."

Toward the evening of the 11th the two men, after a terrible day's tramp in the drifting snow storm, were gladdened by the sight of a hut to the southeast—Matvey—and there they determined to stay for the night. It was a small log hut with a raised hearthplace in the centre. They soon built a fire, keeping it up by putting on the logs of the benches or bunks built round the hut.

"We hated to leave the first shelter we had found since leaving the Captain," Noros says. "We went down to the river again. We had to face the wind from the southward, and we could hardly make any progress against it. We would have to stop once in a little while, unable to move a step further. We began to give it up in despair. At times we felt like going back to the hut and to wait there until death relieved us from our sufferings." But they kept on, walking wearily, with nothing to eat. Then they saw some mountains ahead, and they thought they saw a hut close by, but were not quite sure. There was water between them and the hut, and this they had to wade through up to their knees. They got across, and then found it was really a shelter place, a little *palatka* or round, tent-like hut, built of sticks and plastered outside with mud to keep out the wind. They went inside, but found it was in a very dilapidated condition. Noros thought Nindermann had followed him, but instead of that he had gone a mile further on and had found another hut, a still smaller one. There they saw two crosses stuck up, marking the graves of dead natives.

Here the two men stayed a day and a half, until all the find of food had been consumed down to the fishheads and the refuse, and, though very bad, it seemed to give them some strength. Nindermann says they thought they had then arrived at Kumak Surka, and believed that the course they had followed agreed pretty well with the chart that De Long had given them. But, finding no inhabitants, they determined to press on again and make for Ajakit or Bulun. On the morning of the 14th they again started out on their weary tramp. The wind blew strong from the southeast, and snow and sand were drifted against their faces as they walked, so that they could scarcely hold their eyes open. They did not make much progress that day, and at night they found shelter in a curious opening in the bank, two feet and a half broad, six feet high and about fifteen yards in extent. It was, in fact, a kind of cave funnel, the other opening being on the top of the bank. Next day, the 16th, they had breakfast of Arctic willow tea and portions of sealskin pantaloons, and though the southeast wind was bitterly cold they started out again. They crossed numerous sand banks and small streams frozen over, and toward evening struck the Lena proper, close to the high mountains on the western bank (the place where De Long's party are now entombed). That day, thinking they might find game on the other shore, they crossed over to the mountainous eastern bank of the Lena, where they spent a most wretched night in a ravine in a mountain side. They then crossed over to the western shore of the Lena again. They began to congratulate themselves that the streams were at last all frozen over and wading was now unnecessary. That night they had to camp under the shelter of a high bank, but, failing to find wood, they had neither supper nor shelter, and spent another wretched night. Next morning, the 19th, they started out again after a meal of willow tea and sealskin, going south along the Lena. But they made little progress, being terribly weak. Nindermann says: "We made nearly no progress at all, and every five minutes we had to lay down to rest on the ice." They could hardly drag themselves along, yet they refused to give in, saying they would crawl when they could not walk any further. But assistance was fortunately nearer than they thought. They had accomplished an almost superhuman task already in walking so far with scarcely any food and in the bitter cold. From the place where they had left the Captain to the broken flatboat the distance is about fifteen miles; from that point to Matvey is fifteen or eighteen miles in a direct line, but they had made a circuit of nearly thirty-five; and from Matvey to Bulkoor is officially recognized as 110 versts, or over seventy miles; so that they had already done nearly one hundred and twenty miles. It must have been a terrible walk, and from Bulkoor to Kumak Surka, a known settlement, whither the Captain had told them to go, they had still fifty versts, or thirty-three miles, to go. But on the evening of the 19th, while Noros was walking on the edge of the river about half a mile ahead of Nindermann, on turning a point of land he saw a square hut perched in a gully between two high mountains on the west bank of the river, and going toward it saw two other huts, tent-like structures of wood and plastered outside with mud. These were the huts of Bulkoor.

Noros called Nindermann's attention to the discovery, and both went up to the huts, glad to have found shelter for the night at least, if nothing more. They stayed there two or three days, and then they determined that they would make a fresh start in the morning. They believed the place to be Ajakit, and thought that the next place would be Bulun. Everything was ready for the journey, which they had fixed for the morning of the 22d; but, Nindermann says, on that morning, although they had felt strong enough when sitting or lying down, they felt

TUNGUSES.

hopelessly weak when they stood up and attempted to walk, and therefore decided to rest there another day. This proved fortunate for them. They were cooking their dinner when they heard a noise outside the door that "sounded like a flock of geese sweeping by." Nindermann, who could see through the chinks of the door, said,

"They are deer." He picked up his gun and was creeping up near the door when it was suddenly opened. It was a Tunguse native, who, seeing the gun in Nindermann's hands, dropped on his knees, pleading, apparently, that they should not kill him. The two men made all sorts of signs to assure the man of his safety. Nindermann threw the gun away in the corner to let him see they did not intend to harm him. It was a long time, however, before he would enter, but after fastening his deer up—he had driven up on a deer sled—he finally entered the hut. Noros says:—"He began to talk, but we could not understand what he was saying. We tried to explain to him that we wanted to go to Bulun. We were so glad when we saw him that we could have hugged him, for we knew then that we were pretty nearly all right. We tried to explain to him that there were others of our party away to the north, but he could not understand us. He examined Nindermann's clothes, and then brought in a deerskin and then a pair of deerskin boots, and made gestures as if to say that he would go away, but would soon return. He held up three fingers and we thought he meant three days." Nindermann was for keeping him, but Noros advised that he should be permitted to do as he thought best, the more so as he had left articles enough as a pledge of his wish to assist them, and anyway if he left them they could follow the sled tracks and find him again. Going outside the two men saw four deer, and they afterward learned he had brought the two extra animals to put in a sled which he had left there some days previously, but which had been used by them for their fire.

The two men watched the Tunguse drive down the gully at a dead run and then went into the hut to await what fate should bring them. They waited until darkness came, and then they began to fear that the Tunguse did not intend to return. Nindermann said, "We have done wrong in letting him go." "Night came on," Noros says, "and we had got a little under way with our soup when we heard sleds drive up and saw our Tunguse coming with two other natives and five reindeer teams. The original Tunguse came rushing into the hut, bringing some frozen fish, deerskin coats and boots. We went for the fish. He picked up all our things and put them on the sleds. We put on the coats and the boots and soon started off. This was about midnight. We were driven about fifteen miles when we came to two large tents and many sleds, the deer not being in sight. The natives took us and washed our faces and hands and got us looking a little decent again. They had a big kettle of deer meat on the fire and we were motioned to help ourselves at once. After that they made us some tea, and then spread deerskins for us to sleep on. This was our first comfortable night since the time we left the Captain." The native had brought them to a camp of travelling Tunguses, who were on their way to Kumak Surka from a temporary settlement where they had been staying a little further to the north. In the caravan were seven men and three women, seventy-five head of deer dragging thirty sleds. With this caravan Nindermann and Noros travelled all one day and till four of the afternoon of the next day, when they finally arrived at Kumak Surka on the 24th of October. Here the two men were well taken care of, Noros at one hut and Nindermann at another. Before this, when but a short distance on the road, a native known as "Alexia" led Nindermann to the top of a neighboring hill, and, pointing out the island mountain of Stalbowy, asked if it was there that he had left his companions. He said "Yes," and explained as well as he could that he wanted the sleds to take him there with something for the Captain's party to eat. The native does not seem to have understood him, for he started down the hillside toward the south. They arrived at Kumak Surka during the evening, and, busied with the preparation of meals for a house full of people and with the arrangement of bunks for the accommodation of the guests, there was no opportunity that night to engage their attention to the subject of his errand. The next day, however, he had the field to himself after the morning meal had been discussed. Some one brought him the model of a Yakout boat, which they called a *"parahut"* (a corruption of the Russian term for steamer) and asked if his *"parahut"* was like that. Then, with sticks to represent masts and spars, he showed them that it was bark rigged and moved by steam power also. All this they seemed to understand perfectly and then asked how and where they lost the ship.

Pointing toward the north he made them understand it was very far in that direction, and, with two pieces of ice, showed them how the ship was crushed and sank down into the sea. Afterward he cut the models of three small boats and put sticks in them to represent the men in each boat, and told them, as well as he could, how, with sleds and dogs and boats, they had crossed great seas of broken ice and open water and finally reached the shore of their country. He then got a piece of paper and drew the coast line and sketched the boat, illustrating the manner in which the landing was effected. Drawing in the river from the coast line to the south he showed that they walked down the east bank of the river, and marked the places where they found huts or encamped. He indicated the number of days they had been walking by putting his head down and closing his eyes as if to sleep and counting the number of sleeps with his fingers. He told them as plainly as he could that the Captain, or "Kapitán," as they called it, had sent him to get clothes and food and reindeer, and to fetch them to the settlement, as they were very weak and in a starving condition. He told them he had left the party sixteen days ago and that two days before his departure they had had nothing to eat. He used every effort to convey his meaning to the savages who had befriended him and induce them to go to the succor of the Captain and his party, but was not successful. Sometimes it seemed as if they understood him perfectly, and at others he felt convinced that they had not understood a single thing he had told them. During the entire day he kept talking to them by signs and illustrations upon paper, but without avail. The next day he renewed his efforts and resorted to every expedient to make them understand him. He did not ask them only to go alone, but wanted them to go with him. Prostrated by famine and exposure and weakened by dysentery he was in no fit condition to undertake such a task, but his anxiety was so great that he felt constrained to go. This day, as on the day previous, he at times thought he had been understood, and, again, that it was all a blank to them. They would sigh and look distressed when he described the sufferings and condition of the party on the delta, but when he urged that assistance should be sent to them the faces of his hearers were totally devoid of expression. He then thought of his companions as dead or dying, looking to his return as their only hope for deliverance. Weakened by fatigue, exposure and famine, and feeling how utterly powerless he was when so much depended on him, the terrible strain was too much for him, and this strong, brave man, who has faced death and endured untold hardships without a quiver, sank into a corner and cried like a child. An old woman, the wife of the master of the hut, saw him and took compassion on him, and a long conference was held by the natives, which resulted in their endeavoring to comfort him. Resting a hand tenderly upon his shoulder they told him he should go to Bulun the next day. He had asked to be taken there, hoping to find some one by whom he could make himself understood, and it was to his anxiety to reach that town that they attributed his grief.

The next day he again asked them to take him to Bulun to see the "Commandant," and they told him they had already sent for the "Commandant," and were expecting him. During the evening the Russian exile, Kusmah, came to the hut and Nindermann asked him if he was the "Commandant" of Bulun. To this he answered "Yes!" or at least Nindermann so understood him. Then Kusmah asked, "*Parakod Jeannette?*" and Nindermann replied "Yes!" at the same time believing that he had been notified by the Government at St. Petersburg of the probability of the *Jeannette's* arrival upon the Siberian coast and had been directed to look out for the ship's company. He then told, as well as he could, the whole story of the loss of the *Jeannette* and the history of the retreat, illustrating by his little chart and by sketches. Nindermann soon felt convinced that Kusmah did not understand either the chart or his descriptions. Then he told him that on the journey on land one man had died and that there were eleven alive. While he was telling him this portion of the story Kusmah kept assenting and seemed to understand perfectly. He afterwards found that Kusmah was alluding all the time to Mr. Melville's party, which also consisted of eleven people. He would keep saying, "Kapitán, yes. Two Kapitán, first Kapitán, second Kapitán," alluding to Melville and Danenhower. Nindermann then understood him to say he couldn't do

KUSMAH.

anything until either one or the other of them had telegraphed to St. Petersburg for instructions. Therefore Nindermann wrote a telegram addressed to the American Minister in St. Petersburg, telling him the exact condition of affairs, and that the Captain's party was starving and in need of food and clothing, and while talking, before the despatch was quite finished, Kusmah took it. Nindermann thought nothing of this at the time, supposing he was transacting business with the "Commandant" of Bulun. Three days afterward Kusmah handed the despatch to Melville at Germavelok.

From Kumak Surka the two men were sent to Bulun, a hundred versts further south, where they arrived on the 29th of October. As soon as the "Commandant" learned of their arrival he sent for them and gave them quarters for the day. The next day they were transferred to the house of the priest's assistant, but this gentleman did not appear to know the virtues of hospitality to shipwrecked men. After two days he sent them to the hut of a native, who also did not provide well for the guests. In short, the Bulunese did not show any very praiseworthy characteristics until the arrival of Melville in Bulun, who compelled the people to furnish better food for the two rescued men. Melville arrived at Bulun on the 2d of November, and the remainder of his boat's crew a few days later. He had lost no time as soon as he heard of the existence of Nindermann and Noros in making a move, but it was too late to benefit De Long and his party.

This was the story which Nindermann and Noros related to me on the Lena River. It was the closing chapter of the mournful annals of the *Jeannette*.

YAKOUTSK.

CHAPTER XXIII.

AMONG THE YAKOUTS.

IRKUTSK, *July 29th*, 1882.

RETURNING to my own mission, I was compelled to curtail my visit to the delta in consequence of the prevailing impression that the summer would arrive sooner than usual this year, though the Ispravnik of Werchojansk, whom I met on the road to Bulun, assured me that if I left Werchojansk for Yakoutsk on the 6th of May I would be in time to make the journey on sledges and in from seven to nine days. My anxiety was to get upon the other side of the rivers intervening between Yakoutsk and the north before they broke up and interrupted travel.

I was glad to meet at Werchojansk a Mr. Leon, a political exile, who spoke English quite well, and had been very useful to Chief Melville and also to the Russian officials by acting as interpreter for them. He was well informed concerning the history of the voyage of the *Jeannette*, the remarkable retreat and the sad fate of those who failed to reach the settlements after landing upon the delta. He also told me all that was known concerning Chief Melville's subsequent movements, and furnished me with a chart of the Lena delta, which was as accurate as any in existence at that time. Upon my return to Werchojansk he hurried me off for Yakoutsk very reluctantly, but assuring me that he felt great anxiety already concerning the state of the roads, and feared

I would experience considerable difficulty in reaching my destination. When one reflects that most of the stoppages upon these northern roads are in unoccupied houses it will not be necessary to explain that provision must be made for the entire journey before starting out from a town like Werchojansk.

The stock at these places is very limited indeed, and at the time I arrived provisions were scarce and dear, rendered so partly by the lateness of the season and partly by the fact that Chief Melville, in equipping his search party, was compelled to draw heavily from their limited stores. The articles to provide are cooking utensils, such as a copper tea-kettle, a china or metal teapot, a frying pan and a copper pot for boiling meat; tea, sugar, fresh and dried bread, fresh meat and fish. Then, also, it will be found convenient to have tea-cups and saucers, large spoons for soup and small spoons for tea, plates of iron plated with porcelain, and knives and forks. Many of these articles are luxuries, and may, if found too cumbersome, be dispensed with— as, for instance, knives and forks and plates, for a man can eat with his fingers; tea-cups and saucers, for a wooden bowl will answer. He can do without spoons, for perhaps he may have no sugar, and he can drink his soup from the same bowl which he uses for tea, or he can drink right out of the pot it was cooked in, the same as do the natives; but it is well to provide one's self with the articles named, though perhaps to be abandoned if found necessary. One is not likely to be surfeited with luxuries in this country, and can safely trust himself with the articles I have mentioned. In laying in your stores of provisions it is well to remember that the *yemsheeks* expect a little reward in the shape of civilized food, and though it is not in the bond that they shall receive it it must be a hard heart that can withstand their eager, expectant look as they watch every process of cooking and eating. So if you have not taken this item into consideration you will find yourself short of provisions before the end of your trip.

A proper sled is another desideratum. Dog sledges require to be lighter and to run more easily than reindeer sledges, while horse sledges are more cumbersome than either of the others. In travelling continuously—that is, night and day—it will be found more comfortable to have a covered sled to protect you from the wind and snow and allow you to sleep occasionally. This is seldom allowable, however, with dog teams, as they are not generally used upon stations, but for the entire route, from one distant point to another, where other animals cannot be procured. It is not that dogs are not strong enough, for one good dog team will carry the loads of about six reindeer teams—that is, a single dog can pull nearly as much as a single reindeer. When heavily loaded, however, the dogs travel slowly, while reindeer always trot along at a lively pace. Yakout horses are probably the slowest of all animals except oxen, while the horses upon the post roads of Siberia west of Irkutsk are about the same as those of other countries. I left Werchojansk in the same sled that had carried me through from Sradnia Kolymsk to the portion of the Lena where dogs only are available. It was a light sled, covered with reindeer skins to keep out the wind. It had to be repaired repeatedly, and whenever we halted sufficiently long for such a purpose it was thoroughly overhauled, so that when I say it was the same sled when I left Werchojansk I may make a mistake; it may have been entirely new by that time, for there I had a new cover put on of thin reindeer skin with the hair scraped off. I managed to retain my sled for three stations, the last one being drawn almost all the way over bare ground. After that I had to mount a horse, and experienced all the misfortunes attending such a mode of travel.

The Yakout horses of Northern Siberia can scarcely be called horses—they are a sort of domesticated wild animal. They are small, ill-shaped and awkward, with thick hair and very long and heavy mane and tail. The front lock often entirely conceals the eyes and the whole

YAKOUT HORSE.

front of the head. They stumble and fall in the most unexpected and unnecessary places, and when down make no effort to assist themselves to their feet. They simply stick out their heads to reach for such dried, frost-killed grass or bunches of shrubs as may be within reach until urged to self-assistance by the kicks and voice of their driver. They follow each other in long lines, and it is almost impossible to make a Yakout horse go alongside of another—he wants either to be ahead or behind. This arises from the fact that they are mostly used as pack animals, and are then driven in lines, the hinder animal tied to the tail of the one preceding. Thus also they are harnessed in sledges, with a single trace passing around the bow of the sled and fastened to the tail of the leading horse to keep it from beneath their feet. I don't mean that the first horse pulls his share of the load entirely by his tail. The trace is first fastened to the saddle, and, passing back toward the sled, is attached to the horse's tail to keep it up from the ground when occasionally it slackens. The saddle is always placed by the Yakouts in the middle of the horse's back, is an open tree like the McClellan, with a high, square pommel, often handsomely ornamented with silver and gold of native metal and workmanship highly creditable to their skill in the mechanical arts. The saddle is mounted upon a pad of straw, and the effect when a horse is ready saddled for the road is something like a camel. The natives generally pile a coat or two on the saddle under them, and when mounted are perched high up in the air in what, to one accustomed to civilized accoutrements, seems a very awkward and uncomfortable position. It is quite an art, too, to mount one of these saddles perched in the centre of a horse's back, and the stirrup depending almost immediately from the pommel. If you rise upon your left foot in the stirrup and raise your right leg horizontally over the horse's back you will find yourself ten times to one on the horse's neck just in front of the pommel, and as it is next to impossible to get back over a pommel eight to ten inches high you have to slide ignominiously down over the horse's head to the ground and try it over again. They are perfectly docile—provokingly so—they have not animation enough to be wicked. One could well wish for a little of the mustang or broncho spirit. Their favorite gait is a walk so slow and deliberate that you lose all patience and force them into a trot if possible. Now you have all the exercise you require, for their trot is like unto nothing known to the outside world. They rise in the air and straighten out their legs and then come down upon the end that has the foot on it, the recoil bouncing you high up from your seat and just in time to meet the saddle as it is coming up for the next step. It is for all the world like constant bucking. Soon you have pains in your limbs and chest and hold your breath as long as

GROUP OF BORIAKS.

possible in order to keep it from being driven entirely out of your body. There is no comfort in the saddle upon such horses. The Yakouts, as well as the Boriaks, who are very similar in their nature and habits, although brought up among horses and living upon them in more senses than one—for horseflesh is a delicacy to these people—are not good horsemen. They neither sit well nor manage their horses well. Later I saw many Tartars. They also have many horses and are perfect horsemen. It is a pleasure to see them mounted. They sit upon their horses as if

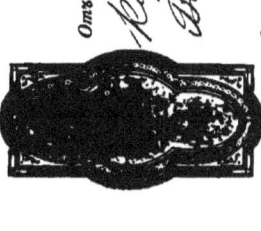

ROAD PASS.

БЛАНКОВЫЙ БИЛЕТЪ.

ЗА ПРОГОНЫ

Слѣдующему отъ города Иркутска чрезъ Вер. С. Петербургъ Карасевскому дерзки Ново-Георгіевскаго уѣзда Госп. Дѣй. Василію Тихѣеву ел. Бубуктычь давать подъ проѣздъ туда и обратно изъ обывательскихъ по три лошади съ проводникомъ за указанныя прогоны и сей билетъ прописывать установленнымъ порядкомъ на сельскихъ станціяхъ. Данъ въ г. Иркутскѣ Июля „ 21 „ дня 1882 года.

Иркутскаго Общаго Губернскаго Управленія № 2557

За Иркутскаго Губернатора [signature]

ORDER FOR HORSES.

they belonged there. Indeed I understand they sometimes sit other people's horses in the same way, as most of them I saw are exiled horse thieves. Beyond Yakoutsk, that is, south of that city, you begin to find horses that have been improved by breeding with European stock and a much superior class of animals. The country is traversed with post roads plentifully supplied with horses that cost but little and are capable of the hard work demanded of them. And when I speak of a plentiful supply I do not mean that on your arrival at a post station you are sure to find horses waiting to convey you to the next post station.

The probability is that your demand for horses will be met with the reply, "*Lorshad naytoo*" (no horses), and you will have to wait for from forty minutes to several hours before you can resume your journey. Between Werchojansk and Yakoutsk it is still worse. It is no unusual experience at the season I passed over the road not only to find no animals at the stations but no station master nor any one else. Nothing, in fact, but an empty house. Several times I had to help drive before us horses that we picked up on the prairie so I would have them at the next station. Finally, after much tribulation, I reached the station of Kingyorak, at the foot of the Werchojansk Mountains. Here were neither horses nor reindeer. Indeed horses would have been of no use whatever on this route, as the valleys on either side of the mountain were filled with soft snow, partially thawed by the sun, which now, in the early part of May, was quite powerful. There was a presumable beaten track made by reindeer teams, which were employed on this route as far as within thirty versts of the Aldan River. Horses travel in this part of the country in single file, as before explained, and would consequently be between the tracks made by the reindeer, which are driven side by side in double teams. Horses, therefore, would sink out of sight in the valleys, as it was only possible to travel, if at all, upon this beaten path. When I found there were no reindeer at the station I at once hired one of my *yemsheeks* to hunt up the savages in the neighborhood and employ some of them to convey me to the south side of the Aldan, some 230 versts distant. I at last succeeded in securing a sufficient number of reindeer from a camp of Yakouts about ten versts from the station, and a promise that they would come for me by nine o'clock.

In the meantime a Tunguse arrived at the station with a team of fine large reindeer, and said he had plenty of them at his camp, which was thirty versts off. He told me he would take me on my journey in case the Yakout team did not arrive, and I would have preferred his escort to the others, as I have always found the Tunguses and Lamoots much more reliable and honorable than the Yakouts. For instance, Mr. Bobookoff, who, with some baggage from Chief Melville's search party, had preceded me over the same road, was compelled to hire teams from some wandering Tunguses in the vicinity of this station, and paid in advance twenty-five rubles for their services. The next morning when they came for him with their teams they asked if he did not belong to the American party that was expected over the road. He told them he did, and had some of their baggage in his charge "In that case," replied the driver, "I cannot accept your money, for the Ispravnik of the district has sent word that we must help the Americans all we can; you are therefore welcome to the use of my reindeer." With this he returned the money to Mr. Bobookoff and proceeded

BRIDGE OF EXILES.

with him to the Aldan. I had a somewhat similar experience with an old Lamoot whom I had employed for fifteen rubles to carry me and my baggage about fifty versts over a very bad road. He received the money during the evening and came for me about midnight, but before starting he returned me five rubles of the money, saying that upon reflection he thought the job was not worth more than ten. It would be an interesting sight to behold a Yakout returning any money he had ever received, whether justly or unjustly, unless forced to do it. I much prefer the Tunguse character and the Lamoot. About the appointed hour my Yakout *yemsheeks* came with a lot of small, thin reindeer, and I was disgusted with them, but subsequently found that they were better for work at this season than the fat, strong ones would have been. It was but ten versts from the station to the foot of the mountains, and yet we did not reach that spot until about four o'clock the next morning. All night long the *yemsheeks* were walking in front of their teams and sounding with long poles through the deep snow to keep upon the beaten path. Occasionally one of them would lose the track and would go almost out of sight in the deep snow. We crossed the mountains as soon as we reached them. As we approached I saw four sleds drawn by reindeer coming down the mountain side, and in the distance they looked like centipedes crawling upon a wall, so steep was the descent. When we met the drivers of these sleds we ascertained that they were the Tunguses who had taken Mr. Bobookoff to the Aldan and were just returning. They reported the road as in a fearful condition, and so we found it to be.

There was one thing that I remarked at this time— namely, the delicious melody of the Yakout tongue as spoken in the conversation with my drivers and Cossack. I had never before noticed this peculiarity, though subsequently it was a matter of constant remark. It seemed to me like a blending of the Irish and Italian dialects, with the crisp, rolling gutturals of the one, modified by the soft musical tones of the other.

Soon we commenced the ascent of this mountain, which proved a sore task. There could be no passengers on the sleds; all had to climb as best they could. I found it impossible to advance more than eight or ten paces at a time through the soft snow, and felt convinced that without the adhesive qualities it then possessed I could not have accomplished so much. When at last the summit was attained there were but six or eight paces before the descent commenced upon the other side, and as I stood there upon the peak looking down it appeared almost an absolute impossibility to make the descent without personal injury. Following the direction and example of my guide, the Cossack, I sat down and worked my passage as best I could, and, at the end of three-quarters of an hour, I found myself about two-thirds of the way to the base. Looking back, I saw that the *yemsheeks* had lashed the six sleds three abreast, with the reindeer astern, and with one man holding firmly on either side, their feet planted forward in the snow, and the reindeer holding back as much as possible, the descent was safely accomplished; but even from where I stood, though still on the mountain side, it appeared as if the reindeer were standing on their heads and the men were sliding down a perpendicular wall. I believe there is no parallel to this pass upon any known road. I have been informed that in midwinter, before the early summer sun has softened the snow, the mountain side is a sheet of ice, and the passage is even more difficult than when I crossed. At that season one is obliged to sit down astride of a stick, which he must manage as a brake, and regulate his speed with great skill or else the descent becomes exceedingly dangerous. From the summit to the valley on the south side the slope is ten versts long, and the gathered momentum of an unobstructed slide from the top may be imagined. There are one or two places in the descent where one can divert his course to a sort of platform and recover his wind and courage to finish the descent. What an opportunity for coasting! I don't believe there is a boy living who ever dreamed of such a lark as to pass this mountain on runners. We found the road through the valley quite as bad as it had been reported, and at ten o'clock were compelled to halt until the cool evening had hardened the surface so as to enable us to proceed.

My *yemsheeks* had refused to bargain for conveying me further than to the station of Beerdakool, ninety versts south of Kingyorak, but before we reached that point informed me that I would find the place deserted and uninhabitable. They said that for an additional exorbitant sum they would take me sixty versts further on, where there was an uninhabited *povarnniar*, near which lived a tribe of Lamoots, who would take me to the Aldan for the regular price—that is, nine kopecks (four and a half cents) a verst. They also agreed to go to the Lamoot camp and bring some of the tribe to me to make the necessary arrangements. I could, of course, do nothing else than accept their terms, as otherwise.there was a strong probability of my starving at this house during the season, when the rivers break up, and there is no communication between one part of the country and another until the water falls. As an excuse for charging me so much for this second stretch they told me that shortly after leaving the station we must cross a river which was filled with surface water to a great depth, and there was every prospect of our being drowned. At this they commenced crossing themselves and praying, and, to add to our other discomforts, the first rain storm of the season set in. I knew the effect of a warm rain upon ice, and felt considerable alarm concerning the condition of the ice upon the Aldan, which I was hastening to cross before it broke. When within ten versts of the little river which they expressed so much fear of crossing these incorrigible miscreants insisted upon stopping in the woods to cook tea, though they had halted for that purpose but two hours before. All my persuasion and threats were of no avail in forcing them to proceed until the little river had been passed until I produced a pistol from my pocket. That was enough. The moment that inducement was offered they exclaimed "*Piadjet!*" (go) and moved off at once. On the trees near the bank of this stream were hung similar gifts to the deities to those described as hung upon the cross between the Kolyma and Werchojansk. My drivers made similar offerings and crossed themselves most fervently before we descended to the ice. I think their appeals must have been heard and answered, for we found less water upon the ice than in many holes in the main road through which we had already passed, and effected the crossing without any difficulty worth noticing. From where we halted for tea on the south side of this river I sent one of the *yemsheeks* ahead to have the Lamoots at the *povarnniar* when we arrived, so that no time need be lost in getting away, and gave him a liberal reward for his extra services as messenger. Upon arriving at the *povarnniar* later in the afternoon I found it a most miserable hovel, the rain streaming through the roof, so that it was impossible to find shelter. It was not altogether rain, either, for that is at least clean white, while this water dribbled through a roof of turf, and was simply mud. The floor was covered with water, and one could only walk around on pieces of wood that had been placed around for that purpose There was no chimney—simply a hole in the roof over the fireplace for the smoke to escape, which it sometimes did. Here I found the sub-Prefect of the police district of the Kolyma, whom I had previously met at Sradnia Kolymsk, with his wife and little girl, of about twelve years. They had been here in this miserable hut for four days waiting for transportation, but could obtain no animals. Here, also, I found my Yakout messenger, who had not been to the Lamoot camp at all. He said there was a deep river intervening and he could not cross it, but promised to make another attempt that evening in company with the other *yemsheek*. The reindeer were sent to a feeding ground in charge of a Lamoot boy; but, much against my desire, they were allowed to put all their effects on their sled which went with the reindeer. I felt convinced that they would make no further effort to reach the Lamoot camp, but would wait until we slept and then go for their animals and drive home. I expressed my fears to the sub-Prefect, or "Promoshnik," as he is termed in Russian, but he and the Cossack both assured me I need have no fear of that, and I, believing they should know more of the character of these people than I, reluctantly submitted to this arrangement. It had been my intention to hold one of the men as hostage, and, in case the Lamoots did not arrive in the morning, to compel them to go on with me to the Aldan. Their reindeer were in excellent condition, and it was only fifty versts to where I would find horses to carry me over the river. If I had been allowed to have my own way I would have been able to cross the Aldan before the ice broke, and been spared much anxiety and suffering; but I foolishly trusted to the judgment of others instead of following the rule laid down by Lieutenant Schwatka, who has said that "a man travelling in the North, or in any unknown country, must depend upon his own judgment and not upon the advice of others if he would be successful." As I had anticipated, the Yakout *yemsheeks* went off home during the night and left me in this forlorn hovel without means of moving, and without food to sustain life until the swollen rivers had subsided and travel could be resumed upon the roads.

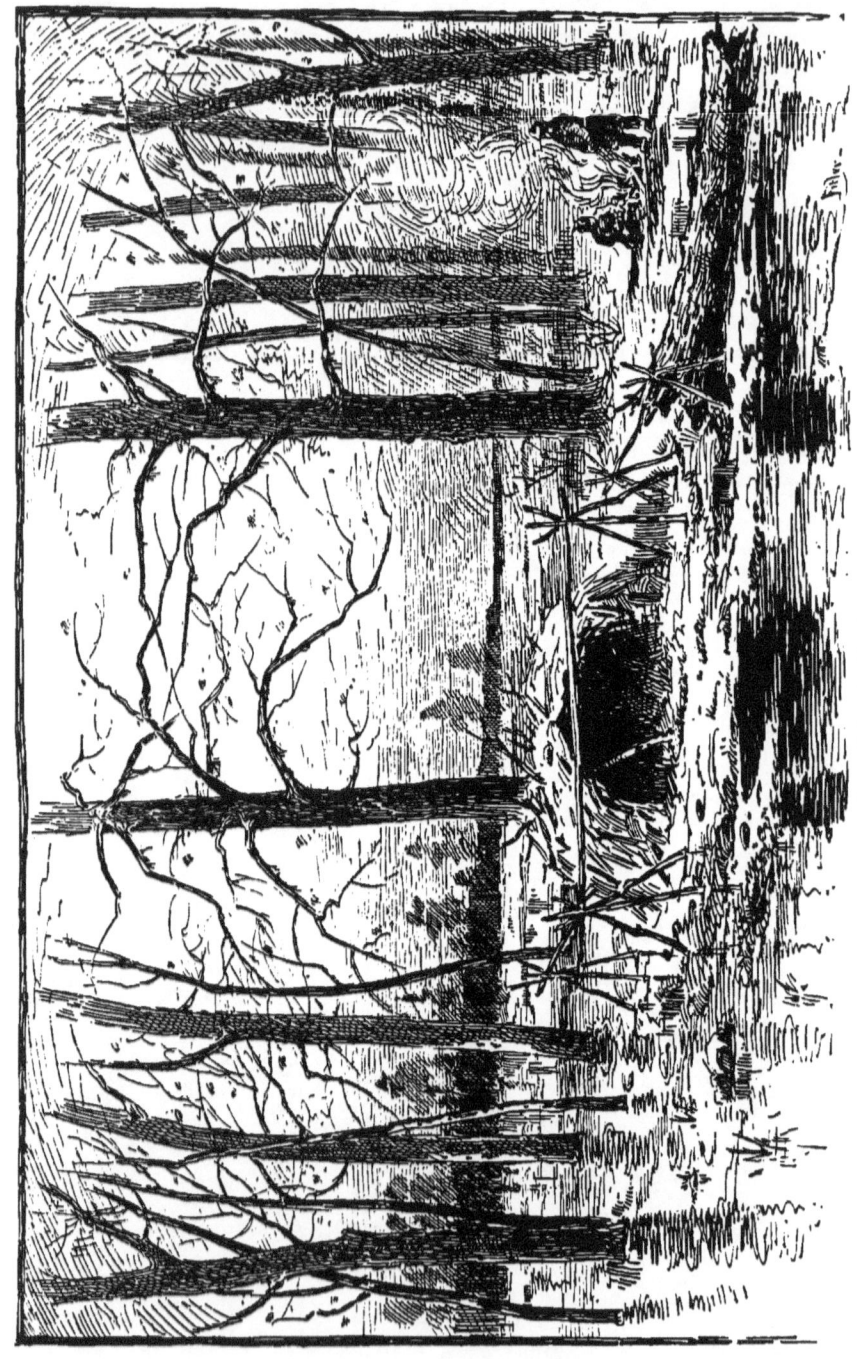

LAGOON CAMP ON THE ALDAN.

CHAPTER XXIV.

CAUGHT BY THE FLOODS.

IRKUTSK, *July* 31*st*, 1882.

DURING the day following my arrival my Cossack took the Lamoot boy as a guide and started for the camp, which was twenty versts distant, carrying with him a hatchet to cut a log upon which to pass the little river if unable to ford it. He returned during the evening with the grateful information that they would take me to the inhabited house I desired to reach that night, if their reindeer returned, which had gone a long distance away to bring home the carcasses of three large elk that had recently been killed by one of their hunters. They did not come that night, but the night following arrived about midnight, while in the meantime about eight horses came from the Aldan to promote the journey. We therefore took all the people on the sleds and left the baggage to be brought on horses. The roads were getting worse and worse every day, and nearly every day it rained, so that the roads were filled with water, and for versts at a time the sled and everything on it was completely submerged. It was such a day's travel that one would be loath to repeat, but finally we arrived at the house, or hut, as it should be called, completely worn out and drenched to the skin. Our baggage arrived later, but the roads were so bad that two of the horses had to be abandoned and the *yemsheeks* came in on foot. At this house we learned that the Aldan, which was now but thirty versts distant, had not yet broken, but that the Lena had, and the ice was moving down, so that the Aldan might be expected to break any day. There was, therefore, no time to be lost, so we started early in the morning mounted upon the six poor horses that had brought our baggage the day before. We could, therefore, only

VIEW ON THE UPPER LENA.

take our blankets, a teakettle and a very small amount of food, only sufficient for the day. We expected to cross the river and reach the station, where we would find sufficient to eat until our baggage arrived the next day. This was a more disagreeable day than the previous, for, though I thought it impossible, the roads were even worse than those we had passed. Almost the whole distance was through frozen swamp land, upon which the water had drained from the adjacent high land, and the horses had to wade through water up to their bellies, treading upon the treacherous icy bottom, and, being without shoes, it was almost impossible for them to keep their feet. The little girl was mounted behind the Cossack. Once his horse fell and he and the horse both rolled over the little one, and I thought she was drowned, when some one riding behind jumped from his horse and rescued the poor frightened creature from her perilous position. Nearly every horse in the party fell several times. Several small streams had to be crossed that were already swollen and we had to seek another than the regular crossing place. Sometimes we would have to leap from our saddles to the shore and help the struggling horses to land.

At last, about ten o'clock in the evening, we reached the bank of the Aldan, to find it already broken up, and heavy ice going down stream at the rate of fourteen versts an hour. Our worst fears were realized. It was now too late and too dark to find our way back to the house we had left, where we could pass the time until the water fell, and we went about three versts along the bank of the river to the point where the crossing is always made, directly opposite the station. Here we cooked some meat with drift-wood, and then lay down to sleep till morning, when light enough to find our way back through the network of little rivers that began to traverse the country in every direction. They told me it would be from eight to twenty days before the ice left the river free enough to cross in a boat, and this intervening time we would have to pass in a hut about ten versts back from the river. We got up about eight o'clock in the morning, cooked some more meat, and then started to return along the river bank by the route we had come.

I noticed that the water in the river was much higher than when we lay down at night, but did not think much of it until we found that our retreat was cut off less than a verst from where we slept. The *yemsheek* said there was another way out by passing around a lake behind where we had slept, but on attempting that route we found we were cut off there also, so we had now nothing else to do but to select the highest piece of ground we could find, and there await the falling of the waters. This was not a very pleasant prospect, with our baggage thirty versts away and with our last meal already eaten. We had a little tea left, and that was all. The highest ground we could find was not much above the general level, and when I saw water marks four feet high upon the trees near us I began to feel a little nervous. We had little time for reflection, however, for there was plenty to do. We cut brush and made a hut that would afford a little shelter from the wind, and covering it with some skin blankets and the saddle pads stopped a good deal of the rain from coming through when we slept. In the meantime I had set a tide gauge, and found the water rising at the rate of twelve inches an hour. At this rate it would only require four hours more to put the floor of our house under water. This was a dismal prospect, but while I was looking around for some place where, in an emergency, we could hang the woman and child up in the trees while we swam around and caught fish for them I again examined my tide gauge and found the water had been stationary for twelve minutes, and soon afterward it was subsiding. It went down as rapidly as it rose, and by evening a fall of six feet was observed. The ice, from one to three feet thick, which had been coursing like a race-horse through the inlet or temporarily submerged land in the rear of our camp, carrying before it masses of drift-wood and tearing up trees in its course most ominously, was now aground. We had six horses with us and had no fear of starving, but felt the need of an axe about as seriously as anything else. Later my Cossack and the Promoshnik rode out to inspect the road to the hut in rear of us and returned with the report that it was feasible. We therefore decided to move there in the morning. Now there seemed no danger of serious disasters, and we slept soundly and comfortably except for a miserable snow and rain storm that drove into the open doorway of our brush hut.

I can in no way better describe the alternate hope and anxiety that were our portion for the next few days than by copying directly from my little pocket journal the pages relating to our lagoon camp:

May 17*th.*—The second day of our residence in the brush. For variety we have had thunder storms all day long, with occasional glimpses of the sun, just sufficient to tempt us to hang out our wet blankets and clothes, merely to get them more thoroughly drenched before we could again get them under cover. Tried the road to the *povarnniar* and found it impassable, and nothing before us but to sit in this swamp until the river is passable. During the afternoon I walked around to where we had slept on the river bank the night of our arrival, and found the ground all wet from having been submerged, and great cakes of ice from one to five feet thick twenty or thirty yards further inland than where we had lain. Stood for some time on an immense cake of grounded ice and gazed wistfully across the three versts of water, filled with moving ice, to where the station is located, not more than four versts from me. We held a council of war after returning from our unsuccessful attempt to retreat this morning, and decided that, as we would be compelled eventually to kill a horse for food to save us from starvation, we might as well kill it now and not wait until starved into it.

Consequently the *yemsheek* was directed to slaughter an animal. I assisted at the operation, which was a novel one. Fastened the horse's hind legs to a tree and then passed a line attached to his fore feet around a tree in front of him. We all pulled on one end of this line, and when the horse began struggling pulled his feet forward, thus throwing him down. His legs were then secured and the *yemsheek* stabbed him behind the ears, severing the spinal column. He was soon skinned and dressed, but as we were all very hungry a piece of meat was cut off immediately from his hind leg and boiled in the teakettle. When I returned from my walk to the river bank I was called to eat and thought I was eating beef; thought it was some they had saved and gave to me, believing that horseflesh would be repugnant to my palate. Don't believe I could tell the difference between horse and cow except that horse meat is harder and tougher. Slept soundly with a full stomach.

May 18*th*.—Breakfasted and dined upon horseflesh and spent the time, as we have done ever since encamping here, trying to dry our clothes, but continued rain and snow storms have prevented. I have been wishing for a change of wind, and this evening it seems to have settled down from the southwest, and blows the smoke from our fire right into the open front of our hut. We may look for better weather, I think, if it continue from that direction. I would like to pass the time writing but dare not open my box in this unsettled state of the weather; it would bring on a deluge surely. Ever since about one o'clock yesterday the water has been rising in the low land behind our brush hut, until at two P.M. to-day it stood six inches higher than at the highest day before yesterday. Then in an hour and a half it settled an inch and stays there without change. There, I think, it will continue for perhaps the ten or twenty days they say it takes for things to settle down after the breaking up of the rivers. In that case we can hope for no relief from behind us, but must wait patiently for the river to clear of ice and a boat can come from the other side. If we could only get our baggage up and have some clean clothes and tobacco, and something else to eat besides horseflesh it would be a relief. Took a walk to see how the river looked, but could not reach the place where we first slept. Returning to camp at half-past six, found the water rising at the rate of three inches an hour and within about two feet of reaching our hut, which is on the highest ground we could find. Looks bad. I don't like this slow and contiued rise.

May 19*th*.—Woke up at six o'clock to find the water rising rapidly and close to our hut. Walked to where I could get a distant view of the river and saw it still full of ice moving rapidly and the water well up on the land all around us. Soon the water reached our fire and put it out, and we had to move it to another spot a little higher, where we cooked some horse meat for breakfast. At half-past seven the water was in our hut. Opened my box and put my most important papers in my pocket and inside the lining of my vest. Moved our place of rest twice and now at a quarter past nine are on the best spot we can find, where we must await events as they transpire.

The water still coming in very fast. Feel the need of an axe more than anything else. I never knew of such idiocy as to come away without one. I saw one slung in its leathern case outside the house before we started and took it for granted they meant to bring it. It must have been forgotten at the last minute. My Cossack and the Promoshnik have crossed themselves and said their prayers and are now stretched out on a big log sleeping. The rest of us are seated on the log, with our feet up on it to keep them out of the water, which now pervades every spot of ground in the vicinity of our camp. I am glad my Cossack is asleep, for when awake he does nothing but scold the poor *yemsheek* for getting us into the dilemma, while I look upon it as his fault for insisting upon going up to the crossing place the night we arrived. I feel more anxiety for the woman and child than for the rest of us, as we can make shift somehow, even if we have to climb a tree. If we only had an axe we could build a raft and cross the inlet to ground from which we could reach the *povarnniar*, which is only four versts off that way. I lose my temper whenever I think of the axe. At ten A.M. the water began falling and went down at the same rate it came up—three inches an hour. This evening it is comparatively pleasant—that is, no snow or rain—and there being no wind all shouted across the river and finally got a response. They sent the fool of a *yemsheek* to talk with them, and he could not understand, though, notwithstanding being a long distance behind him, I could hear them distinctly; but every time they commenced talking he would do the same and drown their voices. There is one good thing about it, however—they know at the station that we are here and will send a boat over as soon as possible. At six P.M. the water has gone down two feet and we can again occupy our hut. The ice in the river seems to me to be looser than before.

May 20th.—A fine day and the river nearly cleared of ice. Only a thin, narrow strip of ice along this shore. This evening, after shouting an hour, got a response that the boat would be over in the morning. Spent most of the day in writing.

By evening the water had gone down as low as I had seen it at any time there, and our anxiety was about at an end. During the afternoon of the next day a small boat came over with two Yakouts, who brought some tea, flour and the awful butter mixed with tallow which is made by the Yakout housewives. The supper that followed was a most sumptuous one—boiled horse meat, with rye cakes, made by mixing the flour with water and baked on a twig stuck in the ground before the fire. Afterward tea boiled in the same pot in which the meat had been cooked and retaining somewhat the flavor of soup. After tea Michael, the Cossack, went back across the river in the little boat with the Yakouts to get some milk, sugar, tobacco and wild geese from the station master. We had been entirely out of tobacco for several days, and had adopted numerous devices to procure a smoke. The bark of the pine tree was chopped up fine and mixed with the stem of an old pipe which had also been cut fine, and, being rank with nicotine, gave some tobacco flavor to the mixture. Our *yemsheek* started back for the house where the baggage had been left to bring it up, but found the land still inundated behind our camp and was compelled to return.

During the next day the big boat came over from the station, propelled by about a dozen men and boys, and bringing an extra horse and a bull with its sled to carry our baggage to the boat. This was the first bull sled I had seen and it was as such a great curiosity. They are used on land devoid of snow, and the driver, often a woman or girl, sits astride of the animal, not upon the sled. I have occasionally met on the road a man mounted upon a bull and guiding it by means of a small rope attached to a ring in its nose. He would have a saddle, too, to sit upon, while his wife walked alongside or ahead of him through all the slush and water. But she was only a woman and he was a man. I found at the station two Cossacks with the post, who had left Werchojansk ten days ahead of me, and another Cossack with a prisoner whom he was taking from Yakoutsk to Werchojansk. I also learned that Mr. Bobookoff was at a house ten versts away and completely surrounded with water. The roads were all reported to be in a fearful condition and travel impossible. That night Mr. Bobookoff arrived, having been informed that I was at the station. I was very glad indeed to meet him, for he spoke French, and since I left Werchojansk I had seen no one with whom I could talk. He told me he had been twelve days at the house where he was now living, unable to get away, as the roads were filled with water and there were several rivers to cross which were too deep to ford. Besides this there were no animals to be had and no boats at the rivers. He had sent his Cossack forward to report the condition of affairs, and expected horses from a village half way to Yakoutsk, and had ordered boats to be taken on bull sleds to the rivers *en route*.

NIJNI NOVGOROD.

CHAPTER XXV.

END OF THE JOURNEY.

IRKUTSK, *August 2d,* 1882.

MY baggage did not arrive until the 26th of May, when I started immediately in company with Mr. Bobookoff, who had with him the box containing the records and relics found with the bodies of Captain De Long and his companions at the Lena mouth. We found the roads in a fearful condition, and bridges broken down. Twice during the night we had to unload the horses before crossing the bridges, which we temporarily repaired. The horse which carried the heavy box containing the relics fell six or seven times in crossing small but deep and swift streams, which beset our path continually, but the larger river, which we had to cross in a boat, was passed without accident, though the current was almost like a waterfall. The horses swam the river, guided and sustained by a rope of twigs made by the natives, and exceedingly strong, though not particularly flexible. All the baggage was transferred on the boat, and, as might be imagined, I watched the box containing the precious relics of the unfortunate heroes from the *Jeannette* with considerable anxiety, and drew a long breath when I saw it safely landed on the opposite shore. We reached the next station at half past one o'clock in the morning, to find it deserted and half filled with water. By making a long detour we managed to pass the submerged land, and four hours later reached a Yakout house five versts from the station. We made a bargain with the inhabitants to take us to the house of the Opraveur, or writer, a petty officer of the Government, living half way between the Aldan and Yakoutsk.

The country here is more thickly peopled than further north, but the houses are of the same construction—logs notched into each other at the corners and a flat roof of logs closely laid and covered with a thick layer of turf. The whole outside of the structure is afterward smeared with manure. The rich Yakouts live just like the poor ones—the same kind of houses, one little end reserved for the family, and the other filled with cows and calves. At the season I passed through this country these people live entirely upon milk, rich and poor alike. The milk is boiled with the inner bark of the pine tree, pounded first to break the fibres. Sometimes this dish is improved with a gallon or two of minnows, caught in traps that are set for the purpose in every lake and stream. I have eaten of this dish with these people in the fashionable style—that is, each male is provided with a large wooden spoon, and the pot is set in the middle of the table, so that every one can fish for himself. When one is hungry it is a very palatable dish, but I cannot understand how great, strong men can be satisfied to subsist on milk when they have an abundance of cattle. Perhaps it is this milk diet that makes such cowards of these people. We reached the village where the Opraveur lives the second day, with the Yakout horses, and again crossed a flood in boats.

We were entertained for the night at the house of a quaint-looking old priest, who was all kindness and attention and brought us such delicacies from his slender stock as boiled beef, biscuit, tea with sugar, and pickled fish. He also opened his heart and brought out his bottle of *vodka* and piously blessed the liquor each time before he joined with us in a glass of the beverage. After refreshment he took a guitar, upon which he played very skilfully, and, for my especial edification, played several negro melodies which he had learned while on a visit to San Francisco many years ago. Afterward he played and sang a number of comic Russian songs in a minor key, each verse concluding with a lively "tol-la-rol-lol," which he gave with great spirit, keeping time to the measure with his foot. Then followed some Spanish love songs, equally well rendered, and I was as much pleased as surprised to hear such good music from so unusual an instrument in the wilds of Siberia and from a long robed and long haired old priest, who looked more like a backwoodsman of America than a musician. But he was a dear, good old soul, and I shall ever remember with the greatest pleasure his successful efforts to entertain his weary guests. We were also indebted to him for some fresh provisions with which to continue our journey the next day. Since my diet of horse meat I had lived entirely upon wild ducks and geese purchased for a nominal price from the Yakouts we encountered *en route*.

Two stations further on I met a newly married Yakout bride and groom, and from my companion, Mr. Bobookoff, who speaks the Yakout language well, I learned the marriage rites of those people. A young man buys a wife from her father for from fifty to five hundred rubles, varying according to her beauty and accomplishments and the earnestness or wealth of the swain. After the purchase the father of the affianced bride again takes possession of her and the lover is not allowed even to see her for a year.

After that interval they are married by a priest and again subjected to an agonizing separation of twenty days, at the termination of which they can fly to each other's arms and none can put them asunder. What devotion must animate their bosoms to outlive such cruel parting without one sly glance to replenish the fires of love! No communication whatever, not even a valentine, may pass between them, for I never saw but one Yakout who could read or write. I expressed my admiration of this sincere love to my friend Bobookoff; but that cynic scouted the idea of love. He said it was simply a matter of money. The young man paid his rubles, and intended to get something for them, if it was only a wife. He says true love would have died for want of nourishment long before the first term of separation was ended. The young man can't be false, for he has already paid all the money he has, and could not afford to be unfaithful. Pshaw! I despise such incredulity, but my friend Bobookoff is an ex-exile, and is, perhaps, entitled to his lack of faith in humanity.

I reached the bank of the Lena late in the afternoon of May 30th, twenty-seven days after my departure from Werchojansk, wearied, hungry and dirty. After crossing the quicksands, where our horses sank nearly to their bellies, we reached a cluster of houses, and there found Sergeant Kolinkon, the Cossack who had accompanied Mr. Bobookoff to the island house where I found him after crossing the Aldan. He had come out from Yakoutsk to meet us, and brought some fresh beefsteak, bread and several interesting looking bottles. He also brought the Governor's greeting to me and a request that I should call upon him as soon as I arrived. The next day we reached Yakoutsk, having crossed the river, which here is fifteen versts wide, during the night, while

TOMSK.

I slept, overcome with fatigue and the happy feeling of relief that the hardest part of my long journey was ended. My old friend, M. de Varowa, came out on the road to meet me and conducted me to his residence, where "*La petite* Nányah" welcomed me with apparent pleasure as an old companion on the road. Soon a messenger came from the Governor with the request that I would call upon him at once, as there was now with him a gentleman who speaks English and who would act as an interpreter for us. To my apology for appearing in my dirty clothes of the road the old General politely replied that he was ashamed to hear an old soldier apologize to another for the accidents of a campaign, and received me with the utmost cordiality, compelling me to stay and dine with him informally *comme à la guerre*.

Our interpreter was Captain Jurgens, of the Russian navy, who was on his way to the Lena delta to establish a meteorological station as one of Russia's links in the chain of stations to take synchronous observations encircling the world within the Arctic. During the period of my stay at Yakoutsk I received the kindest attention on all sides, and there formed friendships that, though they may remain but as recollections, will always be among the pleasantest and most sincere of my life. General Tchernaieff, the Governor, was more like a father to me than a host, and the Lieutenant Governor, Basil Priklonsky, a true brother. Captain Jurgens, though himself a visitor, was unremitting in attention and most patiently performed the onerous duties of interpreter, at all times sacrificing his personal comfort for my benefit.

Seven days after my arrival the search party arrived from the Lena delta and shared with me the hospitality of our friends in Yakoutsk. Chief Melville and his immediate companions, Bartlett, Nindermann and Greenbek were old friends, and but renewed the relations of the previous winter. Captain Berry and Ensign Hunt, of the *Rodgers*, met them, as I had done, for the first time. But all united in feelings of the warmest friendship and deepest gratitude to the officers of the Russian Government in Yakoutsk. On the 11th of June we all embarked upon the little steamer *Pioneer*, and were accompanied to the landing by about half of the citizens of Yakoutsk, including the officers of the Government, who had come thus far to take a final farewell. Many were the warm hand shakings and earnest protestations of enduring friendship, while I, who had become Russianized in Siberia almost as easily as I had become uncivilized among the savages of the North, kissed and was kissed repeatedly by nearly all the—horrors!—men.

The *Pioneer* was a most miserable little steamer, that shed sparks all over us as she struggled up stream against the strong current of the Lena. This was our home for nearly two weeks, during which we often ran unsuccessful races against boats that were being towed along the shore by a couple of bareheaded boys. There was only one convenience in such a craft, and that was there was a place on the cabin tables where you could write at almost any time, for they were seldom encumbered with meals. A little foraging at villages where we stopped for wood added a good deal to our personal comfort, but, much to our surprise, induced the Captain to raise our board.

At Witem we left the *Pioneer* and went aboard of the *Constantine*, a larger and more comfortable craft, where we boarded *à la carte* and fared much better. There were many other passengers than our party upon this boat, and it was a motley group, comprising Russians, Yakoutsks,

Tunguses, Tartars, Mongols and gypsies. Among them were two women who wore a sort of Bloomer costume, which is quite common in travelling in Siberia. The habit consists of a loose shirt, with a belt around the waist and loose trousers tucked into high topped boots. A derby or soft felt hat completes the costume, which is striking and prepossessing.

GOLD MINES OF WITEM.

The scenery along the Lena River is, in many places, most charming and picturesque. Turreted cliffs rise directly from the water's edge, or decorate the wooded slopes, like great feudal castles. Rolling farm lands, tilled with great toil and but little skill, stretch away into the forests, and at intervals of twenty or thirty versts pretty little villages dot the river's banks. In every village are one or more churches of the Greek faith, with the

Oriental domes, gaudily painted or gilded, and giving dignity to what otherwise might be an uninteresting collection of square houses. But I have noticed that a taste for decoration is a distinguishing mark of Siberian architecture. In the cities, the sills and lintels of the windows are ornamented, and even the tin waterspouts that lead the rain from the roofs into the street terminate in dragons' mouths or some other artistic design. Little balconies and corners relieve the monotony of the plain wooden walls, and this, too, with no other material, perhaps, than the cumbrous logs of which most of the dwellings are built. Often you will see the solid window shutters painted in flagrant, gaudy colors, but almost everywhere the attempt is made to beautify one's dwelling. Some of the log church edifices I have seen on the Upper Lena would decorate the finest park in Europe or America.

After five days upon the *Constantine* we reached a station beyond which the boat could not pass. I needed nothing more to convince me of this when I saw herds of cattle fording the river a short distance above us. At this station we took the small boats of the post stations, and for five days and nights were towed near the river bank by horses, which sometimes trotted along the shore, and at others waded in the stream; while occasionally the line was cast adrift entirely until the horses passed around a deep inlet and reappeared ahead of us on a little island, we, in the meantime, maintaining our position against the current or moving ahead propelled by poles in the hands of our *yemsheeks*.

Four days more in carriages took us to Irkutsk, the only real city I had yet seen in Siberia. We took up our quarters at the Hôtel Deko, a commodious and well kept inn, where every effort was made to accommodate and please the taste of the American guests. Another hotel, the Siberian, frequently enticed us to dine, where the cooking was more like civilization than one would expect to find in this country. Cosey little dining rooms, with a really excellent cuisine and fair wines, left with you a feeling that you had passed within the lines of civilization at last.

There was one dish that we found most palatable as well as novel—that was cold soup, a dish truly Siberian. It is made of little chunks of cold meat and sliced hard boiled eggs, mixed with onion tops and sour cream, into which is poured for each individual portion a bottle of "*quass,*" that gives it a most refreshing, pungent taste. Chunks of transparent ice floating in it have a cooling effect. But what is "*quass?*" queries the uninformed New Yorker. *Quass* is a harmless beverage made from black bread and

GENERAL ANOUTCHINE.

yeast, and is so lively when bottled that it must be tightly corked and tied down to keep it. I dare not give the receipt for making this delightful drink, as it is the key of cold soup, or "*okroshka,*" as it is called here, and I know an American who intends to make a fortune in New York with a summer lunch room down town, where nothing will be served except these two articles, with bread, of course, but a strictly temperance house. It will only need an introduction there to secure the patronage of every hungry and thirsty business man, for these are articles that recommend themselves when once tried. Then, to be served by girls in the cool, pretty dress of Little Russia, will have such a soothing influence upon all customers that they will gladly add to the prospective fortune of the enterprising individual who brings this blessing to New York.

The day after our arrival General Anoutchine, the Governor General of Oriental Siberia, returned to town from a protracted tour through his principality to Japan and by the Suez Canal to Europe, from which he returned by the regular post road. He was accompanied by his wife and daughter, who had not only withstood the fatigues of so great a journey, but enjoyed the trip intensely. The entire American party called to pay their respects to the Governor General, by whom they were subsequently presented to his family and afterward entertained at dinner. The whole family, as might be expected, speak French fluently, and Mlle. Anoutchine has added the English language to her other accomplishments. General Anoutchine is quite a young man, though already gray, but a man of considerable force of character. He is polished in his manners and agreeable to all, so that he is exceedingly popular wherever known. We visited the public garden the second evening we were in Irkutsk, and listened to an excellent concert by a small orchestra of stringed and brass instruments. It was an unexpected and brilliant sight to see once more elegantly dressed ladies and gentlemen strolling through avenues of trees illumined with numerous gaudy Chinese lanterns and listening to familiar selections from Wagner and Strauss. In the garden is a summer club house, to which we were introduced by a member and allowed the freedom of the club upon the payment of a nightly due of fifty kopecks each. The club has here a good restaurant and the best wines and liquors that can be procured in town, and here the evenings are passed in playing cards for a small gage. The assemblage is all the more brilliant from the fact that all officers in Russia and its possessions are required to wear their uniform at all times, and, as nearly every citizen, unless a merchant, is an officer,

LAKE BAIKAL.

gaudy uniforms are numerous. But all seemed pleased to greet and be friendly with the American visitors, and they, on their part, will long remember with pleasure their short sojourn in Irkutsk.

Fully convinced that no one who visits Irkutsk should leave without seeing Lake Baikal, I made a trip there and spent two days enjoying its grand and picturesque scenery. At Irkutsk my journey virtually ended, and it only remained for me to get home by the most feasible route. This was found to be over the post roads to Tomsk, a distance of about a thousand miles. At Tomsk, a city of 40,000 inhabitants, I made the acquaintance of the Mayor, Mr. Zoubolski, who in his youth had been a famous hunter and trapper, and later had accumulated enough to purchase an interest in a gold mine, thus becoming one of the richest men in Siberia. From Tomsk, in company with my old friend, Captain John O. Spicer, of Groton, Conn., I journeyed upon a small steamer to Toumein. From this point there were two more days of travel over the post roads to Ekaterinburg, where a short railroad crosses the Ural Mountains, and brings the traveller to Perm. Another steamer brought us in four days to Nishne Novgorod, the old Russian city which has for years been a resort for merchants from all points in Europe and Siberia, assembling for the great fair which is held upon the lowlands on the southern shore of the Volga. Nishne Novgorod is the terminus of the grand railroad system of Europe. Henceforward I entered upon beaten tracks of travel. I had returned to civilization. My mission as a courier was done.

MAYOR OF TOMSK.

www.ingramcontent.com/pod-product-compliance
Lightning Source LLC
Chambersburg PA
CBHW020243240426
43672CB00006B/624